CARRY ON
成 CAR 切
MAKING

*Cover Photo: The famous Huxinting Tea House in the Yu Gardens, Shanghai,
where H.M. The Queen has sipped real tea.*

CARRY ON
成 CAR 功
MAKING

Life in China after Longbridge

成 IAN S POGSON 功

BREWIN BOOKS

First published by
Brewin Books Ltd, 56 Alcester Road,
Studley, Warwickshire B80 7LG in 2007
www.brewinbooks.com

ISBN: 978-1-85858-409-6

A Cataloguing in Publication Record
for this title is available from the British Library

Typeset in Baskerville
Printed in Great Britain by
Warwick Printing Company Ltd.

CONTENTS

DEDICATION

This book is dedicated to my family; my wife Sharon and children Sarah, Ashley and Jessica. Without their support I could not have taken the first step to working in the Far East.

A huge vote of thanks goes to my father, Brian, who has read and edited this entire narrative. Both he and my dear, departed mother Audrey gave me the urge to travel and learn.

To my colleagues and friends British and Chinese go my thanks too, for they provided the material and many of the photographs, expertly selected by Jessica. Proof reading by Señor Muzz 'Pernickety' Williams.

Final proof reading by Nathaniel "Ben" Basevi, so any further mistakes are his fault.

THIS NARRATIVE

In the first period of working in China with Powertrain Ltd, I wrote home many e-mails about life in Shanghai and my view on it. Recipients said that they found them amusing, so why did I not write a diary when I returned? This sounded like a good idea, so wishing to return to the UK with more than just my unreliable memories and some money, I resolved to do so.

What follows is a day-by-day account of life in the Orient. The gaps in the account are when I returned to the UK, as my contract called for three months in territory and one month in the UK, but it rarely worked out like that.

ABOUT THE AUTHOR

Ian is married with three children, all living in Bromsgrove, Worcestershire. This is his first attempt at writing a book. He is a Chartered Automotive Engineer who began his career in 1980 as a Graduate Trainee for Land Rover. He worked his way around the many plants which made up the Rover Group and latterly for Powertrain Limited, the engine and transmission arm of MG Rover. As part of the latter's last-ditch attempt to court an international partner, Ian worked in Shanghai, PRC (People's Republic of China) from the start of January 2005 to redundancy upon the collapse of MG Rover in April that year.

He returned to live and work there over a one year period from June 2005 to 2006 and this is his story. It was written as a daily diary of the ups and downs of being away from family and of the cultural clashes which occurred in trying to teach and guide his Chinese hosts, towards making a National car for China.

It is an amusing Westerner's view on Eastern society as it absorbs and assimilates Western values. Ian is indebted to his Chinese hosts and wishes them well with their venture, continuing as they do towards domination of world manufacturing.

DRAMATIS PERSONAE

Disclaimer

Except for where short sections are accredited to friends Brummie and Winston and some indicated pieces from the apartment offices or the local paper, all the work is my own. Everyone's identity is guarded by a pseudonym and no slur or otherwise is intended on anyone's character; it is all in fun, it is the way we deal with each other at work on a daily basis. Nothing is said here that has not been or would not be said to peoples' faces.

The British "Residents"

Native – a tall engineer

Fraulein – wife of Native and novelist

Let – a tall project manager

Sonnie – a dour engineer

Winston – a chunky engineer

Marvin – a desperately
   dour engineer

Donk – a dark horse engineer

Fluff – a lap-top engineer

Rolf – the oldest manufacturing
   engineer and artist

Doo – wife to Rolf

Gary – a real Welsh leader

Visa – a handsome engineer

Spit – a top boss

DIY – a trading engineer

Turk – an engineer with an
   eastern twist

Clegg – a worried engineer

Tup – a bearded engineer

Ewe – wife to Tup and tennis pro

Lucky – a wife's best friend

Prop – a stout engineer

Scooter – a top body engineer

Flower – a smart engineer

Brummie – a Second City engineer

Hug – a chilling engineer

The British "Visitors"

The Bottom – HR's greatest asset
Fraggle – an old, hairy engineer
AJ – an old, fast engineer
118 – the noisiest engineer
Bling – a posing engineer
Flat-bed – a northern engineer
Loch – a chunky engineer
Gasket – a chef-engineer
Rabbit – a testing engineer
Doctor – the best diesel engineer
Hi-ho – a great photographer
Rumble – the quiet one

Bean – another older engineer
Shirley – a short engineer
Gap – a fastidious engineer
The Body – says he's a top engineer
Milky Bar Kid – a young one
Goose – quiet engineer/fast rider
Uncle Dick – everyone's favourite
Post – a Quality person
Bond – an engines engineer
The PM – an older project manager
One – another for the Lu

The Locals

Hooray – a lot to learn
Smiler – a tested engineer
Boss – knows it all
Pinion – happy chappie
Bassey – top administrator
Oil – legs which translate
Kelly – overlooked
    technical translator
Diva – a goddess in the kitchen
Nimitz – top chef and team leader
Beckham – not a clue about
    the game

Dizzy – not a clue about engines
Test-bed – not a clue about these
Pan – not a clue about girls
Bank – smart and loaded
Waldorf – Statler's heckling mate
Statler – Waldorf's heckling mate
Ruby – top terracotta waitress
Nelson – top barman
Bombay – *sous*-barman
Dennis – bar-minder

FOREWORD

The closure of MG Rover's Longbridge factory in April 2005 was devastating for the people of Birmingham, Bromsgrove and the Black Country. Over 6,000 men and women lost their jobs directly and thousands of others working in the supply chain fell under the spectre of unemployment. Livelihoods were threatened, hopes and dreams were dashed, and the future was made foreboding. Individuals and families suffered but so too did our region, for the closure was a crushing blow to our belief in our manufacturing prowess. For most of the twentieth century the huge car plant, a town within a city, had stood proudly as a symbol of our industrial ingenuity and of our prosperity gained through the making of things.

From its gates had poured the Austin Sevens, designed by Herbert Austin himself, which had democratised car ownership and revolutionised car design; and from here had also poured the Minis that became both an iconic emblem and the epitome of pop culture in the twentieth century. Longbridge and its workers made us proud and gave us confidence. Even through the dark days of the 1970s when the national media, and too often the local media, was knocking the factory and its folk we retained our faith in both. Indeed Longbridge's importance seemed to grow from the recession of the 1980s when our self-belief was badly hit with the closure of so many great firms that had once too made their mark on the world; whilst Longbridge produced cars we could still hold our heads high and proclaim our bond with manufacturing.

In fact the involvement of Honda and the K series engines seemed to promise a bright future, but then things went badly wrong. Starved of long-term investment and a new plant, in 2001 the new owners BMW announced they would be closing down Longbridge. A massive public campaign in support of the workers and manufacturing shocked business leaders and politicians and against all the odds a consortium took over MG Rover. Like the phoenix it seemed that the factory would rise from the ashes into vivid and dynamic life. It was not to be. Everyone knew that MG Rover needed a big partner if it were to survive, let alone thrive. No such partner was forthcoming. Almost as a last throw of the dice, everything was thrown into a link up with Shanghai Automotive and key figures went out to China. One of them was Ian Pogson. But it was not to be. Longbridge could not be saved.

There are many reasons why this is so, but this book is not about them. Instead it is a fascinating and unusual account of one man's life in a country that will soon become the industrial and economic powerhouse in the world but which remains such a mystery to us in Britain. It is a thoughtful, considered and first-hand account of Ian's determined attempts to learn about China and its people and to understand them. Usually such accounts come from the minds and pens of travel writers. The joy of Ian's approach is that he brings China alive in a down-to-earth yet compelling account and he enables us to find out a little more about the country that will come to dominate the world.

Professor Carl Chinn

Introduction

REDUNDANCY 6,000 MILES FROM HOME

Longbridge and China have few similarities, but both are huge places; it is just the scale that is different. I have worked now in both and this is the story of living and working in Shanghai, PRC (People's Republic of China) over a one year period from June 2005 to June 2006. This followed redundancy from Powertrain Limited at Longbridge, part of Phoenix Venture Holdings (MG Rover).

Longbridge was once one of the biggest industrial sites in Europe. From its sprawling acres came 318,475 Minis in 1971. The six engine tracks on the "A" series engine once made 15,000 engines a week. The place supported all the basic processes to make a car and its contents and as there are many books dedicated to its history, I shall not dwell here. If one wished to walk from Cofton Hackett in the east to the railway head-shunt at the tip of West Works, this would be a good 45 minute stroll. To me, it was a big place, never mind the subterranean web of tunnels under its many buildings.

China, on the other hand is mind-bogglingly vast. Estimates put the population at about 1.4 billion souls, with 800 million of these being peasants. The country is about 6,000 miles across and is covered by *one* time zone. Shanghai Municipality supports around 17 million of these people and I only met a few of them! The variety of Chinese faces, shapes, skin hues and dialects is almost unlimited.

What I knew about China before going there could have been written on a postage stamp. Now I may need two. The place is a deep mystery to Westerners, the language I found almost impenetrable, despite loving languages and trying to learn some basic phrases. Chinese people think we are somewhat dim not to be able to speak to them in Mandarin. I occasionally refer to words being in Welsh – in honour of our one-time leader from the West of the UK, this means Chinese!

The people are friendly, kind, easily amused and polite. They are ready to help, (especially if one attempts some Chinese speech) and have a rich history.

This diary raises as many questions as it provides answers for a prospective visitor or even seasoned traveller. The narrative tries to be respectful towards my hosts and wishes no ill-feeling upon them, as with *very* few exceptions they were generous and hospitable.

Except my immediate family, all the characters in this book are disguised by pseudonyms. These characters were in the first instance my work colleagues, but living so close with them both day and night meant that many have become firm friends. We have shared many emotional highs and lows, seen some amazing sights and supported each other through some dark times, but achieved the tough goals we were set.

Our employer during this time is not relevant to you dear reader and as such I have attempted to avoid mentioning any details of the project as these are not exactly secret, but best kept between ourselves who toiled long and hard to make a car in China. I will use the experiences of a friend, Stuart, to relate some of his experiences in China with another company. Work is just a fabric, a canvas on which I have attempted to paint my impressions of a society which is so different from the UK.

Shanghai – recent history

It is a city of stark contrasts, where all road signs are marked with compass direction arrows, with those running east-west generally being named after cities in China and those running north-south being after the provinces.

Shanghai streets have been renamed according to occupying forces and most of the French words have been replaced by Chinese names. It began as a small fishing port, now home to about 17 million.

In November 1941 the last US soldier left Shanghai and the Japanese marched in. Only two Western vessels remained in the Huangpu river; HMS Petrel, with a crew of 27 and USS Wake with 25 seamen on board. Showing superior training and bottle, the British crew scuttled their ship, surrounded by gun-boats, destroyers, cruisers and the flagship of the Imperial Japanese Navy, the Idzumo.

The Nationalists turned up in 1943, ousted the Japanese and settled in.

In April 1949 the Bank of China on the Bund was raided by Chiang Kai Shek's Nationalist forces and the vaults emptied, put on a ship and sailed to Taiwan, where there is still tension between mainland and the island.

The Communists rolled in during May 1949 and the rest is history.

Brummies, Redundancy and new beginnings

As I write this, Longbridge is being demolished, my last office having been turned to rubble last week, but it had been my place of employment for many years in the period from the mid-Nineties to 2005. I had been an employee firstly of Land Rover, then the Rover Group and finally (MG Rover) Powertrain Ltd, for twenty-four and a half years when redundancy came to me in Shanghai.

In late 2004 after several failed attempts to secure a business partner, MG Rover had a last-ditch attempt with a Chinese company to create a joint venture. The reasons for failure are not to be discussed here (maybe that is for a future publication) but in January 2005 I joined colleagues in Shanghai to try and localise the K-series Rover engines for the Rover 75, but 6,000 miles from home. We all knew that this was to be a final desperate attempt to keep Rover afloat, but volunteered anyway. Those of us in the know realised that unless something had been worked out for MG Rover, by March or April the money would have run out.

We left behind in Birmingham a much-reduced workforce of some 6,000 people, some of the finest colleagues you could wish for, enormously capable engineers and some great folk on the shop floor. Very little is or was ever written about the ordinary Longbridge worker, but I assure you that the ones I worked with in Logistics towards the end of my career were flexible, caring, honest, regular people.

Might I just relate one story of the "latter days" to illustrate? This concerns the TU's (Trade Unions) and their flexible attitude to change in East works, the home of Powertrain Ltd. (PtL was a legally separate company from MG Rover, as we had been in BMW ownership for one year longer than MG Rover).

My boss had suggested that we would be looking to outsource Material Handling (Stores operations, Fork-lift truck drivers and line feeders) to an outside company in order to save money and cut headcount. The reaction this provoked in our forward-looking TU was for them to ask if they could also put in a bid for the contract. They did not go on strike, stage a sit-in or anything daft that the media might invent or wish to write about. No, they behaved like business-men and (with some help from us in management, as we wished to retain their considerable skills) put together their own case. In the end, they were competitive and won the day. We re-assigned some people, so "lost the heads" off the payroll group and ended up with a sharper, more tightly-knit function. These sorts of stories never made the news in 2003.

And so I spent three months from the end of January 2005 until redundancy in mid-April working in Shanghai. I did not start this diary until returning in June with my new employer, so the narrative spares the reader many of the initial cultural shocks of those early days. My redundancy was expected, due to the financial situation and the massive media pressure.

We found out about our redundancy from relatives and friends back in the UK, but straight away one of the top Chinese leaders sat a few of us down and asked if we would return soon to continue the work. We were flattered, but knew it would take some time to organise, as we could not work directly for our hosts. In my case, this took six weeks to set up, recruit me and send me back out to the Orient, from when this narrative begins.

Chapter 1

BACK TO A WARM SHANGHAI WELCOME
AND CHINESE FOOTBALL

Thursday, 16th June 2005
This is the life! I was collected at 5.30am from home, care of Regency Cars, driver Bernard. This is all part of the Business Class package, which would never have happened in the old MG days unless I was a director. We picked up my colleague Winston later on and flew via Finnair Business Class.

Friday, 17th June 2005
We arrived on time in Shanghai, but no-one was there to meet us, the wrong information was apparently sent from the UK. We waited for ages, and then hooked up with a taxi hawker and a driver, settling into a ubiquitous black VW Santana, with NO METER! We argued about the fare – they wanted RMB400/£28.60!! After some debate between ourselves, we asked to be let out and transferred to a regular taxi that did not set its meter and charged RMB200/£14.30 – we just couldn't be bothered to argue any more.

We were not expected at the allocated apartment hotel, the "Pent-Ox Metropolis", due to further poor communications. We even went to the wrong reception and ended up doing a circuit of the building! We were tired by then. "Just get me to my room", is the thought familiar to those of you who have travelled long-haul. (Photos p.II, p.III).

Reception finally sorted room 21G for Winston and next door 21H for me. The rooms were fine, but had no Internet access and featured a depressing view of the cement bagging and storage yard below. The pool on the roof was not as in the brochure – it was all green and slimy with debris floating therein. I think a full diving dry suit would be required.

The neighbourhood is not as friendly or quiet and green as JinQiao, where we lived when in the Diamond Court apartments during our first visit here; no café-bars in the Western style, just a crazy Chinese busy main street

– Pudong Da Dao (Avenue). No DVD-Man either, like we used to have in JinQiao! He would sit outside the café with his mate, at the foot of the steps selling DVDs for RMB8/50p each. (Photo p.IV).

However, free Internet access is provided in the lobby via two terminals.

Sadly, unlike at DC, I do not possess a walk-in shower and there is no clothes line or washing basket – what a tragedy?! The room was not ready, no loo-roll, or towels in place. However, I have a bigger guest bed and air-con with remote controls!

We are nearly all unhappy with the state of the area compared with DC where we were in MG Rover days; were we spoiled?

As a consequence some of us went to JinQiao by taxi and walked in to applause from the staff at the Mawdesley, our old local bar! There we had a few drinks and dinner, then a quick shop in Carrefour, a massive Shanghai outpost of the French supermarket chain.

Saturday, 18th June 2005

I was woken at 10.00 by Winston and the IT man to fix the internet connection – but it was still no good. We taxied out for lunch at East-West, a small café in JinQiao opposite DC and whiled away the time. Then it was more Carrefour shopping and back to the Mawdesley for dinner.

A wedding party landed at the Coffee Beanery (another café in the same row as the East-West and the Mawdesley). There were very few guests and an ugly groom, who was on his mobile phone most of the time! They took video and stills on the decking with us in the background, then down on to the pavement for more pictures.

In the evening, we went to "Luna", our favourite haunt in the group of bars and restaurants known as Xintiandi in the old part of the city.

Our favourite band, "Friction", was in full swing – there were big smiles to see us and they played loads of great music.

Beer is now RMB45/£3 per 0.3L bottle – it's RMB3 in Carrefour. We left at the end of the show, about 1.30am.

Sunday, 19th June 2005

Jet-lagged, I lazed about all day until 7.30pm when I went to the Mawdesley for dinner with Rolf, Sonnie, Brummie & Winston. Complimentary melon cubes and red vodka cocktail in a jug were served, with an illuminated stirring stick, poured into plastic shot glasses with flashing lights in the base! Naturally being engineers we had to find out how the lights flashed and how to turn them off. The presence of liquid caused a contact between the two terminals moulded into the base of the glass and set it off flashing. We rapidly drained our glasses and set about trying to dry the base to extinguish the lights. Small things, they say!

Monday, 20th June 2005
The first day in work revealed no computer, but a desk in Powertrain Engineering, working for a Chinese Team Leader on "Accessories" (by that they mean things like water pumps, oil pumps, filters, about which I was seen as an expert!). Everyone seems very pleased to see us; there are lots of formal welcomes and "Glad you came back" comments. There are plenty of issues to sort out as we expected. I sat in with the team, next to my colleague Native. I was given a "Monthly Performance Appraisal Form" with objectives set by my Team Leader. This was quick! I was even asked to advise on "possible suggestions about starter motors sourcing in China" – not an area of expertise for me.

After a day working, we were worn out. We went out for a meal to the huge Super Brand Shopping Mall opposite the Oriental Pearl TV Tower in Lujiazui – 8 floors of shops and eateries plus a cinema. It was RMB58/£4 for a bowl of noodles with one prawn and some beef – good, though.

On the lower floor was a crazy fashion parade with traditional costume and stick-thin long-legged models (and their Mums supporting!) showing off the clothes.

We descended to the basement food hall for Rolf to buy some cereal – it was like a subterranean Kwik Save. Beyond the tills, we spotted a "Trouser Prune" sign for clothing alterations – sometimes translation is so funny.

Tuesday, 21st June 2005
I enjoyed a Pent-Ox breakfast and then it is a 30 min taxi ride to work with Rolf, who says he has been painting again! He sorted himself an alloy easel for next-to-nothing, so he's happy. Like all of us, he doesn't know how long he's going to be out here; it is the longest he's been away from his family and he is nearly ten years my senior! He always avoided travelling for our old Company.

We managed to fire up my PC and start working today, and I have a phone too. The Chinese keep coming with lots more obscure/varied questions. I felt stretched a bit as my speciality is not engine design. I was given a carton of Chinese leaf tea by my boss, which was very kind!

We dined at the East-West for RMB40/£2.82, and then moved onto the Mawdesley for a swift one – which turned out to be on the house!

As this narrative develops, I shall try to spot a non-job of the day, something you just would not see back in the UK.

So, here is a first non-job – several blue-overalled, coolie-hatted women were sitting on the grass or little stools, picking at the grass outside a company HQ. They appear to use forks or very small tools and spend ages on one patch of ground, supposedly weeding.

Wednesday, 22nd June 2005

Today was another hot one. We dined in the small Puxi Pent-Ox restaurant at the base of the six-storey admin building, (atop which is the closed swimming pool), where we spent a mere RMB60/£4 for a variety of dishes selected from a menu, much of which was "off"! We could only select that which was ticked! It was, however, great when it came. We were slightly worried, as there were only staff dining there when we arrived. I managed a whole box of orange juice to myself; it does not seem to come by the glass!

Tonight there was much noise in the dock-yard again, but I finally managed to sleep sometime after 3.00am. Curse that cement yard below and the clanging, crashing trucks. We are really bothered by the incredible noise.

Thursday, 23rd June 2005

25 to 30 minutes seems to be the time taken and RMB28 to 30/£2 for the 11km distance to work from here. It is still incredibly hot, well into the 30s. In the evening, we ventured out to Super Brand Mall for a meal in "78". It is a very cheap and cheerful restaurant chain – RMB60/£4.

Down in the Lotus Supermarket I bought a pair of trainers for RMB99/£7. We walked home, as no taxis were available, taking a good 40 minutes as no-one wants to rush in this heat. I watched TV and read until 2.00am; this is the single man's life! (Photo p.VI).

Non-job of the day is a guy brushing the grass on the central reservation with his stick-broom. One reason for so many trees and bushes on the streets here could be that the street-cleaners use the foliage to make their witch-style brooms.

Friday, 24th June 2005

More heat, more sweat. I came back to the Pent-Ox and went out to the East-West for a RMB50/£3.58 meal. I was given a free green tea in the Mawdsley! I made it back at 1.00pm; my body clock is now adjusted to Shanghai fun-time.

Non-jobs of the day – in our favourite JinQiao bar (the Mawdesley) there were four customers (us) and twelve staff! The "terracotta waitresses" as we call them in their brown uniforms were stood in pairs at their "stations". There is a real sense of progression through the ranks of the waitresses even here in this tiny neighbourhood bar. The new girls are not allowed to serve directly, but must carry trays to the guests, who are then given their food by more experienced operatives. There is a new pair of girls who stand by the end of the bar nearest the kitchen, where all novices start and they squeeze close together, holding hands or inflicting "Chinese burns" on each others' arms. They part some time later, rubbing sore limbs, giggling. There is a lot of touching in this society, even occasionally amongst the engineers at work.

Conundrum for our colleagues – we complain about our accommodation, they listen and say that we have "special quarters". We find out many share up to eight together in about 100sq.ft. apartments. We enjoy 110sq.ft. each. Colleagues poles apart, in the same office.

Saturday, 25th June 2005

The cleaner came in at 09.15! That was a rude awakening.

Today was our twenty-second Wedding Anniversary and Sharon had packed a card in my case, with punched out hearts aplenty spilling from the envelope!!

Just for a mad thing to do on a hot day, Rolf and I went to Century Park. We walked across the park, by a Musical fountain and hired a side-by-side cycle for RMB100/£7.14 deposit and RMB40/£2.82 per hour. We spent two hours sweating away! Amusingly there were loads of workers from the "Family Store" in yellow tops playing team-building games, such as playing catch with bottled water and "trust-falls" (where one "falls" backwards and trust colleagues to catch you).

We caught up with them in the coffee-house at lunch-time, where they were sprawled about in the cool, air-conditioned room, some sleeping, still clutching the bottled water! When all of them left, there remained only about six of us who had actually ordered and paid for any food. A good plateful of sweet-and-sour pork with a drink was consumed for RMB50/£3.60. It was hardly an over-crowded place; but compare this place with real China just outside the gates – even the hallowed surroundings of JinQiao, where there are people living in shanties. The park is RMB10/70p entry and RMB40/£2.86 an hour for a bike, when a cheap-and-cheerful bike can be bought for RMB200/£14.30.

Everybody seems to be coping at home, but I am missed for helping with building the new deck and the ironing and a few other things, such as DIY and just being Dad.

Tonight was spent in our favourite bar, Luna – I set out walking on my own as the others had gone for dinner in JinQiao. On Pudong Da Dao (the road where we live) I passed several "pink hairdressers" with pretty young ladies sprawled about, idly watching TV. Not a lot of hair was being cut. Everybody is out on the pavement, playing mah-jong or drinking tea. There are lots of bare-foot youngsters lounging everywhere. There is quite a community spirit here. Many people choose in this heat to sleep out on the pavement, despite the roar of the traffic.

I was fried by the time I reached Eton Place apartments, just ten minutes down the road, so I hailed a taxi (air-con is such a luxury) and we beat our way through the weekend traffic to Xintiandi. I toddled down to the lake to cool, but no such luck, it was just as warm by the water. I took up my place on the front row in Luna and waited for the boys. Friction, the band, did a superb first set, with some Santana and "Alone" by Heart really pulling at the heart-strings.

The boys arrived after the first set. I collared Marissa (singer) and Andrew (bass) in the break and passed on a request card. They did a brilliant version of Bryan Adams' "Heaven" for Sharon and me and our 22 years together. (The last time I had heard Bryan play that, I was holding my wife's softly swaying hips as we watched from the VIP area in Cardiff Arena). A Yorkshireman, Michael, came up and said it was a really commendable thing to play a song for an absent lady. We made it back to the Pent-Ox for 3.00am and I telephoned Sharon again. I think she was pleased with the dedication.

Sunday, 26th June 2005

I managed to sleep in to mid-day, and then went out for 1.30pm to lunch with Winston, Brummie and Donk. We stayed until 5.00pm. I found a note under my apartment door from the recently arrived Marvin, so we met at 7.30pm for a meal in the larger Pent-Ox restaurant, which is in the Sichuan (spicy) style. It cost RMB114/£8.50 for six dishes and two drinks. It was really good food, but I ate too late and had trouble sleeping.

I called my friend in the UK, Richard Trundle before turning in and enjoyed a very odd, three-way with his wife, Lesley and my best mate, Stuart Galey. They were in a car on the M6 travelling up North for our oldest friend William Morgan's Mother's funeral. Richard and I were using Internet Telephony on our PCs, me in Shanghai and he in Warwick. It was great talking with them all. It might not be such a bad funeral after all. Lesley promised to keep my Father company at the meal afterwards, as they all love him and he enjoys their presence too.

Conundrum of the day – how can such a bicycle-oriented society not know about "ankling" when one pedals? This is where one places the pedal under the ball of the foot, thus using more muscles in that limb. Most of them stick the pedal hard against the heel – not good for the many high-heeled lady cyclists, scraping away at their shoes.

Monday, 27th June 2005

Two huge boats turned up at the docks – will we have a noisy few nights? We caught the new shuttle bus provided by the apartment in the morning, a new air-con mini-bus, but it took ages.

Shock news – our contact and organiser of everything in HR, a real whirl-wind of talent and character is leaving to go to Warner Bros.

Non-job of the day is the guy who comes around the office, waters the plants and cleans the pots. He also does a great job pruning.

Conundrum of the day – how can such a race of clever people with horticultural skills treat so many areas of grass and trees so badly?

It appeared to be firework night in the side-street of the apartment block, but I cannot see anyone enjoying them, they appear to emanate from the guard-house. Each salvo sets off the alarms in at least two cars I can see. The local fire-station is within rocket range, just around the corner. Back home this would have been stopped by nosey neighbours or the authorities.

Conundrum of the day by my Father – who asks, "Who therefore has the free society?!"

Tuesday, 28th June 2005

I had a really good sleep, but was woken at 5.30am by a big ship unloading cement in the dock – that will be there for a while. Marvin despairs over the Pent-Ox as well; he is in a lower-level temporary hotel room, which means he has no kitchen access. He and others looked at apartments in Green City yesterday. On the way to work we saw old folk ballroom dancing on a pavement in the shade along Zhangyong Lu, some with partners, some alone. Apparently Latin dancing is a big hit here to keep fit.

It was good to speak to all my girls by telephone this afternoon; I even miss Sarah moaning about her job. It is the small, everyday things you miss by not being there. However, for me and some of my colleagues, this was the only decently-paid job on offer at the time. Other, good people are having real trouble finding anything back in the UK.

Every cloud has a silver lining; the recent rain has curtailed all cement-loading activities out in the docks! I suppose the down side is that they will work that much harder to empty the massive vessel currently tied up outside. Wonder what the crew do when it is like this?

Toddled off into the city (Puxi) tonight by walking out into the refreshing rain and on down to the "spitting ferry", so-called because of the propensity for the men to use it as a huge, floating spittoon. This is about an hour's walk from the Pent-Ox. By the time I paid my half a Yuan and scurried down the slipway, I had just missed the ferry, so I had to wait a whole 5 minutes or so for another. Never been across the river in the dark before; even largish vessels disappear or melt into the lights as they show very few lights themselves, just a mast-head or two and the old green port and red starboard lanterns. A few cabin lights show, but you only see them along the side. The low barges are almost invisible.

Once over the Huangpu I legged it for the Yu Gardens to catch a couple of stalls, but all was being locked up. So I resolved to do a loop, enjoy the exercise and lights, return across the river and slide into the welcoming air-conditioned haven of Lotus Superstore under the Super Brand Mall.

Non-job of the day – the guy in uniform (hat and white gloves) who stands at the side exit of the underground car park to the Super Brand Mall and when the siren sounds, he stops pedestrians from being run over by exiting cars.

I bought some groceries and the mug I was after with a sieve to catch all the foliage (tea-leaves), then caught a taxi and collapsed in my apartment. Winston was just leaving his room as I appeared – you should see his legs – horrible!! – and that's without the monster bites thereon. He is really badly blistered and red. He bought some cream to put on them. Reckons he was attacked when they sat outside the Mawdesley one evening.

Today's conundrum is a question from our work colleagues – "What is this new B&Q store? Why would you want to paint your walls different colours or put paper on them?"

Wednesday, 29th June 2005

So, once more we went out for our mid-week excitement and ended up at the Super Brand Mall again, in search of food. I was not too keen as we had already eaten lunch at our local mosque-look-alike hotel. Our vouchers today entitled us to a plate full of spaghetti, mushrooms and Spam, (cue for the Monty Python sketch).

We found an amazing restaurant whose name we do not know as it is all in Welsh symbols, but for RMB60/£4.30 we dined like kings. The prawns in scrambled eggs were amazing. The beef rolls were like nothing you would see at home. The mutton pieces (about the size of beans) came in cases shaped like flowers made of fortune cookie type pastry. Two drinks and "lashings" of green tea were included.

The waiting staff were looking at us giggling into their hands all the time. Quite what we have done (apart from massacring their language) I do not know. We are as different to them as they are to us. The waiter who helps us through the menu, pointing at the photos and exclaiming "Pork" or "Fish" is openly abused by his female companions, a slap of his bum and verbal jesting. He retires to share a joke about us in the kitchen. Staff from there come out to look and laugh. Have we ordered a strange combination of food? One of the beans turns out to be a chilli. Brummie coughs and his eyes water – perhaps that is the joke!

Our next stop at the river-side Bianjin Paulaner German "Brauhaus" was RMB65/£4.20 for a beer. Western fare, Western prices. As a supermarket bottle of beer can be yours for RMB3/21p, that is taking the river-water. One tequila sunrise and I was ready for bed. Besides, I felt as if the mosquitoes were biting.

Conundrum of the day – how does a race of people so adept at art with lights and who adorn trees, bushes, buildings and even the outside retaining walls of flyovers with flashing strip lights with so much skill, have such dull domestic luminaires? I look into so many dwellings, rich and poor and the prevailing light source is a ring or strip fluorescent tube. Why? After the hours some of these people work, surely some relaxing lighting would be welcome?

Non-job of the day – *three* uniformed guards at attention for hours outside the fire-station on a dais.

Thursday, 30th June 2005

We endured yet another taxi driver, another different route to work. Haven't mentioned it before, but it always amazes one to see very young children stood on the running board of a scooter or moped, hands on the bars, generally with no helmet, gaining some early training in collision avoidance. Often there will be three members of the family on one two-wheeler.

Today's interesting manoeuvre was synchronised "U" turns – two people pulled such turns at the same time in the same spot from opposite directions. How did they not collide? The girl whom I saw closely did not even appear to look anywhere except straight ahead.

Driving deserves a complete section of its own. So many close shaves, so many cars and bikes. Down the centre of many of the important thoroughfares there is a steel fence, to stop people crossing. Tonight we were driving next to it in a ramshackle taxi and there was some scooter-mounted deviant coming towards us – we nearly shredded him through the fence. Our boyo in the driving seat even found it so unacceptable he found time to roll down his window and remonstrate with the offender. It takes something for that to happen here.

I was in a taxi one night where the driver was negotiating one of two notable roundabouts (the only two I've seen) and he was confused, the road had been "washed" and looked like a skid-pan and he was aimlessly wandering about like only a Chinese driver can, so he stopped, was almost rammed by a fellow licensed bandit and proceeded to berate the other guy! Not often you catch some road-rage; the offence has to be heinous.

The huge freighter which has been off-loading lime or cement is shut up for the night and the yard is quiet – maybe a chance of some sleep. Tomorrow is promised to be the hottest day so far and the day the pool opens. I reckon it will be essential to don your goggles and drink a can of coke after to avoid eye irritation and sickness. It looks clean; they have even moved some plants onto the roof.

Stunner of the day – I had to explain to a colleague how a transverse engine creates a front-wheel drive car. This is basic automotive knowledge. It's a long haul.

Obvious comment for a Thursday – we discover that HR departments are inept the world over, even here. Lose one good person and they fall apart. So many Personnel functions are staffed with young girls who have never been anywhere and have no idea of what it is like to be 6,000 miles away from a spouse and children. Give me the grey-haired ones anytime who have lived and loved and been somewhere.

We ate on the way home in JinQiao, just relaxing in the fan-heater type of wind blowing down the boulevard that is Biyun Lu. More messing about with the waiting staff at the East-West, we put one of them off so much she caused "bicycle-dominoes" as she attempted to wrest her rusty steed from the pile outside. Why do they bother locking them? Their English is improving; I wish our Chinese moved along quicker.

Friday, 1st July 2005
Even hardened Shanghai taxi-riders in our contingent suggest it would be worth mounting a video-camera on the front of the shuttle-bus to capture the insanity of the driving. One wag suggested that the Daily Telegraph would still not believe us.

Most of today was spent in a five-hour meeting with three Frenchmen and my colleagues, so there was English spoken for my benefit, although I took the chance to polish up some of my rudimentary French. We took lunch late in the works canteen – the faces of my Gallic visitors at the meal was a picture. Or three pictures.

It was an interesting culture clash, the detailed, experienced French with real knowledge of the parts in question and massive technical back-up; the Chinese, still with some good questions and points, but wanting it all fast. There were lots of rolling upwards of French eyes and raising of hands in protest. I did my best to present a united front with my Eastern colleagues, but also to appreciate the deep technical nature of the European presentation, from which my new friends could learn and grow. Good move by the Europeans to appoint a local Chinese Project Manager. That really helped and we came away with a good proposal for progress to suit all.

Once back at the apartment, I was desperate after all that time in deep technical and cultural water to sample the now clear water of the hotel pool visible from my balcony. It is not obvious how one ascends to the heights of the 6th floor. Foolishly I tried the stairs and came out into the back of the kitchens. Not pleasant.

Once up there via the correct lift, the pool was clean, about 15m long and did not smell strongly of chlorine. The Germans were there, had collared most of the chairs and tables, but were not forming pyramids and frightening the children!

Non-job was awarded to the "medical team". A "medical" was required before I could swim – not a check on my ability to negotiate the pool without drowning, or dive for a rubber brick on the bottom, but a check of my blood-pressure! That was it, medical cleared and I could slip into the cool water. The medical "team" consisted of one "nurse" to do the pumping and listening, one to write out the "Medical card" and a third to pass the drinks – for the other members of the team!

I talked to a Swedish girl who worked for Siemens, as did most of the Germans in this place. We Brits must be quiet as she had not known we were there. She was pleased to talk to someone who was not German.

Tonight was a late one again; we went to the Super Brand Mall again to re-visit our table from Wednesday. The Maitre d' was really pleased to see all six of us. We had to queue to get in, which left Marvin shuffling and itching to move on. Nonetheless, the meal turned out to be well up to standard. Brummie, Winston and I then had to suffer him in the expensive Paulaner bar.

We stayed there heckling the band, another bunch of Philippinos, whereas most other guests almost ignored them. Chito who plays keyboards is also a mean sax player. Singers Janet and Joy sat down with us during their breaks and we learned something about their life and loves as a touring group. One has a French boyfriend, the other a Danish guy who was there.

It is quite cultured and a great place to observe the rich Shanghainese as well as lots of other nationalities. The view across the river to the Bund is spectacular; I spent ages just staring. Drinks are Western prices, so I only had two in four hours!

Waiting for us in our rooms when we returned was what I assume is the response to the Customer Questionnaire which we were urged to complete. Maybe our whinging at HR has reached the ears of people here. Anyway, pretty soon there will only be a few of us here, as most of the long-termers are taking up apartments closer to work.

I record verbatim as follows the message left for us in our rooms:

'2005/7/1
Dear residents,

As the reason of the unload-working carried out at the shipside in the front of our Building A at midnight nearly. Meanwhile the noise of unload-working awakened you. We are apologising that such unhappy things happened and awfully sorry to disturbed you. Our general manager has commanded OGM to negotiate with relevant department to avoid same things happen again.

We are sorry for what happened and any inconvenienced caused. We sincerely hope you stay here pleasantly and appreciate that you give us understanding and supports.

Yours Sincerely
Front Office,
Shanghai Xing Tai Hotel Management Co, Ltd.'

Now that is a lot better than any Chinese I could ever write, but such service and a genuine desire to please! The people here are really helpful and friendly, they do try hard. We must sound like a bunch of whinging Europeans. We have massive rooms, air-con and two TVs. Just around the corner is what one could only describe as a shanty-town, the people probably driven from their old residences by a city planner desperate to build more high-rises on the piece of waste-ground now at the back of their shacks. Progress has its price.

Saturday, 2nd July 2005
My cleaning ladies are in at the moment; it is 10.30am and the dirty mop has been out on the living room balcony, on the handrail first then on the tiled

floor. It is odd to sit here and not jump up to help. I opened the door to them in just my £1 shorts, which are too small really to go out in, I only went as far as the pool yesterday wearing them.

The cleaners have gone now, all done in about 10 minutes. My washing has dried on the bedroom balcony in one hour. The heat of the sun, coupled with the exhaust from the air-con unit generates serious drying conditions.

As I am in the mood for translating, I present some more classics from Chinese to English, provided by one of the Assistant Engineers (he will be fully-fledged in just under four years as there is a recognised five-year period to train). He has collected these for me and they come from across the country. The Chinese love their slogans, which hang in prominent places, sometimes in English.

Laughable slogans in different provinces:
- To rob a police car is illegal! – HENAN
- One woman has the surgery not to procreate, the who family is glorified! – HENAN
- Set fire on the hill, set your life in prison! – GUIZHOU
- Lie on the railway, guilty even if not dead! – GUIZHOU
- Nation's rise and fall, everyone's duty; planned procreating, husbands' duty! – ZHEJIANG
- Bore fewer children, grow more trees – ZHEJIANG
- Foster fewer children, feed more pigs! – BEIJING
- No copper in cable, condemn the thieves! – SHANDONG
- People die but loan doesn't rot away, sons give the fathers' back! – ANHUI
- Sort the rubbish, start from me! – SHANGHAI
- Families break up rather than the nation for our planned procreating policy! – SHANDONG
- One over creating, the whole country get surgery! – HUNAN
- Tax dodging and evasion, punished to be nuns in eternity! – OUTER WALL OF A NUNNERY IN ZHEJIANG
- Beside national highways: "Quicken our reforming *(domestic policy)* and opening *(policy to abroad)* step" – BEIJING
- "Go along the Chinese Characteristic Communistic Road" – BEIJING

To these I will add one I saw on the underground:

- "A first under on, do riding with civility"

Today's entertainment was to be a mass Brit visit to a local football game. One of our work colleagues, Beckham, advised us on how to reach the stadium on the other side of the river and where to meet. He and others were quite concerned that we should be able to find our way there, but we did not understand the fuss, we negotiate our way around here all the time, often not knowing where we are precisely. In the two years he has worked here, he has been to one game (we had taken him to be a real hard-core fan) and only once into Xintiandi (where we planned to meet later). The difference is due in some part to money (although tickets start at RMB10/70p for the footie) but also that old British exploratory, inquisitive nature. We do not feel threatened by the unknown and go out to search for it. Is it just a cultural thing?

The football was amazing; the stadium a very modern, bright affair with loads of seating. As ever, it was the details which caught the eye, such as the refusal to allow us up the steps to enter the stadium with our 0.5L bottles of water, yet at the top of the steps, you could buy bottles, tennis rackets and baseball-bats!

Now I am no football fan, the last and only professional game I have ever seen was years ago when my cousin, Paul Mariner played for Plymouth Argyle against Blackpool, my old home town. I prefer rugby with its need for deeper thought as well as stronger muscle and also the order which generally prevails upon the field of play. Soccer always seems to be 11 overpaid captains playing in a pantomime, with ponsy hair-dos, a huge propensity for what my Mother used to call "dramatics" until they get their way and silly dances and mass cuddling when a goal is scored. Chinese soccer appears to be no different. At least two guys were stretchered off the pitch and then as soon as play resumed and was going their team's way, these previously mortally wounded combatants sprung up and jumped around to be allowed back on the pitch.

The game was played between a local Shanghai team, Shenhua, and a bunch of boyos from the north. The home fans were very much in the noisy majority – it must have been quite a journey to the ground with all the brass instruments and big bass drums being blasted out for all they were worth. The away fans, both of them, were way up in the cheap seats. We had treated our Chinese colleague to a really good seat with us. All he paid for was the hastily consumed water. We were something of a novelty, with a couple of professional cameramen photographing us and one ordinary fan clicking away. Many other fans and officials looked amused by us.

Just before the game commenced, the riot police (all four of them) took a tour of the pitch perimeter with their black combat gear and shields. Then came the camouflaged dog-handlers and their charges, the biggest and most numerous canine group I have yet seen here. Their circuit done, the regular police arose from their seats, donned black helmets and visors and made their way to the tunnel mouth in anticipation of the teams' entrances. Their colleagues from the other side did the same to form an impregnable line of defence should the massed fans leap over the barriers to assail the opposing side or lavish praise on their home heroes. One of the constables came leaping back to his seat, because he had forgotten that crucial ingredient of every impregnable police cordon; the blue and white striped plastic tape! Duly armed, he was able to complete his duty and unravel the barrier, job done.

The game started after we all stood for the raising of the national flag of China and a not-so-rousing chorus of the national anthem, an issue of some current debate in Hong Kong, especially.

It was obvious from the start that one team was physically bigger than the other and had better hair-stylists. They were also the best at dramatics. They ran away with the first half, popping the goals in for 2-0. We leapt up at the appropriate points as naturally we had decided before the start to support our boys from Shanghai. Someone said two of the players reside in our hotel block.

The final score was 6-1 and I began to get a bit bored by the middle of the second half, it may have been better were the teams more closely matched. As it was, we had a great time, there were no riots (the tape came out again at the end, but Constable Wang remembered his package this time) and Beckham had a great time, but almost every question we asked about the game or teams he had to consult with another! He also objected to our nickname for him, commenting that the real Beckham was a great player and had a beautiful wife, yet the same could not be said of him. Like with Americans, irony seems lost here!

Like any mass-exodus anywhere, we had a devil of a job hailing a taxi, but our determination paid off and we picked up two towards Xintiandi, (pronounced Shin-ti-an-dee, with a raise of inflexion on the "dee". This is most important, apparently. We will jump in a taxi, say Xintiandi, chie-chie (pronounced she-she, with a short "e", as in "end") and the driver will repeat what we have just said quizzically. We will say it again and he will repeat joyfully the destination, as if he now understands. You must learn Chinese, we are often told! It is so subtle; our tiny British minds cannot cope. Rumble suggests that they speak in "dolphin", so our ears cannot pick up the higher frequencies of speech!

Xintiandi is a collection of old French-inspired two and three-storey buildings of impressive architectural merit, containing the site of the first meeting room of the Chinese Communist Party. Now it is a playground for the rich of Shanghai and a tourist honey-pot. Amusingly for us, it has a lake on the outside edge of the property, beyond which one can see the looming neon sign for Price Waterhouse Coopers, the administrators for our old employers.

The buildings were bought in disrepair by a wealthy Hong Kong businessman and re-developed to feature shops and restaurants galore. Our favourite haunt is "Luna", where the obligatory Philippino band plays six nights a week, only resting on Sunday. We love their music, their abilities with several instruments each and the way they throw themselves into every performance with undiminished gusto. Naturally there are two beautiful female singers and we make lots of noise by way of appreciating their performance.

We have become quite friendly with them (which does not appear to be difficult with Philippinos) and always generate smiles when our eyes meet. As they play mainly Western cover songs, we know them all and shout out requests which are usually met.

Monday, 4th July 2005

Good day, lots of meetings with useful progress. Hero of the day was an old guy who was transporting a very old upright fridge/freezer on the pedal of his bike, leaning the assembly into himself and struggling down the road. He looked all-in on his legs. Later we passed a trike full of crates of beer being assisted along the road by another bloke on his moped pushing the laden trike with his foot!

"Welfare" today was a cup of ice-cream, with an insert cup containing the ice-cream and secreted below was a plastic "collectable" figure. Marvin commented that he was "getting a bit hacked off about having only half a cup of ice-cream" when he realised that the figures were being immediately and excitedly collected by the girls in the office. Someone knows their target market in Nestlé Shanghai.

Apparently the HR girls have a ball selecting the day's welfare from the Nestlé catalogue.

Took a walk down to Lujiazui, and followed some roads parallel to Pudong Da Dao, where life gets a little more interesting. There is a fair share of real Chinese city life on the main road, but it is noisy and busy. Some of the side roads are quieter, but no less colourful. There is a huge, mosque-like building (a spa) from which emanates bright searchlights, and outside of which one can peruse row upon row of china vases. Just what I need for the apartment, but not now! For some reason, there were a number of tents erected on the pavement around the display of pots. No-one was evidently in, so I could not see why they were there. I have seen tents stood inside buildings which are being renovated, obviously a place to put your head and keep the flies away.

Tuesday 5th July 2005
Enjoyed a walk into town, leaving behind a bedroom whose temperature was 32°C!! The sun just streams in during the day.

Could not wait to get back for a swim tonight; it is so pleasant on the sixth floor pool level, with the sun going down over the river, the twin towers of this place symmetrically either side and monster new buildings going up around. The builders must look down on us with resentment, or perhaps not – maybe these people do not feel that way, it would not surprise me.

Rolf and I strolled in the evening heat after a swim, to Lujiazui, where the Oriental Pearl Tower rises like a rocket from Pudong and went across the road into the Super Brand Mall, fourth floor to sample, oh, what shall it be tonight……….? How about Thai? Thai it was and just to make sure, the eatery was called "Thai, Thai". In case you missed it first time. RMB65/£4.65 secured one drink and six different dishes and we were stuffed, so much so that we had to stroll the 40 minutes back to the Pent-Ox again to let it settle. Even at 10.30pm one can still buy taps and other sundry sanitary ware from at least two shops along the way; have your hair cut and other services performed by young ladies in about five establishments; be served by six people in the pharmacy, (for what you caught whilst having your locks trimmed, I guess); and eat at any number of places from "this is horrible" to "How much?!"

Wednesday, 6th July 2005

We were amused by the "Traffic Assistant" we call "Littering Lil". She just blatantly screwed up some paper and threw it to the floor. That is how it works here. They would throw rubbish on the White House lawn, the belief being that there is always a blue-suited person sweeping up; that or no sense of personal responsibility, which is what we find at work. When challenged that due to an individual's inaction the project fails, that individual believes the blame lies with his or her leader. Another breakthrough is that bearing in mind these people's love of lists, if you wish to promote your own agenda, just take their list, add to or modify it, present it back and they love it! Things happen.

There is also a strong belief in the process and following it, without question. In this trait the Chinese are in with the Germans. The process is king, which in a manufacturing environment can be just what Herr Doktor ordered. We often said with BMW that if you asked them to mow the grass this way then that way to produce a pattern, he or she would set to and follow the instruction. A British person is much more likely to try to find any way around the job so he can slope off for a beer/cigarette/snooze. Even if he does the job, it will not be as instructed; he will have found his own way of completing the task. Either that or he will have sub-contracted it out whilst he slopes off for...........

Today's hero was a guy with not one, not two, but FOUR TVs strapped to the pillion seat of his moped. Absolutely stunning. Even beats the other contender, man on bike with four big (30kg?) gas cylinders.

Dinner was again at our favourite Chinese, the "Old Shanghai" in SBM, where having five or more makes it worthwhile ordering several dishes (about twelve, actually). They love to see us there and the one waiter always leaps over to serve us, with a delightful, round-face. We take the mickey; no doubt they do too, so everyone is happy. This is service with so many smiles.

In the Paulaner later, we roared our approval for the band at the appropriate points and sang along as we drank. It must be quite hard to concentrate as a performer in China, because those bodies on the dance floor had simply *no* sense of rhythm. There were a couple of women clapping along and they just could not keep time! So off-putting. The "lone-groover rubber-band-man" (lone flexible dancer) was not there this time; his place was taken by another elderly man who moved like a stiff boxer. However, the sax-player in the band, Chito came over to us and blew his best; he is really very talented. We were again last to leave the establishment, but not before disputing the bill, whereby they tried to charge us for 3 beers we most definitely had not consumed.

Fashion victim was provided by a girl at work, who sported the most awful, Nora Batty style, thick yellow tights. It is over 30°C and she had tights on. Her skinny legs looked like a chicken's.

Thursday, 7th July 2005
Today's hero was a guy I saw hanging from a harness over the edge of a building at 7.00pm, screwing a neon sign framework to the side of a building. He was drilling and plugging the wall whilst stood on the ladder he had just installed. Trust your own workmanship time.

Today's transportation accident waiting to happen was a tie between Wang, Fang and Zhong who were racing at speed down Pudong Da Dao on their scooters with noisy pipes – not a stitch of protective clothing nor a whiff of fibreglass to cover their bodies and heads – and the Wang family: Dad and three kids all on one scooter, with no helmets at all.

Every day a close shave is witnessed from the bus or taxi, eliciting gasps from the occupants. There is a definite belief in either divine intervention or simply that if one does not look at the approaching heavy vehicle, it will not hit one, or perhaps these people have 20/20 peripheral vision – they certainly do not look much to left or right. Side windows are often blacked-out anyway.

I took another swim tonight and placed an entry for the non-job of the day award. There were seven pool attendants and little me. Their weather has gone all grey, so the Germans won't come out, only crazy Brits who are used to it.

At Lujiazui I caught the cool underground train to emerge at Hong Kong Plaza to catch the Cybermart before it closed. This is a monster mall, featuring hundreds of computer, component and camera shops on several floors. It is not somewhere you can take in on a first visit. I'm an old lag now, so I walked up to the first likely looking stand and haggled for a headset and mike so I can use the internet VOIP (Voice over Internet Protocol) telephony facility to call home cheaply. I also scored an MP3 player really cheaply. How long before they are old hat? (Photo p.X).

Next stop was the Xiangyang fashion market for visit number two. It was closing and I managed to haggle hard and secure a "North Face" jacket for a friend. (Photo p.X).

I gave an apple and a couple of RMB to a semi-naked old beggar man lying prone on the Huahai Lu. I probably have more money in my back pocket than he will see in a year, yet there he is on one of the most affluent roads in town.

Walking back to the apartment, the number of people sleeping on this most noisy of roads is increasing daily. Then I saw a sight which made me very sad – dog mess on the pavement. Oh, dear, these people are being encouraged to view dogs as pets, not food and more appear daily. But as with every other piece of litter, the Chinese will just leave it where it falls. Shanghai used to be great to walk around because you did not see dogs, therefore no mess. I predict a growing public health problem.

Friday, 8th July 2005

The news back home was all about the London bombings. It all seems so far away, yet close at hand.

Winston, Let and Sonnie passed their driving tests yesterday. They never once sat in a car, but went from place to place and desk to desk, filling in forms and paying money. It appears that holding a UK licence for over 3 years exempts one from a practical driving test as our driving abilities are held in such high regard. Local people practise and it appears are tested off the highway, driving around cones in underground parking areas. This possibly explains the way they drive around pedestrians and other objects.

The British contingent first had to report to a police station local to our apartments. When they and their guide from HR turned up, it was the wrong place; the Pent-Ox is under another station's jurisdiction. More forms. The test itself was undertaken way south of the city and began with more form filling, money changing hands and a list of questions and answers to read, upon which they would be tested later in the day. All of it would have been unintelligible without a local guide and there was a lot of "chopping" or stamping of forms with a flourish. All in all they saw about ten people.

A hearing test was conducted and then a multiple-choice test, where most of the questions featured the usual "silly" answer and a couple of other possibilities. Winston scored 100%, not bad for a bloke from the Maypole area of Birmingham, where men are men and women are wise to avoid them.

A fine sight today was the arrival of three colleagues from the UK, almost doubling the head-count of experienced UK engineers in our part of the project. Welcome to Flower, Turk and Native.

Today's fashion victims were a husband and wife team with flip-flops and pyjamas on. He had the decency to wear his Y-fronts. Modesty prevented me from checking on her undergarments.

Saturday, 9th July 2005
Conundrum for the day – how can one explain the difference between Japan and its close neighbour, China? Japan achieved economic greatness by taking on European and American quality philosophies and really taking them to a fine art through the works of Quality "Gurus" like Juran, Crosby, Deming, etc. This involved efficiency; the use of the minimum time and resources to perform an operation, minimising waste and all the other good techniques. China has achieved its economic aims with massive inefficiencies, hence my many observations on "Non-job of the day". I know that in many cases the non-jobbers are paid peanuts, but they are still themselves consumers and part of the chain.

We even hear of Korean manufacturers re-locating production to China as it is so cheap, yet everywhere there are inefficiencies.

When will it all end? China is in many ways emulating the rise of Japan, so when will the Chinese consumer start to emulate their Western counterpart, wanting more of everything and driving prices up?

When will the first car plant open up in Bolivia or Madagascar? BMW already builds cars in Vietnam and Triumph motorcycles have a plant in Thailand, so the Eastern economy grows.

I read today in the excellent local English-language "Shanghai Daily" of old traditional houses in the Jinan area, where I have often wandered, having their sewage and sanitary facilities renovated by the City, as these dwellings, designed for one family, (with bathrooms measuring one metre square, according to the paper), are now supporting five families!

House prices are rocketing here and more are being built all the time. Someone is making serious money.

This morning I was awakened by fireworks at 7.45am. Why? Possibly because we complained about the noise! Had breakfast with Donk and admired the non-jobber in the Puxi Café – her job was to stand by the door and make sure all diners signed the book. That's it.

The cleaner did her thing again. Why change a bed I haven't slept in? She was quiet and unaccompanied this time, but it seemed to take her as long as it did last time when she had a mate doing the job as well. That word efficiency again. Or am I just a boring engineering type?

Looking back on the week at work, I cannot write much as that is commercially sensitive and best left in the office. However, quite satisfying, I made some progress, Brummie felt he had made a difference too and Gary always galvanises them into action, he is born for this. Winston is well integrated into his team and Rolf and Donk, being alone in their specialisms are essential to the project's success. There are others too and more arrived Friday. Our hosts are picking it up, but how they are organised is still a mystery.

It is a pleasure to work with some of the local "grey-heads" (who still have more dark hair than I!) who have been involved in manufacture before. They ask good questions, challenge anything one is insufficiently specific about and generally make life interesting. With the language barrier it is even harder. One may not understand the question though and because one is operating from a position of knowledge and experience, assumptions are made about certain things which we have so far blindly accepted. One cannot do that here, the best way is to imagine explaining it to a teenager at home who has no idea of the product. Keep it simple.

Our product has many features which we accept because we know it works, but in a basic engineering sense they are really unusual and still unique, so these generate many questions.

Conversely, some of the younger "engineering assistants" require even more tutoring as their base engineering experience is not there and they have not seen test-beds, not driven a car nor played about at home with basic tools, DIY or anything practical, as far as we can tell.

I enjoyed lunch with Winston and Brummie, it is always a laugh with the waitresses, making a mess of their language; hopefully they will remember us as friendly English gentlemen. We fooled around Carrefour supermarket looking for odds and sods, most of which is stocked by this French shopping outpost in China. I picked up a litre of French gin for £3 and Blue Bols for £5!! Hope I can get it home.

We decided to eat Western tonight and struck out for the "Blarney Stone", which is naturally an Irish bar with Guinness on tap and I could not resist my favourite – bangers and mash. Three bonus items appeared to complement this height of Western cuisine: HP sauce, baked beans and gravy with onions! Tuck in, chaps. The others had similarly stodgy fare. So filling was it that they had trouble seeing off their beers before we left for "Luna", our favourite night spot.

We were not to be disappointed, as the band were mostly sober this time, despite the ever-present "Sonnie" (merchant banker type) and the endless supply of his Black Label Johnnie Walker on free vend. They played a new selection of songs, until I suggested a choice of eight or so tunes and Winston had a soppy one played for his 20th Wedding Anniversary to Karen back home. Marissa does a real good Tina Turner (dances better than the lady herself) and "Simply the best" was belted out. Later on Madeleine sang "Alone" by Heart for me and mine. As we shout loudest, we often get our way.

As usual, a great night, although some faded crooner with long, grey hair in a pony tail and a leather Stetson popped up on stage with his mouth-organ and sent both Winston and Brummie to the gents in disgust. They gave him a hard time; he may have been famous once and we just don't know it. So ended another "stay to the end night" and 3.00am tumble into bed.

Sunday, 10th July 2005

I started off into town to sort out my head-set, so I could hook back up to the "Skype" VOIP service. Neither Winston nor I could squeeze any sound out of the headphones, nor use the microphone, so off I went back to the Cybermart where I had bought the things. Naturally a young lady pops up as the English speaker and general PC whizz. It took her some time, but she fixed it. I told her Chinese girls are smarter than English blokes, and she wouldn't have it, but she proved her worth. On my walk down to the underground I saw more arc welding on the pavement with no screens, no mask and an end result of blow-holes, rust and uneven lumps.

Another shop on the way is the local branch of what we knew in the Midlands as "Deritend re-winds". Here the local electric motor armature re-winding service is open all hours. You never know when you re going to need a re-wind. An amusing observation by DIY is the large number of holes drilled into the pavement outside the shop. Imagine what glazed paving tiles did to the drill-bit – why did they not do what we would do and put some wood underneath?

The fashion statement disaster has to be the funny little socks the women wear. They are made out of normal tights material, but unlike "Knee-highs" or "Pop-socks" which are worn with trousers, so the top is hidden, these are ankle-high and look awful. Why do they wear them with often pretty sandals? Leave them off, girls! Almost as bad as men wearing dark socks and sandals – a fashion nightmare.

In the Mawdesley we watched the British Grand Prix. Jensen "I'll be on the podium" Button cruises home in 5th. Still, it was good food and good company.

Monday, 11th July 2005

Today's hero was a guy with *twelve*, yes, twelve bottles of water on his scooter. We reckon in old money, that is about 600lbs. A serious load and his rear tyre didn't even seem to be flattened out!

Top amusing comment of the day was the discussion we had on contraceptives – don't know how it started, but one experienced traveller remarked that many hotel rooms he had used in China supplied sheaths in the mini-bar. He reckoned them to be fairly unreliable, of dubious quality and probably Chinese rip-offs. Hoots of laughter. OK, so you had to be there.

This brings me around to today's conundrum. I read two different local news publications and both featured stories on sex and the young. One bemoaned the lack of quality sex education in schools and observed that most girls and boys became sexually aware around the age of 15, but did not engage in any serious activity until 25. I had to read it twice, once myself and then to Brummie to believe it.

I then read in the other source that Beijing had a new problem, whereby students who had been renting off-campus apartments had been ordered back by national decree to university dormitory accommodation to control their sexual forays, in the name of "spiritual cleansing". Naturally market forces combined to produce a supply of rooms called "Rizufang", available by the hour (sometimes in family residences), to satisfy rising demand for somewhere to discuss politics, amongst other hot subjects! A national survey of students reported 42% had experienced sex without contraceptives, according to Beijing Today.

How does one have two reports so far apart, in two publications I look to for accuracy?

Subject change – called my Dad to wish him Happy Birthday. I wish he could just sit on my balcony and watch the boats go by, he'd love it.

On the subject of family, I am looking forward to returning home and the simple pleasure of driving to Stratford-upon-Avon with my wife and just listening to her talk.

Tuesday, 12th July 2005

The shanty-town near to the hotel had woken up this morning as we passed by and glimpses of the insides of the makeshift huts were gained – they are not more than garden shed size and feature a rough sheet of ply or other wood upon which the residents sleep. "Washing" on the line looks as if it were dunked in river water, which is probably what happened.

Bicycle repair man on the corner was busy as usual with a seated, waiting customer. We were imagining the conversation out loud "…..best price…." "….look at this lovely inner-tube, all black and rubbery……… to you only RMB10…" The guys looked up, saw a bus-load of foreigners grinning back and returned the smile with a wave. Back home the same exchange between a couple of street-workers and rich folk in a bus would probably have generated all manner of ugly gestures and a different atmosphere altogether.

I chose to eat lunch in the company canteen and was glad I did so, as apart from being luke warm, the tastes and textures were good. Sitting opposite one of the female interpreters was also rather pleasant. The alternative lunch for us Brits was the walk around the corner to the hotel restaurant, but as this had been spaghetti for days, I decided to avoid it. This turned out to be a good plan as they were served up yet more Italian stringy pasta. Amusingly, we had been sent the lunch-time menu by HR, (on the ball as usual), which promised a fair variety of dishes. Reality and HR's world were as distant as ever; they were unaware of the domination by spaghetti of the menu. We told our contact three times before she repeated that "It was spaghetti again?!" and finally accepted the point. There are so many Monty Python-like moments in any one day. (Photo p.V).

The evening's entertainment was begun early on the shuttle bus when our driver decided to take on a far larger coach, bearing down at some speed. He just brazenly pulled across its path, eliciting real gasps from the passengers. No horns were sounded in anger, no abusive gestures or doubting of parentage. Amazing and so close.

The evening proper was to be a "Farewell" do for one of the most competent people we have met here. So we organised a meal for twenty of us and met at the "Blue Frog" for a few bevvies before descending to the Turkish restaurant, also in the same "Green City" complex designed to make Americans feel at home. Some had eaten in this grand establishment before and relayed lurid tales of the waif-like belly dancer. How can you belly-dance with no midriff?

It was half an hour before our drinks arrived – the dancer had been out twice and failed to convince any customers to join her gyrations. We had some cold starters which arrived without the bread necessary to accompany them. A further hour passed and we still had not received our main course. The second round of drinks ordered at the same time as the first finally landed, took twenty minutes to appear and then only one came for Brummie, who thought he had best order again for us quickly to prevent mass dehydration.

We opted to leave and Turk took the manager and chef aside to explain a few home truths about service and managing staff. We shuffled off to the Mawdesley, where we knew a welcome always awaited and food is never a problem. And so it came to pass, with the usual surfeit of terracotta waitresses and new boy waiter who stood there and grinned a lot.

Wednesday, 13th July 2005

Another classic drive into work with our boyo at the wheel constantly on his horn – he likes driving the big Toyota Coaster bus as it has a bigger horn than the smaller Mercedes. Why he thinks he needs to sound it so many times, I don't know. He presses it even when it is obvious that we cannot make progress. Perhaps he feels he just has to get his payload of ghost-faces to work on time. We would rather him have a more peaceful journey.

Another dip in the pool – I wonder if my regular swims account for the gut-rot I have experienced recently. As usual for a rainy day, the pool was devoid of sun-bathing Germans occupying one end of the roof-top area and all the attendants were huddled under shelter of the changing rooms. One was also laid out on the bed which lurks at the head of the stairwell. So again it was non-job time with six of them and one of me. A pleasant swim was endured by all.

Mid-week thoughts turn to a late night and so it turned out to be. Again we sloped off into the Super Brand Mall where we are inexorably drawn towards our favourite restaurant, which means a good tip for the staff and a great welcome for us.

Following this again it was on to the Paulaner bar, where again we are regulars and welcomed. Big smiles appear on the faces of everyone from the lavatory-cleaner (because we notice him and say "Nee-hao"), up to the manager, including naturally, the band – Janet, Joy, Chito and the Osmonds guitarist. We always make a noise for them, heckle loudly and generally appreciate their attempts to cover Western songs.

Tonight, the girls were very sexy and we were almost overcome, persuading Janet to text Winston that they were performing naked as it was so warm. He was most certainly overcome.

Watching the locals at play is always amusing – how can three women in one party sat next to each other all clap out of time with each other and the music? It must be so off-putting trying to sing whilst your audience is so disconnected. There was the usual "lone groover" local male dancer who sincerely believed himself to be an Oriental character from "Grease". He was truly amazing, a rubber band man with some top moves designed to impress the ladies.

There was quite a hive of activity from the cleaning staff to mop up their nice floor following a colourful display of vomiting by a couple of locals. Like real troopers, Janet and the team had kept singing, but pinching their noses in real discomfort, admitted later on that it was hard to look and sound sexy with that smell wafting across, propelled by the air-con!

Later on, when the place had been restored to Teutonic order (it is meant to be a Bavarian Hofbrauhaus!) the other cleaner was doing her normal rounds with the ubiquitous mop and she gave the area in front of the stage (i.e. the dance-floor) a good slap with the wet rag, nearly sending the Lone Groover into a spin and then wiped over the stage as Chito the sax-player was trying to give "Danny Boy" a good tooting on his instrument! The guy had to step back and the girls looked at the cleaner in disbelief, shaking their heads! When questioned later, she believed some projectile vomit had made it to the stage and so it *had* to be mopped.

We left when they finally turned on the lights at about 1.30am. A great night of entertainment. Why can the locals just not feel the beat? Why is it so hard to step in time with the music?

Fashion statement was the local with smart white shirt, white knee-length trousers, but disaster! He was sporting dark blue socks pulled up to his knees and black town-shoes!

No pose. No points.

Thursday, 14th July 2005

After work we were treated to a meal by our Departmental Head, who is a really genteel fellow and a knowledgeable chap to boot. He is also a Party Member. He used to run an engine research facility here in Shanghai, which is now being used by our employer and appears to be waking from a long slumber.

Several notable things happened at the meal, which was held in one of fifty rooms in the restaurant at the base of the building where we used to live, Diamond Court. We discovered that there are no tenses in Chinese, which explains why (after all this time) phrases like "Will you do this" or "Have you done the other" are met with quizzical looks. How does China function?

We also asked about names; what do we call the leader? What does his wife call him? (At this point Marvin stupidly called out something derogatory. Why does he have to sound like a prat so often? He has a good brain and is an excellent engineer; he also knows how it should be done. He just does not always engage brain before jaw).

It turns out that there are several ways of addressing people at work, depending upon their experience. Almost Germanic, that notion. His wife calls him by his family or a "pet" name, rarely his given name.

Just like the HSBC advert about being aware of local customs, we kept eating, so the food kept coming! Just when you thought it was safe to say "War hung bow-luh" (my phonetic way of writing the words for "I'm very full"), the dumplings came out! We managed to struggle out of there and repair to the Mawdsley for a swift half. Again, though, Chinese food does not lie as heavily as Western fare.

Friday, 15th July 2005

This was an odd day to start with, as we were prevented from coming to work due to a power cut in the JinQuiao area where we normally toil. So today was "an early Saturday", which would be followed by a normal Saturday and then we would attend work on Sunday.

I struck out for town to shop for "orders" taken from home and walked the three miles or so to the spitting ferry, paid my half a Yuan (about 3p) and enjoyed another smoky crossing of the Huangpu river. Shanghai would really be so much better with emissions controls on the trucks, buses and the ferry. Even the locals walked away from the stern as a cloud of black smoke curled up from the tail-pipes (if that is what you call them on a boat). I just reached for my ever-present towel as a mask. (Photo p.XII).

The girls on the stand in the YuYuan tourist shopping centre were really amused when I walked up, pulled the right money out of my wallet and proceeded to expertly select 10 ladies' garments of differing colours for my girls.

I followed this purchase with a Mao Tse Tung T-shirt, always a good conversation starter in Shanghai, as many who discuss his life with me believe him to have been a great man!!

I hid for a while in a typical Shanghai park. It always amazes me how a few sticks of bamboo and some grass can shield a volume of noise.

Native joined us for the usual meal and Paulaner visit, and in his excitement at meeting the girls, swept his beer dregs over Brummie's lap.

He left before us later on and didn't leave an RMB for his drinks! Some mate you are! We do tend to live out of each other's pockets here.

Saturday, 16th July 2005

A quiet day, with a late start due to a late night and then I found the local CD/DVD shop. What a great place! Double CDs for RMB16 and the usual

RMB7 DVDs. I might as well have a music library here for the amount of time I am going to be in Shanghai. As is so often the case, a ledger is made by hand of purchases made; bar-code scanning is a little out of the question here.

The whole experience cost me under RMB200 (£14), for six DVDs and six CDs.

I met Brummie on his way back from the same place, and he had a decent catch of DVDs. We agreed to a night in by the TV and opted to watch "The Exorcist" new version with extra footage. What a classic film; shaking bed (moved by a fork-lift truck behind the wall) and green pea soup for the vomiting bits. We just sat there in his room and chilled. Went to bed warily, but separately!

Sunday, 17th July 2005

We trundled out to work in a very quiet JinQiao economic area. Power shortages are a real problem here; the country just cannot keep up with the demand for energy. More factories and more houses are being built every day across the country. (Photo p.XXVII)

Many Chinese attend work on Sunday anyway, so that would not be out of the norm for them. You see them in the offices and shops, spread-eagled asleep on desks in the hot temperatures, but there anyway.

Today's hero is a tie – either the drivers of the non-air-con buses or the pilots of the FAW (First Auto Works) tipper trucks. The latter are slow, very noisy and belch black smoke from not just the exhaust. You can hear the drivers fighting with recalcitrant gearboxes and heaving on huge steering wheels with no power assistance. The former are not much better, except that the driver has some more company on the journey. Many of these buses are packed with commuters like sardines in the glaring sun.

As Winston was back amongst us we fell into the Super Brand Mall trip and attempted to veer from our normal restaurant, but it was no good, the food is tasty and the service excellent. And there is only one place one can go after that, yes, the Paulaner bar. Sunday is obviously a quieter night and the band is asked to play more schmoozy stuff during happy hour(s). The girls were dressed in very fetching dresses and were as usual very pleased to see us. The waitress with whom we had endured a battle over charging us for beer we did not consume was pressed into handing on a request to Janet from Scooter. He wrote "Do it naked!" on a serviette, which caused much hilarity on stage.

Monday, 18th July 2005

There are many noises around this building, most of which are unwelcome and some even unnecessary, but occasionally the sound of a bird will rise above all the other sounds. Could have been a thrush or similar, but what do I know? I repeat my observation that there are so very few seagulls here – back home a river would be full of the things, following vessels and leaving mess everywhere.

There is a patch of waste ground just down the road from the Pent-Ox, and I am sure that tonight I saw bats swooping and hovering, looking for food. I have also seen many butterflies along the same stretch, the only other place being outside the East-West café.

Conundrums aplenty here – if you are waiting for a chance to cross the road, stood at the ferry terminal gates or even in line at the supermarket, there will be some local squeezing past, to gain very little advantage. The whole driving experience is all about positioning your bonnet ahead of the next one. Then there is the opposite behaviour on the escalators on the underground. Whereas in London it is stand to one side (right?) and a stream of desperate lemmings filter past; not here, people just stand at random on the stairs and wait for the ride to finish.

Having been given shopping requests from home, I enjoyed the usual swim then tripped off into town to catch the Cybermart before closure and the same at the Gift Market. More walking away from stands with sellers hanging on my arms, but I did negotiate some good prices! All theatre and all good fun. One does see some dreadful sights on the market periphery; beggars and people with distorted or no limbs. Very sad. To give or not to give. I often do. Right or wrong, I don't know, but I do have more than they can ever dream of.

Tuesday, 19th July 2005

Woke up this morning (cue for a blues song..........) and all I could hear was the birds! What a treat! No mechanical noises from the docks, just natural song. A very pleasant change.

Always amusing is a translation from Chinese, so I record verbatim a memo about the lunch arrangements.......

Hi, everyone

I am so sorry for your lunch. I've called the manager of the restaurant about the lunch. After enquiry, it is said that the chef is newcome and has few experience of cooking western food. Now they fired the chef and have a better one. They feel guilty for it, however, I must take partial responsibility for unqualified coordination among you, restaurant and me. From tomorrow on, they will strictly stand by the menu, hoping you can give them another chance.

I will enhance communication with people from restaurant. For any further suggestion, pls let me know. Any request should be directed to me.

The very helpful lady in HR (Human Remains) was true to her word and lunch had indeed reverted to plan today, complete with a battered piece of "chicken" inside a greasy bun, chips, pickled gherkin, tomato and watery mushroom soup!

An interesting phenomenon amongst the female populace is a tendency to cover their faces with their hands when giggling. This even extends to the cleaning lady who doubles as a card-swiping monitor (non-job of the day?) when we take lunch in the company canteen.

Most of her compatriots tend to ignore her, even when she dishes out the welcome "welfare" ice-cream on hot days. Every time I speak to her, she lights up with a smile.

We had observed ourselves that it was a bit odd men visiting each others' rooms; a bit of a girlie thing to do, but heck, why not, we are all living out here long-term, we might as well do some "neighbouring". So we took our beer (and gin in my case), to Brummie's room along with some of Mr Cadbury's best and watched several episodes of the classic series "The Office". Yes, we can recognise colleagues past and present.

Although we still press for a move back to JinQiao, the view from Brummie's balcony is quite simply stunning; a long-shot of the majestic Jinmao Tower and the peak of the Pearl Tower beyond some rapidly soaring new buildings. The down-town financial district is there, with the Marine Tower and Bank of China visible on a clear night. This is the sort of view favoured by American movie directors to show someone of wealth living above the plebs. Even the constantly busy river is an endless source of interest if that is what turns you on.

Something huge is passing by now, I can hear it through the open patio door. I do not have to rise out of my chair to see the vessels gliding by. My father would love it – "Very romantic; all those ships lit up at night – where are they all going to and from where?"

Wednesday, 20th July 2005

Two days before I see my loved ones again – I cannot wait to bury my head in the curls of my wife's hair and give all the kids a huge hug. Last time I returned home I remember the tears as I visited Sarah at work. Other shoppers and staff were crying at the sight of an emotional home-coming. At least I am not flying home to redundancy this time.

A couple of amusing coincidences here, one is that the dialling code for Shanghai is 021, which used to be the code for Birmingham and the Shanghai Internal Combustion Engine Research Institute (SICERI) is still open for business, whereas the British version of a similar acronym (BICERI) is gone forever. Ironic progress.

From my room I have just noticed that I can see the massive Yangpu Bridge, whose deck must be about 80 metres high and is supported on two wishbone-shaped uprights, I would estimate to tower another 80 metres further on into the sky. This is a real statement to the world that Shanghai is here. There are three other principal bridges in the area, all of which are quite amazing.

Lunch today was again amusing; the spaghetti was certainly absent, but it was "Club sandwiches", which had many of the same ingredients as the previous day's burgers. Again it was bread, tomatoes and pickled gherkins with fries, the chicken burger being replaced by fried egg and Spam. The bread was regular sliced stuff, which I can't really eat anyway. The soup was the same, but elements of fish were lurking in the murky depths of the bowl. Quite why we were served four bowls of ketchup, I do not know. The staff seem to over-correct to criticism. We had asked for more drinks and now the cups runneth over and the ketchup too.

Pictographs and characters

The earliest writings in Chinese, which can be traced back 3500 years, were pictures carved on oracle bones. They are known as pictographs. Over the years they developed into characters which are formed of brush or pen strokes.

Altogether, there are about 50,000 characters. In the 1950s and 60s, China went through the language reform movement and 2000 characters were simplified. These are known as 'simplified characters' as opposed to 'complex characters' (also known as 'traditional form'). All the characters introduced here are simplified characters. You need around 2000 characters to be able to read and write.

Chapter 2

A RIVER CRUISE AND WE BUY

CHINESE BICYCLES

Tuesday, 23rd August 2005

"The Body" and I flew back to Shanghai on SAS SA997 which was punctual and the cases took no time to tumble off the baggage claim. Before we made it to the carousel I was really pleased to note we were back in China. There were three give-aways:

A mop-lady carrying the dirty tool of her trade; a device used for moving dirt from one place and spreading it over others.

A bunch of guys in the car park bouncing a car out of the way following a typically Chinese piece of precision parking.

Slender bottoms and legs – on the ladies – before any of you get the wrong idea about me!

The Body and I were met by a likeable company driver and driven efficiently to drop him off at Diamond Court (Jealous? Me? Just because that was the original place in which we stayed and almost anything after is a come-down, unless it is 4 or 5 stars). I continued on to the Pent-Ox (Pent-Ox Metropolis Hotel on Pudong Da Dao or Pudong Avenue) and amazingly I was expected. I had asked for a room above floor 22 and side A or B. I scored with 25E – nearly there. It was a good room having said that, but I wanted a lounge view of the downtown financial district as Brummie had enjoyed. I could have swapped rooms I supposed, as he was leaving the next day, but I just wanted to settle in and freshen up. At least I have no view of the cement yard, just a panoramic one of the main road. Will it be noisier? Time would tell. Rolf, who is still here a few floors above my old room in 25H, has moved into his spare room in an attempt to shut out the worst of the docklands cacophony of trucks, alarms and ship's horns.

Once freshened up and smelling vaguely human again, I decide to relax on the couch and "chill". Exhaustion and jet-lag took over and knocked me out for an hour or so. Feeling not much better I determined to slide in to work and say "hello", catch up with Brummie before he leaves for the UK and find out where the project is along the time-line of progress. I try not to say anything about the project here as it is commercially none of your business and may well bore some of you. Enough said, I will continue to pick out cultural issues which are not project or company-specific and are reported by others working with the Chinese.

After a month of not being there, little had changed. Frustration had set in and the project had a "stalled" feel to it. That is what politics, delving into too much detail and indecision does for you. The lawyers had moved in back home and that meant everything slowed right down. "My people will talk to your people". Give me a break, as they say. What could be simpler but sorting out the mess of MG Rover??!! As a car salesman once said to me, "Only Rover could cock up its own demise". And so a waiting game began. We carried on doing what we had to do, watching the slow-motion debacle unfold back at Longbridge.

Wednesday, 24th August 2005

More insights into the Chinese psyche appear at work ; full of contradictions, but some definitive impressions come through from time to time. Their feeling of being independent of time (very few people, men in particular, wear watches) shows through in many of the work activities. They seem to wait until it is too late to act. Forward planning is almost non-existent – this is shown in their driving quite starkly.

What a taxi ride home tonight?! Mario Andretti Wang was determined to make me, as front seat jockey, soil my pants. He was also a white line sitter, straddling two lanes until the one with the least traffic opened up. We had flashing headlights behind us and horns blaring as we cut people up left, right and centre. He would "accelerate" into impossible gaps without changing down, the engine complaining and "pinking" as the cheap fuel gasped through a worn intake system. He "block-changed" up from 1st to 3rd, as 2nd must have been worn out long ago.

We made it home in record time, but all three of us could not wait to be out of that wreck of a car. He did not wear a seat-belt either. Quite a change from the driver the night before who showed consummate skill and did plan his route beyond the car in front, although the girl listening to her MP3 player on her bicycle nearly had us as she just pulled across our speeding vehicle on one of the fastest sections of road. What did girls do before the advent of small electronic devices like mobiles and music players?

Another interesting comment from one of the locals followed his questioning of me over my recent holidays. He listened to my account, asked some more questions about my accommodation and declared that "I am very jealous of your life-style!" I'll bet he is. We are under no illusion that we operate on a totally different plane to those with whom we work.

Thursday, 25th August 2005
Fantastic! For once it was a case of right place, right time. After another day learning cultural differences, but not necessarily how to bridge them, we were in a very clean taxi when Lucky announced that tonight there was a free river cruise staged by the hotel. We leapt up to the reception desk and slapped our monikers on the list. A quick shower and down for dinner with Rolf, having paused in his room on my floor to admire his pen-and-wash Chinese style water colours. He is a talented guy. "Can you guess what it is, yet?" Superb artistry.

We tried hard to spend a lot in the restaurant, but only managed RMB48 for five dishes and a litre of orange juice with green tea! It was fabulous food, on the ground floor of the Pent-Ox. We were regarded with some amazement or interest by the waiting staff, being rare Western visitors to an under-used facility. It was excellent food and we stuffed ourselves for RMB48/£3!

We strolled through the "Robby" and into the coaches. Naturally ours sounded very sick just ticking over, or idling I should say, as ticking brings to mind the regularity of a clock – not so on this charabanc. The bus was filled as 65 were booked on the trip and it seemed most of the "tourists" were staff.

Had this been a British works outing, alcohol would have been mandatory. Not so with these people. They can hang loose and enjoy themselves without any muscle relaxant.

This was my first opportunity to meet Lucky's girlfriend who gave him his name in this narrative, as she is neither old, nor ugly, nor a bad cook.

The cruise boat was moored near the "spitting ferry" (so-called because of the habit in which most male travellers indulge). It was clean and bright and there was a typically pointless rush for the doors to gain access to the upper open deck. On the tables in the lower accommodation were bowls of fruit and a bar was on hand. Cans of "Coke" were fetched on board and passed around.

There was a wandering Chinese troubadour on the boat, who was picking out couples and serenading them. As this was not too fruitful, he tried to appeal to some of the individuals amongst the young people who formed the majority of the cruisers. One of the girls from Reception, Yuki, warned us that it was to be his pleasure to play something for us later. I had audio visions of a Chinese version of the "Birdie Song" or something equally dreadful. What did he pick to dedicate to our wives? Edelweiss. In Chinese, of course. It does not gain any appeal for me in this language, as it has very little in German, being my least favourite film. My dear Mother took me and I ruined it totally for her, as I was sub-9, I think, when it came out. I kept asking to go to the toilet or cringing noisily in my seat. It took me thirty years or more to "enjoy" a musical (excepting, of course, The Blues Brothers, 1 & 2) when Sharon coerced me to go to London for "Whistle down the Wind".

As he was strumming his way through an awful rendition of an awful song, I turned to Rolf and told him I was feeling all choked up and that I had always fancied him and........! As usual, humour was my only route out of embarrassment. I showed my family photo to Yuki, who (as is the usual reaction for single-child policy Chinese) said "San? Three?". "Yes, three, san", I replied.

At this point we were intrigued to be passing a building we can see from the Pent-Ox opposite, which is a long, low building in a sort of Venetian style around the windows, but has castellations along the roof-line. "It is a water-factory" we were informed. "From here?" said I, pointing down at the dirty water below. "No, no!" said Yuki. That was a relief.

A feature of any Chinese outing, as anyone who has visited Stratford-upon-Avon or London, or any UK tourist hot-spot will know, is the Photo Ritual. Everybody in the party has to be captured on film or disc, in several combinations. We found ourselves wrapped up in this. The crew-man, who had been smiling wandering around passing out fruit, had earlier given me a banana, which I had saved, being full after dinner. This I had stashed in the folds of my jacket, tied by the arms around my waist, it looking very threateningly like a.......... Banana.

Fruity-man then indulged in another favourite Chinese pastime. Touching other men. This they do regularly, and with no pretensions of homosexuality, which is OK if you are, but unusual in everyday conservative British society. He ran his left arm around my back and pulled me to him, then his right did a sort of patting dance around my right side and around the front until he grabbed my, my,…….. banana! Well, I didn't know where to put my yellow skin. He then ushered Rolf and I into a photo-call with the girls. With much relief I stood by them, babbling nervously. So gentle and funny, these folk.

The cruise was from the mooring to the western bridge of Nanpu, to the Yangpu further down river, about 6km between the two, having started about 1km short of the former. The river is a busy place in the day and even at night vessels are rolling in from the East China Sea and out there from all points inland along the Huangpu. We passed the floating repair dock with a ship inside and men still busy. A spooky, burnt-out passenger ship was moored to the Pudong side, awaiting attention. Other pleasure boats and the regular ferries passed by and of course, the highlight of the tour was a grand river-view of the old Pent-Ox. We stood to attention for a second and tried to see the sign which said "Please sound your very loudest ship's horn, as there are Brits trying to sleep in here", which we were convinced had been erected following our earlier complaints!

Altogether it was a fine evening, which ended with a return to the Pent-Ox, three hours after we had left and all free. My Dad would have loved it, apart from the staggeringly over-powering sewerage smell by the Nanpu Bridge, right by some working boats all moored up for the night. Someone must have had a rough noodle-soup.

Friday, 26th August 2005

Sometimes work brings a gem of humour to our otherwise dull lives. One can usually rely upon HR for a good one. Today's was a very useful and well written guide to living in this fair city of the Orient. I have said before that Chinese is a most difficult language and my knowledge of it is scant, although I will have a go. So one should not mock them, when our hosts torture the Queen's English. But this just has to be shared with you, dear reader. It is a section called "Stories", which talks about the famous Xiangyang gift market, the haggler's favourite spot.

Ever had a wet dream about a shopping haven where goods are plentiful and prices are low? Ever wanted to bargain for an item to the point your 'opponent' vomits blood while you savor the victory of the battle? Let me introduce you then, to one of Shanghai's (you could even say the world) best shopping spot. Flocked by people from all walks of life and from every corner of the earth, Xiangyang Market is the answer to your prayers... paradise for shopping addicts.

You can just ask any cab driver to take you straight to the Xiangyang Market, whack the driver if he/she gives you a blank expression and pretends not to know.

Brilliant, priceless prose, but nonetheless a useful guide, including some things of which I was unaware and must sample.

Tonight's excitement, organised by Marvin was to go to the kart racing track. I hastily photocopied Native's map and foolishly did not have the address written in Chinese. So I consulted the excellent "City Weekend" magazine and found the address, but only in English. Hailing a taxi outside here at 6.00pm on a Friday was hopeless, so I resolved to be cool and native, walk to the Taidong Lu ferry south-west of the Pent-Ox, cross the river and taxi from the other side. It was a great ferry ride, spent answering a text from friends at home about my son's excellent GCSE results (all A's and B's!). On the other side there weren't too many taxis, but I managed to find one who had some English and wanted paying in UK currency! He was great, and as usual for most Shanghai drivers, really tried to find the place for me. It wasn't easy, but we found it.

On the open-air track, two-strokes were to be the power-plant of choice, with three levels of performance, so we selected middle. Sadly, there were no gloves and as Marvin commented "the worst of the worst helmets". Suitably kitted and having parted with a mere RMB150/£10.70, we strutted to our machines. I was usefully reminded by Marv that the track was a hairpin turn to the right out of the pits (not logical), but the first squirt of the pedal was enough to convince me that fun was about to be ladled out in the two-stroke fumes of a Shanghai night.

Marvin & Native left me trailing quite early on, as Native is something of an accomplished Sprint driver back home and Marv was really pumped-up about the event. There were no marshal's flags and very little instruction except for pointing at the engine and making "HOT" signs! I suppose it was assumed that three Brits could drive anyway. As usual for these sorts of events, I was amazed at how quickly other people could drive, but I had fun competing against myself. Once I had mastered the accelerator action and slid around a few corners, I was happy. It was huge fun, but over really quickly, though long enough to make one's hands quite sore.

I hope I didn't look as sweaty as Marv following the event – he must have put his complete being into it, never mind heart and soul.

Afterwards it was a case of "are we hungry?" The nearest restaurant was a soup specialty place. Not sure what province the food represented, but it featured a recessed burner in the table heating a big bowl of broth with floating knuckles of beef.

We had some appetizers, which were difficult to identify, except for the nuts and we may have eaten diced chicken feet. It was rather chewy. The nuts were good practice for using chop-sticks! There was also some salty fish to be going on with. Like the broth, this all turned up quite quickly.

The menu was a little hard to decipher and we were fawned over by an over-excited waiter who was desperate to practise his broken English on some rare Western visitors to his restaurant. We were also stared at from the moment the "Welcome girls" greeted us and for a long time afterwards.

The waiter, desperate to show his colleagues (especially the girls) how good a conversationalist he was in English, would always precede his speech with "Excuse me, sir". Marvin, never one to be patient with anyone not being perfect or up to his own standards, kept going on about his interruptions. Credit to him, the guy was trying his best and as I reminded Marv, his command of English was better than ours of Chinese. When he tried to tell us that there was free beer with the meal, even this took some time for Marvin to accept!

Into the bubbling broth on the table one sank the vegetables which we had ordered, so in went the raw potatoes, spinach, mushrooms and some thinly-sliced beef. All this could be removed with the supplied sieve or ladle when cooked. At times a waitress would amble up and top up the broth from a kettle. It was all rather good and very hot.

Next came another surprise – a straw and plastic glove. We were wondering what these were for when the waitress demonstrated that the idea was to sieve a knuckle out of the pot, put it on one's plate, put on the glove in order to hold the knuckle and use the straw to suck out the marrow, which naturally melted the straw! This was unusual but rather good-tasting and again well cooked.

Once we had all eaten sufficiently, Native decided that to be a good husband he should take some broth home for his good lady who had been less than well for a few days, unable to eat much or keep it down. So he asked for a take-away container. The "Excuse me!" waiter returned really pleased to help and understand English with a couple of those polystyrene folding white take-away clam cases! "No", we said, "for the broth", pointing at the liquid. He fully understood, apologised profusely, almost genuflecting in his desire to serve, and went away again. This time he produced plastic bags. Much rolling of eyes from guess who and Native decided to take the issue into his own hands, literally and used a suitable container to hand – an empty beer bottle.

This he had to fill with his ladle – not easy, but he's always up for a challenge. There were looks of amazement on the faces of all around – another crazy "ghost-face" (as white people are sometimes called). "Excuse me Sir" waiter came and tried to take over, but he was cack-handed and the just-off-boiling liquid gave his hand some grief. His gaffer appeared and forbid him to make much more of a fool of himself. So that was it, we had paid some ridiculously low fee for the meal and we rose to leave. They gave us the old bottle-top and this together with the bag from earlier made carry-out broth a possibility, the bottle at this point reaching the temperature of the contents.

Saturday, 27th August 2005

Today we had arranged to head off to the "Giant" (a Taiwanese make of bicycles) shop in Hengshan Lu, where many of the top bars are located. But today was not for drinking, it was for things of beauty on two wheels – no, not Chinese girls, but the machines themselves. Many of us engineers love the simplicity and grace of a bike. Native and his gorgeous wife, Frau came to the Pent-Ox and we all walked down to Lujiazui in order to catch the underground and re-appear in Hengshan Lu. Rolf had his first experience of the German-built system and loved it. The shop is not far from the underground stop and we were amazed at how busy it was, with a whole Western family being kitted out and PDIs (Pre-delivery inspections) being carried out at record speed. The choice was bewildering.

I think that the cheapest machine was around RMB400 and they went all the way up to a carbon-fibre, disc-braked job at RMB24,400. There were some reasonable component parts with that magic name of Shimano on the box. (e.g. Shimano 105 bottom bracket for RMB250, a top-notch frame for

RMB900, Rock Shox Pilot forks RMB 980 and a disc-brake kit with billet-machined calliper for RMB900). £1 = RMB14.

I thought that my two colleagues were just window-shopping, but there was serious intent to purchase going on in their heads once they saw the excellence of the welds and the componentry. We established from some other Westerners that there was no haggling with Giant, as it was not Company Policy, so the marked price was it. The guys had some fairly specific ideas about what they wanted to buy, with a preference for no suspension, but to suit their large frames, a long piece of cross-tubing was required. This, plus the need for a fairly upright riding position and speed (i.e. gears) pointed them to a bike called a Hunter.

Hunters were pulled out of stock and set up for my tall colleagues to rest their bums on and try. Despite the front suspension, which came with the larger frame and ideal riding position, these seemed to fit the bill. Meantime, I had been examining all the alternatives, including the two styles of folding bikes (RMB900). The one was really clever, with a sliding main cross-tube, rather than a folding one – a really good piece of engineering. However, the small wheels and the need to occasionally ride over rough ground cut these out. A look at the sports-style bikes revealed inferior components to the Hunters, especially on the gears and brakes (unless you paid RMB1000 for a decent one – Hunters are fitted with "V" brakes).

So deals were struck, PDIs were started (it was a race between the two mechanics; one was "BMW" and one "Minardi" in Formula 1 racing terms). The bikes came with free ruc-sacs and for RMB12 one could register them to oneself and address. Some extra bits were bolted on, such as bottle-carriers and pumps. Nearly all Chinese bikes come with rear luggage racks, for the lady (or mate) in your life to ride side-saddle.

It was quite an event, leaving the shop, photos having been taken and off they shot into a busy, rainy Shanghai Saturday, without a backwards glance. Quite funny, really, as Rolf had said to me that he did not want to go out into busy traffic, but just pootle around the local roads to the Pent-Ox on a Sunday morning, to get himself back into the swing and used to the cycle lane discipline. And there he was, off down the Hengshan Lu, in the rain, on a Saturday. Brave man, which was good, because that left me with the lady! I actually got the girl! So we repaired to a local café and splashed out on two fresh fruit juices, expensive at RMB30/£2.14 each! But it was very good.

We then retraced our steps on the metro and split up at Lujiazui. I walked back up Pudong Da Dao, and into the apartment for the swimming gear and back down. I met a returning Rolf in the lobby – he was gibbering like an excited child with a new toy. He loved his new bike so much he had been way off the direct line home and was waxing over its smooth operation, comfort, speed and looks. Some level of customizing was to be carried out – he reckoned a louder bell and some form of light luggage carrying device, together with a place to put map and specs were required. This is after all to be a functional device for doing the odd bit of shopping.

Sunday, 28th August 2005
I managed to sleep in until 10.30am, but I had been up at 2.00am calling home as I could not sleep – managed to reach my brother Alan and have a good chat with the family who were naturally at 7 hours behind, having dinner. I was quite jealous of him sat there surrounded by his nearest and dearest, just being English.

I knocked on Rolf's door and wandered in to see how the latest art was progressing. It was very impressive, he was trying out a "pen wash", which is a technique much favoured by Chinese artists and he has bought quite a few books on how to draw, Oriental style. The painting was of a bridge in front of a town, backed by mountains. The reflections on the water were proving difficult, but he had painted the trees rather well, with shadow and contrasting colour picked out.

His bike was sat there in the room, gleaming, urging me to go to the local shop and say "I'll have one of those, please". So off to the shop we went, him on two wheels, me on two legs. On the way I just glimpsed the first real accident I had witnessed here – a scooter rider was running down the cycle track and some dope in a blacked-out Buick RV was turning across the lane from the Da Dao. I heard the noise before I saw the result, so I don't really know how it happened, but it was nasty. A crowd gathered, though people were more ready to stare rather than help, as at home. I was impressed at how quickly the ambulance came.

The local Pudong shop was nowhere near as big or well-kitted as the Hengshan Lu place; no air-line and no stands for the bikes whilst one set up the gears, just young Wang, the shop lad holding the bike.

45

They had the same bike in the same colours as Native and Rolf had bought, but also one in an odd ochre sort of hue. I wanted to be different, so that was my choice. They had run out of pumps, so I could only have a bottle-carrier and bottle as extras.

In no time I was handing over the RMB (1,008 of them or £78) and on my way, with a request to return on Tuesday for the licence plate. The bike was as smooth and easy to ride as Rolf had declared and an ideal riding position. The cycle ways are smooth for the most part and astonishing progress could be made, compared to a car going in the same direction. I enjoyed hacking around and we kept up a fair lick along the way.

We were heading for JinQiao and the East-West café. Even a bit of rain could not dampen our enjoyment of being able to ride around Shanghai under our own steam. We strayed onto the main road where the track was dug up and mixed it with the traffic, then dived off onto a side road. Using the massive, stately King tower as a land-mark we navigated our way to the café. We proudly parked our steeds in the bike area and sat down to order. Soon we were joined by Fluff, who had taken the easy way out and taxied. We passed a pleasant few hours in the sun eating and drinking. It is so much more pleasant in that district than near the Pent-Ox as there are trees, space and less noise.

Non-job of the day goes to Ping the tree-bander, whose job it was to cycle around the district with his stool, loosening the thick rubber band fastening the new planar trees to the wood-effect concrete support posts. There are always plenty of non-jobs around here. So he stood on his stool, loosened the band, moved it up the post and let it out a bit, then re-secured with some wire. The authorities really look after this area.

After this, we decided on a shop to Decathlon, the sports store down the road for some hopefully cheaper bike accessories. This is a great shop, with some temptingly-priced gear for all manner of sports. We picked up all sorts of bargains, including gloves and repair kits, extra locks and inner tubes. We are now all set for Shanghai roads.

Monday, 29th August 2005

Today is a very sad day for me, as it is the 24th anniversary of the passing on of my dearly beloved Mother. Now *there* was a lady who brought sunshine to many a dark day and many a down person, a real Christian soul and the best Mum one could ever hope for. Even though it is long ago, I still feel down almost without noticing the date and waking up to its significance. She was great, we loved her so and my Dad must be so lonely sometimes without her most amusing, warm presence. Bless you and all you did for us, Mum. Hope you are pleased with your children.

It was a fairly boring day at the office – these folk just won't ask for help. They also make life more difficult for themselves by wanting to change things they do not understand. They also do not understand shades of grey – it is all black and white. Experience paints the shades for you. We know that because we have made engines and we know that an engine is an unforgiving cold piece of metal.

A dose of shopping should sort us out, so we taxied to Carrefour and went to experience the new "Megabite" eatery. This is a revamped version of the old one, which we used to patronise regularly, where meals can be had for as little as RMB16 (just over a pound) and a drink for RMB6. The choice is bewildering, with about a dozen different counters vying for your business as well as a Japanese Teppanyaki. The noise is amazing, with lots of shouting from the counter staff to buy from them. Purchases are made via a smart card, which adds to the other two I have for the taxi/underground and the apartment.

We were really full afterwards and managed a good shop, finding more accessories for the bikes at a cheaper price than Decathlon. The whole of JinQiao must have been in that shop, it was packed. Where did they go before it was built?

Tuesday, 30th August 2005
I spotted lots of fashion victims about – there are still people wearing pyjamas out on the street, which is quite frightening.

It was an interesting day at work – attending another no-notice meeting. At least it was an interesting subject with one of the most capable suppliers we are dealing with. They are French, with a JV (joint venture) over here. This is the first situation with a supplier over here when I have heard the magical phrase "back-up plan". I love that phrase, it shows some sort of forward planning in an unstable market. It could imply that they are expecting failure, but it also implied prudence.

We even seemed to manage to hold on to most Chinese attendees all the way through the meeting! Only the Logistics guy left after he had said his usual sensible piece.

Another interesting work-place culture clash is reported by my friend Stuart at another company. He regularly wonders aloud why he has to tell the Chinese the same thing time after time. We do too. He was giving one of the engineers (who apparently grins irritatingly all the while one is berating him) a lecture on quality and how to work his way out of the situation where a large quantity of parts were non-conforming. He showed him how to solve his problems, but the local just made life worse. Does he want to fail? We are paid for our advice, we give it, they do what they want to do, fall over and then if we are lucky they ask for help. Not an unusual Western/Chinese experience.

I agree with Stuart who says that it is quite irritating to give so many warnings that his project is in deep, deep mire and be grinned at, which many of them do. Is it a defence against being told bad news? But the message does not seem to sink in and they do not seem concerned. At least when we worked for BMW, if you had no success at one level, one just kept working upwards until someone would take an interest and usually only one was necessary. They were interested in the project "Reds" or stoppers and the "Ambers" or issues. Not these people. There seems to be, (and this is reflected in driving), very little personal responsibility. It is the "Leader's", whoever it may be. Those at the very top seem burdened, but the levels we meet seem oblivious, or are we missing something?

The driving illustration is back to the pulling out from a side road. One sees so many vehicles pull out into traffic without a look to the left. Nothing. No eye or head movement. It is not their responsibility to look out for themselves, but on-coming traffic must take evasive action or sound the old horn, which just keeps me awake at night.

Excitement tonight was the return to the bike shop for my licence plate. Big grins as I appeared in the doorway. Even more as I bought a rear flashing light (just to give Shanghai taxi drivers a better target). Light and plate fitted in no time and off I vanished into the dark streets on my way to Carrefour for a new mobile phone. Rolf and I are the only ones without. He was stuck at work with a supplier, so I pushed a note under his door as to where I was going.

The route I took brought me out at the new Carrefour in Yuanshen. I thought I could find just what I wanted in an unfamiliar store. Wrong. I wandered around not knowing my way, so I bailed out and headed for JinQiao, and familiar territory. Amazing "Bloodhound" Rolf found me squinting at phones. Luckily for me an English-speaking lady had just translated my requirements and I had made a purchase. We then walked off together for a "Megabite" as the check-out queues were staggering.

Yet again the eatery provided top-notch food at knock-down prices; another RMB22/£1.57 total! We were both pleased with our choices, though it was a bit late to eat. After that it was time to sort out Rolf with a mobile (which was better than mine – a Nokia – which turned out to be more intuitive than my Motorola and it has a torch in the end. So if you get bored talking, you can look for another person to call in the dark).

It was an absolute hoot riding in the dark – we were regularly presented with empty cycle lanes and so could speed along. Sometimes we were unsure as to whether to proceed or not at red lights, but most other cyclists just rattled on. As ever it pays not to hesitate on the road – you could risk being hit up the back. I feel slightly odd, wearing a helmet and gloves, but one is an English gentleman and one should be correctly attired for the road. One might make contact with it at the speeds at which one travels! Very few Chinese wear any protection, even on motorised scooters and bikes. They do not care or know the dangers or are charmed. Perhaps that is the key at work! Don't worry or prepare or plan and failure may not come to visit.

Cycling rule no. 1 – if crossing a junction and the lights change, don't be an "amber gambler"! I set off like a rat out of an aqueduct, eager to show a clean pair of pedals to the mass of Chinese riders behind and I looked around the bus to my left for people who had jumped the red coming across us. Good job I did, because as usual there were several. Not one, like there might be at home, but *several* who believed themselves especially charmed. It was close, but I was ready and I have "V" brakes – so I can stop on a half-RMB coin. They carry this "It won't happen to me" belief on the road, in the work-place, everywhere. It is tiresome to watch, but occasionally funny.

Wednesday, 31st August 2005
Today was different; we had appointments with PWC in Xintiandi, a very fashionable part of town, to receive some advice on our tax situation working here. I had walked to Lujiazui, some 30 minutes stroll before boarding a metro train and walking from the underground to PWC. I was dressed in shorts and trainers with a pair of long trousers and shoes in my bag. The look

of sheer disgust on the faces of the pretty, prim receptionists was a picture. I nearly dripped sweat on their clean desks.

Three of us, Marvin, Native and I opted to join our separate hour-long appointments and use each other to bounce ideas around and make use of three heads at once. Initiative and not following the rules, is occasionally a strong-point of we Brits. I could not see Germans or the Chinese doing that.

It was useful, but depressing. Simply, we cannot escape punitive Chinese tax, which begins at the appallingly low level of RMB500/£35.71. So not only is bank interest about 0.05%, but you get taxed to death. The UK suddenly looks appealing. Why we were not told all this before coming out here I do not know as our employer has an office here. We now could be liable, having been here for some time, to pay penalties for non-payment of taxes!

From the PWC office (which is the same PWC administering our old company!), where 1500 people work in Dilbert-style cubic offices, air-conditioned so the shiny suits do not see any perspiration, we had a grand view 11 floors up of the old Shanghai houses below where the poor people lived. Almost every house showed evidence of rubbish DIY repairs; they just do not seem capable. We are in the wrong trade – PWC even charge Western rates for their services! In China, a low-cost country! More fool those who pay.

An interesting problem here is one I never really saw in the UK, but is a real issue here. "Poison hands" as they are known, belong to people who sweat profusely and whose leaking fluid contains acids and salts which attack metallic parts of engines. A crankshaft which had been assembled into a block yesterday was now rusty, despite being oiled on assembly. Corrosion was forming under the oil film. This was amazing and even beyond dressing with emery paper. One could see a hand-print in the brown oxidisation mark. It is a real problem for us.

One of the engineers near me wants to change a process essential to the integrity of our engine, which has been settled and sorted for 15 years – he must know better, we have been doing it wrong all these years. What he says is logical, but wrong in practice and we know.

I record below the e-mail trail between HR in the UK and China and myself over our accommodation. See if it tickles you as much as it did me.

Dear girls,

Well, it is great to be back in China; I have now been back one week. I have joined the locals with my own bicycle, which is great, as Shanghai is designed around cyclists.

Before I came, I asked if I could be housed in a floor above 20 and in an A or B room to avoid the docks. However, when I booked into the Pent-Ox, I was allocated 25E, 'by order of the management'. So, except the ships' horns, (which I can still hear), I have traded dockside cacophony for the crashing and banging of a 24-hour building site and the thunder of the traffic and mostly unnecessary horn-blowing on Pudong Dah Dao. As this is China, there is no let-up for the weekend, so at 6.00am Saturday and Sunday I was woken by the crashing of scaffold poles and guys hammering rag-bolts into concrete. I estimate that I manage about four hours sleep each night, so if I fall asleep at my desk please understand.

Hi Ian,

I am very regret that you did not have a room in 'A' or 'B' side, I did ask the Pent-Ox to provide you a room in 'A' or 'B' and they said 'no problem' at that time.

I called Pent-Ox again, and they told me at the moment there is no available room in 'A' or ' B' until Sept 6. But they promised they would transfer you to the other rooms as soon as there are some flats available.

Of course, it does not mean that HR will stop to search alternative flats for you, however, I have to say it is not so easy to find a suitable alternative in BIYUN area with good quality, good facilities, good service and within the budget.

Anyway, we will arrange Rolf to visit those flats without service. After his tour, maybe we could find out whether it could be a feasible choice or not.

Any questions or suggestions please let me know.

The next part of the string flows thus:

Ladies,

Accommodation:
Further to your note, the room 25E is OK in that I do not hear any cement yard noise, just the thunderous road roar. Take your pick which is worse – the yard is 24 hours, the

road calms down a bit at night. I fancied an A or B room as they had a great view of down-town from the lounge and it is not at the back against the docks.

Bad news is that the pool closes tomorrow after only two months – a short summer and it is over 30°C today. This facility is one of the few redeeming features of the Pent-Ox and we are all to lose it. Public swimming is hard to find here and I come from a long line of aquatic creatures; it is one of my passions. This was another plus point for Diamond Court and Xinhe Gardens. Even Shimao Lakeside has a facility but it cost about £25 a week!

Tax:

We have just returned from our tax session. Judging from the offices and personnel figures, this is the business in which to be.

I am singularly chagrined that we were not given this tax advice before coming out here. We are now technically due to be fined 0.05% per day for late tax payment. We are basically to pay tax in China on everything and should have started to pay as soon as we came in territory. All the time the Company and tax advisers cannot come to an arrangement on payment for the latter's services, we are still overdue on taxes and the fines are mounting. The tax advisor was effectively speaking for the Chinese government in her answers and not looking for ways to dodge the system as a UK advisor would. I am very worried about this.

So adding all this up, I shall not be able to sleep well, nor swim and will be a taxation criminal. Life's a bowl of cherries.

Thursday, 1st September 2005

The drive to work is still bordering on the suicidal at times; we come within a hair's breadth of being rammed almost every day. We see the odd crash, but not as many as one would expect. There are scrapes on lots of vehicles, testimony to lots of not-so-great driving.

Today was no exception. Wang, the taxi-driver on the way home was another lane-hopper, desperate to make up two cars here, three trucks there. I am still not used to the last-second turning left across the road – they just keep coming even in the face of oncoming traffic running straight across. It is apex to apex cornering; the shortest distance.

Probably the worst part for me is not the driving style, which is OK, as they are all equally bad, but the fumes. One great way of improving Shanghai at a stroke would be to instigate a "smoke test" on buses and trucks. Almost all would fail, for clouds of black diesel smoke are belched from pipes everywhere. The sad part is that the locals do not seem to be offended by it, as it is the norm. Life would be improved immeasurably by tightened emissions regulations. Many thousands of vehicles would be outlawed overnight, however. If you think about it though, we were in a similar position with "smogs" not that long ago in the UK and we have only adopted stringent European emission regulations fairly recently. Tail-pipe emission checks are a recent addition to the MOT test for a vehicle.

One amusing incident at work involved Rolf, after three months of asking, being "awarded" a personal assistant and translator. Sadly not a female, which is the only bit which pleased Gary when he found out, as being our team leader he has been after the same (only female) since he first started back in late 2004!

Tonight was a sad sight out of my room window. The pool is shut for autumn, no more cooling swims to look forward to after a hot day.

Rolf had been out to see three alternative apartments today, so our mission tonight was to return to the one he thought was the best and for me to see where it was. The location turned out to be ideal, at the west end of the Biyun Lu, on which is located Diamond Court and Carrefour, so we would be well served by all the necessary shops and restaurants.

We cycled out and made a circuit of the block, which would place us close to some of the other ex-pats. It looks really quiet and there is not too much building going on around it. So we could try and move HR towards setting us up in there and out of the Pent-Ox, which for me has now lost one of its great appeals (the pool).

Happy with the potential new neighbourhood, we popped over to Carrefour for yet another Megabite. This time it was RMB20/£1.57 – we pushed the boat out this time! I had a superb chicken, rice, onions, and sweet corn dish, sizzling on a cast iron platter, spitting away as I carried it from the counter – delicious.

We had a good, fast cycle home and arrived, dripping and tired into the lift at the Pent-Ox. We had successfully negotiated our way around Shanghai again, dodging the traffic and avoiding crazy cyclists and pedestrians intent upon being mown down by us.

Back in the apartment after a cooling shower I took not one but two calls for Rolf, who was having trouble answering his new mobile! Looks like he is off back home on Saturday for at least a week! Almost last minute, but home is home.

Friday, 2nd September 2005
Aren't we lucky not to be in New Orleans? The unfolding tragedy of that great city in one of the poorest States of the Union is hard to watch, how awful must it be to bear? Army Engineers who should have completed repairs to various flood defences were re-deployed to Iraq, but even that may not have stopped the flooding. It seems like the poor and some of the most desperate ones are left committing horrible crimes amongst the vulnerable. The old US gun culture backfires again.

China too receives its share of torrential rain and consequential flooding, not far south of here. It is of some concern that where we are now is very few feet above sea level and much of the area is reclaimed land. A rise of a foot in the sea would cause major problems for millions of people.

We must take even some limited video of traffic at junctions for showing back home as they cannot fully appreciate the horrors and close shaves, the risks and liberties. As a road user, you do need eyes everywhere, especially as a pedestrian. It is still the pulling out slowly into the traffic flow and making no effort to match its speed that stuns me. Our driver today changed up when he should have held the gear whilst overtaking on the wrong side of the road.

Non-job of the day has to be our office cleaning lady and her pal. They sit together at a table just inside the door to the staff canteen and chat and watch the card-reader machine. That's it. They sit and watch hundreds of people file past and hold their card to the reader and wait for the reader to "beep" in recognition. I always bid them a polite "Nee hao" and watch their little faces light up, under those funny asexual hair-cuts that they and many of their like seem to sport. I wonder what province she is from, as many of the menial working women seem to have similar shaped faces and hair-cuts.

Saturday, 3rd September 2005
I tried sleeping in the spare room as it is so much lighter and inviting than the main room when I come back from a day's work. It sounds stupid, but come the morning, I realised that an appealing-looking room does not guarantee a good night's sleep. The noise from the Da Dao was staggering, as the spare room has a full-depth, ill-fitting patio door. Typically Chinese, it

seals the same way any ill-sealed Chinese door doesn't, so all the road-noise comes right through. The main bedroom does not have such a leak, as it is an ordinary window. The roar of morning traffic had to be heard to be believed. It creates a thunderous wave as eight lanes of traffic set off from the lights outside the Pent-Ox, right below my 25th floor window. It was a huge volume of noise, but I manfully slept a little bit more once it had woken me!

Today was another bike-buying trip. This time it was Marvin's turn to become native and go for two wheels. We rode over to the Giant shop just off the Hengshan Lu where Rolf and Native had got theirs. Marv selected a similar steed and was soon sorted out. We then took refuge in "Planet Shanghai", a fairly good restaurant, with ace air-con and a menu in English for lunch, which was really good and reasonably priced. That end of Hengshan Lu is a planar-tree-lined avenue and has some really interesting looking bars.

We had a deranged ride back to the spitting ferry, as it was not possible to stay on the road we had picked out on the map and ride straight there, as we had on the way out. Signs prohibited us from cycling at various points and we had to circle out and back. Nonetheless, we managed with one stop to look at the map, (assisted by a local security guard), to find our way. It is a real buzz riding along Shanghai streets – there was one narrow road, where people were coming from all directions, completely random movement and it demanded that one be highly observant. They pull out without looking even on bicycles and cut across your path, or even just ride on the wrong side of the road towards you. I was faced at one point by two women who just pushed a guy in a wheel-chair straight out in front of me. Good job the brakes are powerful.

It is great fun to race people on bikes, especially the powered ones as they go so slowly and pull away with no real verve. I swerved around so many people, it was great fun – I felt about fourteen again – a real two-wheeled hooligan. Then you realise why locals do not sweat; they go nowhere quickly.

Sunday, 4th September 2005

I had more chores, such as ironing to do, then a real need for some speed, so it was off to the "Ka-De Club", a well-stocked music and film DVD shop which is a honey-pot for tourists here. Americans come by taxi-load and I saw one guy snap up RMB700 worth – about 80 discs! They come with lists and just buy in bulk. Myself, I was content with a couple of music CDs and four films. It was a great ride there and back, although my legendary sense of direction worked as usual and I rode around in circles before finding the Ka-De. Interesting, but there are moves afoot to outlaw pirate video copies by the Chinese Government and the fear was that it would go underground, but the Ka-De now has a second branch. As usual, issues in China clouded by mystery and conjecture, which we do not understand.

That evening we watched the Formula 1 race at O'Malley's, (yes, an Irish pub), which I found with the usual amount of circling and wrong-turns, despite my writing instructions and drawing a map. Those who know me well would see the fallacy of these precautions. However, I reached the beer garden at the appointed time and found Marv, Native and Frau already there and their food ordered. I was recommended a beef in Guinness, which comes served in a small cast-iron cauldron (made in S Africa, by the way), so I chose Cottage Pie to be different. It came with beans and a roast potato, which was a mistake, as there was far too much there for one as svelte as I, but having had no lunch, I tucked in and ended up full.

The race was OK, as Formula 1's go, old Montoya scoring another McLaren Mercedes win. Amusingly, Marv had a "friend" turn up, your typical female Chinese thirty-something. Long black hair she stroked seductively, perfect legs and a size 8 maximum body. Stunning, the sort you could take home to Mum and be the envy of all your mates down the pub. Apart from being fairly fluent in English, she also knows some Norwegian, having studied there for two years. Nothing like picking a "cheap" European country in which to study!

Non-job of the day was the plant-carer in the underground. I am sure if we had pot plants in our Underground stations, they would be either nicked or used as footballs. Here, none of that carry-on; the plants were lovingly tended by plant-carer man; pots watered and leaves polished, dead ones swept away.

Monday, 5th September 2005
I woke up and felt awful – had endured an appalling night's "sleep" tossing and turning and alternately shivering and sweating. Perhaps it was the sun yesterday. I nearly passed up the chance to go to work I felt so bad and looked it, apparently. We then endured the worst taxi-ride ever. When you feel so lousy, you just want to reach the end of the journey safely and what you do NOT want is some impatient, badly trained driver honking his stupid horn

when all it does is annoy. DIY suggested that we put out some mis-information that excessive horn use drinks fuel!

Today, I managed 40 winks in trap 2, floor 3, where the toilet-roll dispenser is at just the right height on which to lean one's arms. I just felt so bad. I secured some Chinese medicine from Bassey, which seemed to do the trick. Hooray told me today that in many Chinese cities it is accepted that people have a sleep during the hot part of the day for one or two hours! I could enjoy that. He says Shanghai is too intense and busy and does not allow for that. This does not stop one seeing heads on arms sprawled over desks in many places!

Yet another two meetings happened today with a moment's notice of each. One was a session just amongst us Brits, so that was reasonable, just a complete supplier change debate; the other was pre-planned. They must have known about it for ages, as a couple of the attendees were from Japan, one from Beijing and the other local. All I got was one minute's notice and the subject was not my own, either.

The journey home was horrible; all I could think about was calling home to find out what was to become of my favourite furry friend, our dog, Nala. She had been going downhill all week fast and we suspected a tumour or something really dire. Her back legs had been failing her, she had been sick and now her front legs were shaky. I called from the apartment, fearing the worst. I connected with a very distraught wife. The awful reality hit home and we both cried. I put the phone down, broken-hearted. No more walks in summer, with Nala chasing rabbits and squirrels. No more walks in winter, cursing her long hair that had to be washed and brushed and dried. No more noisy welcome home barking.

She was a friend and confidante, a constant companion on so many walks, on so many days at home for her mistress. I suppose tomorrow will bring the final news of her demise, as when I called, Ashley had yet to be consulted, but as Sharon had said, she was not herself anymore, she was miserable. Farewell, old friend, my company on all those days of redundancy walking the local lanes, wondering about life without a job.

I tried to say a few words – to a dog over the phone. It sounds ridiculous, but I could not let her go without saying something. Sharon said that Nala pricked up her floppy, hairy ears and listened. I hope so, but I could not say much for choking up on my own sadness.

Tuesday, 6th September 2005

A good day today, at least some learning – now I know broadly how the "hot end" of an exhaust system is made, having seen it at a plant near the new and huge, Shanghai Formula 1 racing track. I hope I was able to inject something extra into the discussion about a subject not my own. The introduction to the Westerners at the JV (joint venture) factory could not have been easier – two of them were born in the same small seaside town in the North-West as I!!! Never before have I met a fellow "Toffee-nosed St Annie"! The accent was a give-away for all the guys there, one from Alabama and the rest from the Lancashire coast.

Winston had returned during the day and so we went out for a quiet dinner. Very pleasant to see his ugly face again and hear about his holiday in Mexico, swapping my stories of a Roman holiday followed by lazing about in the English Lake District. He was relieved to find things had not changed much, there was still little progress on some of the pay and condition issues which had plagued us from the start.

On the way home I spotted the day's non-job and also conundrum. Non-jobbing were the ladies in the coolie hats washing the metal barriers between the traffic rushing by at up to 40mph and the cycle lane! Civic pride, as sponsored by the City, is prevalent everywhere; yesterday we saw the tree-pruners at work. (Note here that it has become very hard to find Shanghai tree-surgeons as so many of them have perished or been injured falling out of them that they are now short of volunteers). I can just see the poor hapless lumberjacks sawing off the very limb upon which they stand – common sense is not common here, nor is self-protection.

So the conundrum is that as those ladies clean some metal barriers, why do they allow black-smoke-belching buses and trucks and let the ordinary people just view the road as a rubbish bin? I thought that the average British male could not hit a bin unless it was within reach, but these guys take the biscuit. After the biscuit they throw away the wrapper on the floor and being China, the biscuit is double-wrapped with layers of unnecessary packaging.

Chinese men are not what my wife would call refined gentlemen; they are the noisiest eaters it has ever been my displeasure to sit with. There are many smokers amongst them; dental care is not what it is to the Osmonds and they wretch and spit at the slightest excuse. Long nails are a fashion accessory, which are often dirty and/or yellow, used for cleaning the ears.

Date, any of you girls out there? Oh, and did I mention the bad breath and leaning on you?

Another interesting conundrum is that we are fast becoming a real "nanny state" in the UK with do-gooders and government at all levels deciding what is and what is not good for us to eat, drink, see, hear and do. The element of personal responsibility is being removed from us in so many cases. More and more clumsy idiots are suing authorities for tripping up when they should clearly look where they are going, for example. Playgrounds are losing traditional games over fears of kids hurting themselves and parents who won't play with their own off-spring then suing the school, rather than let kids scrape the odd knee, as part of the normal process of growing up. Yet over here we are continually bemoaning the lack of personal responsibility for actions. So who, if either nationality, has it right?

Wednesday, 7th September 2005
Dogs seem to be on the increase as pets here, but a city is not the place for a pooch, really, unless there is plenty of open space to release their energy and people ready to accept responsibility to clean up the resultant mess, which is not the way here. It took us years to drum that into even a small proportion of the dog-owning population. Of all the dogs one does see, the vast majority are yapping little "hand-bag" dogs, with bulging eyes and a fearful expression.

Back on to more mundane matters, the manner in which a telephone is answered still amuses us. The engineer in front of me just demonstrated appropriately; he picked up the "bone" and said "Wei" (which Sharon tells me is Cantonese for "Hello") three times, before recognising the person on the other end, or they announced themselves appropriately and he got down to a normal "Nee Hao". What a waste of time! Why not give your name out when you pick up? Some sad types have counted the number of times "Wei" is spoken before conversation starts and we have had instances of five!

The office is largely empty today, so the works bus must have expired. I hope that is all. Some of these people spend two hours on a bus to reach here. Imagine that with smoking, sniffing, coughing, slurping men, ladies? Oh, and the guys have started wearing vests, now! I am still running round at 10.00pm wearing shorts and a tee-shirt, yet still requiring a post-walk shower and these men are donning underclothes. When Winston moaned about the pool closing he was told that Shanghai open air pools only open for two summer months and after that it is too cold for locals. Hang on a minute, this country stretches across so many climates and they survive in deep winter, but cannot manage being in warm water outside!

Native and Marvin have just come back from a top-class supplier and reckoned that along with the two guys at the plant, they were the only Westerners in the town.

My mate Stuart was joined on a visit by a couple of Chinese engineers from his office here. He made several interesting observations:

There ensued a heated argument about changing drawings and why the locals would not do it. Lots of excuses, but it boiled down to the fact that they do not have the desired capability here. It will have to be supported from the UK.

Their Western hosts stated that they have been in virtually all the Chinese engine plants and have yet to meet anyone who really understands engines and knows what they are doing.

They commented that our engine is so highly tuned that it would take a much larger unit of anyone else's design to compete. They also doubted our ability to make it properly here. We'll show them.

Conundrum – Many Chinese people will avoid buying home made if at all possible, believing it to be inferior. Indeed, one of the translators visiting the UK spent huge amounts on what she believed were "genuine" shirts, blouses and jewellery. Stuart's Party card-carrying confidante here has a US lighter he paid silly money for, a Japanese camera (despite "hating" them) and a European mobile phone!

Another weird thing which I may have remarked upon before is the propensity for suppliers to wander unchallenged about the corridors here. They peer through the glass, see whom they want and stroll right in. Back home there is a strict control of visitors to the office. Opposites and extremes.

Office life here is as ever accurately reflected in the famous UK TV series, whereby most minutes are sheer drudgery and people are working away, with just the occasional spark to brighten life. The Chinese office also has its own duds, bullies and pranksters, bores and wits, pretty girls and some devastatingly quick-witted ladies.

Tonight was a chance to visit Frau and Native's apartment in Shimao Lakeside, a truly huge development in Green Bridge (JinQiao). There are several large 30 or so storey blocks, surrounding man-made lakes, with bridges, canoes, trees and landscaping. A gym and swimming pool is available for £25 per person, per month! Barbecues can be hired and placed on the garden roof of the sports hall.

The view is amazing from their 30th floor room and it is very airy as there are windows on both sides. Other ex-pats from our company have taken root there as well. Again, typically Chinese, there were 9 bulbs which did not work when they moved in, out of a total of about ten times that. The shower is one of the biggest I have seen outside the US and the sofa can accommodate two adults full length without touching. Settee intimacy requires an intense orienteering, logistical and mountaineering exercise in order to find one's partner, have sufficient food for the journey to get there and actually make contact.

Amusingly, the spare room mattress was British. Many of the appliances are European, except the TV.

Thursday, 8th September 2005

I have a cold, which came on yesterday, resulting in the usual uncontrollable nose. I had to find the "Max strength" powders from the first time since I was here in February.

The temperature has taken a noticeable fall here; it is no longer necessary to have the air-con on full blast with the windows and doors shut. Naturally, being Chinese, they open the windows and still turn on the air-con. So much for energy conservation. It has gone sufficiently colder for the first fashion victims to be spotted – men with vests on and women with the old thick, yellow woolly tights. Following SARS, the government decreed that all buildings should be aired twice a day.

Non-job today was reported by Flower – he spotted a lift-operator; all day, just sat on a seat pressing the old buttons. I reminded him that not that long ago, (well, thirty years to be precise!), I remember old Ron in the lift at the department store where my Father worked. He had bottle-glasses, a brown cow-gown and worked the lift.

Many of us seemed to end up today at the Mawdesley for dinner. Very pleasant it was too, recalling past exploits of notable ex-Rover employees in China and comparing notes as to who ended up where since redundancy.

The new "bring 'em in" deal at the bar is an all-you-can-eat barbecue for RMB98/£4.43. So I didn't have one. One of the guys had complained last time about raw meat in his chicken leg and had seen the BBQ chef struggling in the dark to see if it was cooked, before serving him uncooked poultry. They have a light out there to illuminate the sign, so why not a little one for the chef? Typically they had not listened the first time and there was still no light for the guy with the cooking tongues and yes, there was the pink meat visible!

Friend Stuart says he has similar experiences all the time. There are no doubt some very clever people in his host company, but there are also others who do not know one end of a car from the other and could not distinguish good quality from poor. He tells them his expert opinion, which is why he's there and he is largely ignored. Many issues are really coming to a head and tempers are fraying. We know the feeling.

Chapter 3

MOON FESTIVAL TEAM BUILDING

AND A WEDDING "IN THE FAMILY"

Saturday, 10th September 2005

I am writing this quickly as I do not want to soak the lap-top with my sweat; I left work early yesterday as I felt so ill. Luckily I could, unlike the Chinese, I suspect, although I did wonder if I should have gone in the first place.

I spent much of yesterday in bed and slept all night; today has been lounging around the place, drinking the few remedies I have here. Three of the guys have called to see how I am; supplies should be on the way.

The view from my eyrie above the Da Dao shows a steady stream of traffic, with lots of vehicles showing no lights at all. When will they get the idea? There must be so many accidents, as I cannot believe that the myopic taxi drivers I have been with can see perfectly in daylight, let alone darkness. The two-wheelers have a death-wish especially. How can anyone on a bike not try and be seen? When you see the manoeuvres they make, it would be as well to have a search-light on them so they can be spotted.

The building work goes on across the road as if the workers have not heard of Saturday night out with their mates, although as many of them live on site, and there is no local pub to go to, I suppose there is little else to do *but* work. When I turned in last night about 10.00pm, there was a lone welder at work opposite, who must have been thirty floors up, still at it. How could he see his target in the dark? I wonder if he had a mask, as they seem optional here. It is 7.30pm now and I can still hear the sounds of clattering scaffolding poles and there are lights on at various levels.

Back to the pub thing, they just do not exist here as such in any number. Drinks with friends and family are taken on the pavement here on the **Da Dao**, with small tables and chairs placed to create makeshift gaming places for the benefit mainly of the men.

Today I read an interesting piece on local architecture, which gave a description of the *Lilong*, where '*Li*' means neighbourhoods and '*Long*' means lanes, so a Lilong is a combination of the two, many of which can still be seen here in Shanghai. The piece went on to say that per hectare of ground, a traditional average-sized Lilong can support 15,000sq.m of housing, which is the same as the density of many modern high-rise projects. This sounds crazy until one considers all the extra land and open space which needs to surround the high-risers so light can reach all.

Some of the Lilong have been converted into expensive play-places for tourist and the rich, such as Xintiandi, and this just pushes up property prices all around, with the result that some of the surrounding Lilong have been demolished. Many were erected by rapacious developers in the thirties and had a design life of maybe 50 years as tenement structures. They were not built well and the density of population has multiplied, especially since 1949, so families have doubled up and added levels to the shaky structures. As previously noted, Chinese DIY is not good, so who knows what state they are in structurally? The sanitary conditions cannot be good and the ones I have walked among have running water – outside – in a stone sink.

So if I am right about Chinese DIY, how can we explain the rise of the DIY store? B&Q has several branches in Shanghai alone. The clientele were not all Western, so there must be some Chinese DIY going on, but I have never seen anyone wielding a paintbrush inside or outside their property.

For example, it was comfortingly sad to turn up in the toilets of a restaurant I had not visited for some time to find that the taps were still turning on their base and wobbly. Maintenance – what's that? We have been warned that when it comes to air filter change time the Chinese technique is to throw the element away and put the lid back on without a replacement! Who needs several layers of cleaning fibre anyway, let that engine breathe……… and suck in all manner of dirt, sand and airborne grime.

Light relief was provided by Mr. & Mrs. Native who brought round some drugs to combat my ailing body. They had searched quite hard for these and they were "Night and day cold-relief capsules" of some sort. I reckon they did the trick. It was good to have my first visitors, but all they needed was a drink of water. Good job, as I had not much else to share!

Sunday, 11th September 2005

Today was going to be fairly boring from the start, as I was still recovering from the illness of the previous days, so I resolved to stay in and sweat it out. Not a pleasant thought, but it was all I could do. The mind was willing, but the body reluctant. It was a good job that medicine had been brought to my room, so I did not have to venture far.

Later on in the day I decided to sally forth and pick up some fruit and telephone "IP" cards. These allow one to access cheap calls outside China and it can be as low as RMB1 per minute, if you know where to buy them. The best deal so far has been the lady in the basement of the Super Brand Mall. I did not fancy walking all that way, so I picked the nearest card retailer on the Avenue. Amazingly, being Sunday, there were a few closed businesses, including the usual telephone place.

Having returned and feeling much improved (must be something in those Chinese drugs) I opted to join the others at O'Malley's pub garden where the Formula 1 Grand Prix racing was on the big screen again. This time I sensibly ordered bangers and mash, which was excellent and made a fine accompaniment to the torrential rain hammering down on the roof and tent in the beer garden. A real English meal feeling, with appropriate weather.

The night passed pleasantly enough and I had spent more than many local residents earn in a day. It transpires that one of the engineers here earns about RMB80 a day. He regards me as a rich man, because I travel in taxis.

That night we experienced a real typhoon, which had tracked along the East China coast and was ripping into coastal towns causing damage and loss of life, the final count being 12. I thought that the single glazing in the building was going to blow in, but not even a dribble of water passed into my rooms, unlike those in the newer, Shimao Lakeside apartments, where poor door seals allowed huge quantities of water to flood marble or wooden floors. Even ramming tea-towels down the gap did not prevent Sonnie's rooms from being under water. He mopped up two bucket-fulls before giving up.

Monday, 12th September 2005

Tonight was the unofficial "stag night" for Prop and we gathered in the Mawdesley for a few sponsored drinks by the big man. We lounged around until stomachs started rumbling for food and the power went off in the bar, making it difficult to pay! There was a drinks salesman trying to promote his wares, so we were naturally asked for our advice on beer choice. A sample of Boddingtons was provided and we had to give direction on how to open, pour and settle. It had travelled quite well all the way from the Rainy City of Manchester to Shanghai. It looked like there were either new owners in place, or people installed to run the bar for Helen and her husband who had run it so far.

On to the nearby Indian Kitchen restaurant we went, which is renowned for several things; one is giving Native the runs on 100% of his visits, and the other being slow service, with a tendency to serve courses randomly and not necessarily in the order of Starter, Main, and Dessert. So strict instructions were given to ensure we only ordered Starters and then gave the menus back, which worked, so we retrieved them for the Mains.

Two non-jobs: one was the young lad whose job it was to stand by the food lift from the kitchen and wait for the light to illuminate showing food was on the way. He looked bored out of his skull. The other was the girl in the (very small) loos, whose job it was to turn away when one walked in! I do not know what her function was. I have been met by toilet flunkies before, even in the US, where in Planet Hollywood in Minneapolis there was a person dispensing eau de toilette, cologne and other smellies free from an immense collection. Always a little off-putting, someone watching one urinate; some guys can't even do it with a non-participating audience (it's a guy thing, ladies)!

Tuesday, 13th September 2005
An interesting discovery today was the system of favours/relationships, or *guanxi*, which proliferate in this country. If it was an African state it would probably be called corruption, but here it is above board and all around.

My friend Stuart found out that one of his Parts Quality Engineers who was investigating quality problems at a supplier was actually employed by that supplier! He even identified his office on the factory tour. So there was no chance that he was going to get particularly excited or would press for change and improvement. He would give his old company an easy time. He found that the company he is supporting is composed of a large number of people on secondment from other, less busy parts of the parent company's empire. So these companies are hardly likely to lend out their best people, which is what we find.

It also explains why there are so many late and poor quality parts there. A regular report produced by one of Stuart's team showed the status of the project. There is little preventing progress, it just needs action and fairly simple actions to bring it back on track. In his experience he had never seen a project so far off track and not corrected. We are not at the point of meeting seemingly insurmountable technical problems; we just need parts of good quality in on time.

In the evening I elected to cycle down to the usual Dongchang Lu ferry (the "spitting" ferry) and enjoy a dash across the darkening river as dusk fell. As always the atmosphere is busy, congested and noisy on the water, with dirty, low barges scurrying up and down the Huangpu. Their pilots stand in dimly-lit wheel-houses which do not appear to have any glass, squinting out at the gathering darkness. To the rear, or aft of the load, is a form of living accommodation. This seems to have a TV, air-conditioning and a reasonable amount of room, but will hardly be 5-star digs. These barges are rough vessels used for cheap transportation of low-value bulk loads.

My end aim was a travel agency on the Yan'An Lu, in the Jing'An Temple district. I had not been to this part of the city for some time – it was the first place Native took me when I came to Shanghai back in January. I remember the assault on my senses as we rose out of the subterranean world of the metro system, up into a cold, bright, staggeringly noisy district. The Jing'An Temple is a famous place in Shanghai and a very old community, even if the temple building is not (most of it is concrete). It is a huge place, with many shrines within, as usual for a Buddhist temple. I have been in a few now and find them beautiful, fascinating but serene places, with room to accept all faiths, as well as the casual tourist.

Chinese streets are reasonably easy to find in Shanghai, as the signs are good and each has the compass direction shown. I surprised myself with how far west into the city I had cycled, keeping up such a high speed, that I overshot my intended turn north by some distance, necessitating a back-track. The thrill of riding at speed through dense traffic and finding my way around has not faded at all; the bigger the intersection I have to cross, the more fun and sheer terror is felt. On some of the one-way roads, bikes can still ride in a contrary direction, but riding into someone's headlights is not for the faint-hearted. The Chinese cyclists do not give each other much room and spread right out across the pedestrian crossings at junctions, making it really hard for those on two legs to pass through. They push and squeeze to make the front row, and then set off really slowly in the wrong gear, with me almost pulling "wheelies" in my haste to pull away. Neither do they seem to like queuing behind me; I just do not push far enough ahead, but then again, I leave them all for dead at the start, including the powered two-wheelers. Most of them take ages to catch up again and the process repeats itself.

Once I found the right address, it was too late to conduct any business, but I was happy to have found it myself, with no special maps or guidance. I downed some by now warm water from my carrier and set off on the return leg, this time determined to follow the Yan'An elevated highway as far as possible to the river. This was quite easy at the start, and then fell apart as the entrance to the tunnel loomed and I was diverted off south-east. Again, my high speed worked against me and I slipped off much too far in that direction, thinking that things didn't look right, but stupidly carried on. Even if I wasn't a stupid, pig-headed bloke, if I had stopped to ask directions, the chance of understanding them would have been so remote, so I continued blindly on. This route dealt me way down into the south-east corner of the city, by the Nanpu Bridge, an immense structure spanning the river. That was a sure sign to try and cycle north and quickly, before I ran out of road or I drifted into dark and potentially dangerous dockside areas.

As ever, I was full of the good intentions noted above yet still managed to end up down a dark, dirty and dead-ended dock road. The smell was appalling. I think I had stumbled upon the same area as we had sailed past on our river cruise, when our noses were so violently offended. I turned the bike around and set of for the brighter lights and finally found a familiar road leading to the ferry terminal. I was, as usual, squeezed onto the ferry with bikes and bodies pushing behind me as if their lives depended on their position on the boat. I always try to create room around me to prevent being crammed into too small a space. Over here there is little concept of personal space, so I try to protect what little I can.

Once off the ferry, I rolled around to the Super Brand Mall to try and park the bike under the building and so walk into the Lotus Supermarket. This was prevented by several uniformed guards at each entrance. "Mayo" said one, meaning that I was not welcome down there. So I locked it up at the side of the road and worried if it would be there later.

The evening's purchase included a photo album of old and new Shanghai shots by a local photographer. Most of the shots were presented as the "old" (meaning up to 1980) and "new" showing the dramatic development in this city. The photographer's story was a sad one; he had been an eldest son of poor parents and when his brother fell ill, he resolved to go out and find some medicine for him, or a way to make some money to help. He did both, selling mushrooms he found in the countryside. He developed into a lover of the local flora and fauna, determined to try and capture its beauty as it disappeared under the pressure of people moving in.

His story developed into something that must have been typical of many people in this vast country; where his love for nature, the arts, and writing poetry highlighted him as a Party threat. He had to burn his photographs, which he had by then started to take, and suffered persecution in labour camps. Only after the country opened up did he pick up a camera again and began to record what he saw changing through the lens.

The book is an amazing series of contrasts, which is its point. Many of them I recognise from the modern shot, but so many then and now shots are separated by only 10 to 15 years.

The other significant purchase was a kettle for £5!

Wednesday, 14th September 2005
Another day, another Yuan, as they say. More issues arise surrounding guanxi, or favours/relationships, depending upon how one translates it. The practice goes on here and it does not always benefit the project.

The evening was pleasant enough; Winston and I enjoyed a Thai meal in the SB Mall and strolled on down to the Paulaner bar, for I had gifts to distribute. Before I left for the UK in June, the girls in the resident "Blue Heaven" band had requested a box of Weetabix and a stick of white Toblerone. I presented these to grateful, but surprised girls, who thought I would not remember. Their gratitude duly expressed, we settled into another night of watching the Chinese at play and the international community mixing with them. There was only a brief appearance by the "Lone Groover" who had consumed sufficient to be there on his own on the floor. Later the dance floor filled up well and the night passed drinking expensive liquid.

We learned a little more about the Philippines from our hosts, who missed the sand, sea and palm trees of their island homes – a far cry from the noise and grime of city life. They were not looking forward to moving out of their apartments near "Times Square", a vibrant, brightly-lit group of shopping paradises in Pudong, and shipping out to the "barracks" as they called their new accommodation in Puxi. It sounds very Chinese. Many of the waiting staff at the Paulaner are Philippinos as well, so they live together, 8 girls and one lad. "Lucky guy" we observed to one waitress, but it sailed over her head. "He has a separate room", we were told with a straight face.

Thursday, 15th September 2005
Today was the day of our "Moon or mid-autumn Festival" Team-building event. Thankfully, the Chinese suggestions of reading or sleeping had not been taken up and we were bussed in the afternoon to a local sports centre to join people we do not work with (so how is that Team-building?) and play some badminton. HR had pulled out all the stops to ensure we were umpired by a national coach and a lady Company badminton champion. There was a singles and a doubles competition. It was obvious that there were "dark horses" on our British side that we did not know we had. Their weapons were not so secret, apart from the guy doubled up with me, they were mostly hot-shots. We managed a doubles win, with a local boy and Native claiming the trophy, but the singles was a Chinese victory.

I shall let Winston take up the story:

No fatalities, no bruised egos, at least to my knowledge, there were one or two serious faces but in the end the Chinese were just too good for us.

Sonnie beat Marvin in the 3rd place play off of the singles and for his trophy he got to play The Company's champion (3 years running). He appeared to hold his own for the first few points but she (yes she) was only toying with him – she then proceeded to 'wop his ass' with a big grin on her face without breaking into a sweat.

The 2 expert umpires or referees or whatever you have in Badminton were the afore -mentioned Company reigning champion and a national coach. They must have been told that 'Team GB' was in town!!! The national coach took the first few games really seriously applying the 'Queensbury' rules to the letter, but then the penny dropped and he then lightened up a bit and applied a liberal sprinkling of British 'what the @#$*'.

Can't remember too much about the doubles. I think that Native and Barclay won with Turk and another Chinese super star as runner up.

Me, oh I was given a bye in the first round (luck of the draw) and got hammered by the guy who was humiliated by the Champion (Sonnie) in the second round. Quite pleased to get off the court with all my hamstrings and bits intact!

Whilst sitting on the side lines (for most of the evening) I was quizzed by the girls from HR on my knowledge of the Chinese language. There was a lot of giggling and chatter, not sure whether they were impressed or taking the P!!!

The after match buffet was good – nothing too disgusting to eat, with a few speeches about how well we all were doing and how it was appreciated that we were doing such a 'spiffing' support role. Maybe hypocritical as we are still not being listened to. A little bit of sentiment crept in as it was remarked that we were all away from our families at Moon festival which is a very Chinese family orientated time or the year. Cracking food and a few beers but no Gambei (challenges to down in one). Proceedings ceased at 8.00pm with carriages home.

Ian managed to bore the pants off Bassey (not literally), he was talking to 3 of the Chinese girls and Temple gave up the will to live after 10 mins. As soon as Ian stopped for a breath (maybe ½ hour) they all got up to get some fruit in the hope that he would go away. It worked!!!

So you can see how my colleagues view me! Whilst trying to entertain the girls (no-one else had a go, by the way) I remarked to a Chinese guy on the next table that he should leave smoking to his test engines. I was reminded by one of the HR beauties that a Chinese girl would never ask a man not to smoke. I tried to incite revolution and promote more women's rights. It was at this point as Winston observed that they ran away for some fruit!

The whole evening was a great success and passed off very cordially, but would have been much more effective if we had been playing with office colleagues, not people we had never seen before! This was classic; missing the main point completely.

Another observation was being watched in the changing room, by a non-jobber attendant who showed us the way to the showers (as if it were not obvious from the wet floor and steam), who then stood and watched all the *gweilos* (foreigners) undress and change! Strange, but perhaps he had not seen naked white guys before and wanted to know if the stories about us were true! We are gifted, but only with a sense of humour to take the Mick out of him.

Amusingly, in the foyer of the sports centre was a medical station, with a man in a white coat, a hairdressing salon and about three places to eat! So you were assured of a prompt response if you had one too many spring rolls after your sports exertions. A new hair-do could then be created to complete the experience. Food and hair are two of the biggest industries here, judging by the preponderance of purveyors of these activities on the streets, followed closely by sign-makers and bicycle repair shops.

Friday, 16th September 2005

Today is my son's 17th birthday. I noticed on the 'phone his ever-deepening voice. Autumn has certainly arrived here and also apparently in the UK. The trees here are starting to drop leaves, keeping more street-sweepers employed and the flowers at the roadside are losing their glory. There have been some very colourful displays all around this city; someone in the authorities has planned several impressive displays along key boulevards here. There are, of course the people to tend them and keep the bushes trimmed, the flowers watered and the borders well-maintained.

The evening's entertainment was to be another foray to a Chinese football stadium, this one quite close to our apartments. For the princely sum of RMB30/£2, we were able to secure a pick of the grandstand seats as there was hardly a capacity crowd. We were entertained by a team from the capital, Beijing, challenging a local side, who fancied their chances as the home "hip-Shanghai" team against the boys from up north. The game was interesting, being dominated by an early goal by Beijing in the first half and then much Shanghai dominance. The second half saw the boys from the capital resurgent and went on to win 2-1.

On the way in to the game, bearing in mind that at the last match we saw we were prevented from taking in our bottled water, we saw two locals carrying a car battery. Attached to the battery was a rail with three horns on it! So no water, but a full-size lead-acid battery was OK! During the game, when Shanghai scored its only goal, a red firework was ignited amongst the home crowd opposite us. The red matched the strip colours for the side. Very quickly the security boys waded in to much jeering and jostling to extract the perpetrators.

There were some good dramatics as ever, with theatre on the pitch and players sulking after rebuke, with one send-off for a bad tackle and a member of one team's management being given a yellow card for interfering with the ball. Empty plastic drinks bottles were hurled at the tunnel as the match officials left the pitch – how very sickeningly European.

Following the match, we decided to make a visit to the bar at the side of the Novotel. I had not darkened its doors before, but Winston had been a couple of times and had remarked that there had been more staff than punters. The frightening lady manager had asked him for advice on how to turn the place from night club into Sports Bar. Winston had duly obliged, but she had decided to try and attract as she put it, the local "Pyjama crowd". We were ushered up the steps by her, dressed as she was in high-heel black suede knee-boots, a tiny yellow mini-dress and her long black hair in ringlets, topped by a face which will keep Max Factor in business.

Inside, some stairs led up to the Karaoke rooms, complete with one's choice of girls in yellow dresses. Downstairs the place was dark and the music pumping. Against a huge video wall was projected a film of what looked like the Chengdu fetish disco dancing championships – lots of skinny girls in dodgy clothes.

It was a typical Chinese place; loads of blokes (and many girls) smoking from both sides of the bar. I think that the next time someone asks me if I mind their filthy habit I shall reply that it is up to them if they want to smell and die early, but I would rather not. No-one asked in the bar, of course. So one drink was all I could stand.

We were treated to a live performance by the manageress and her friend, who formed a girly-duo on keyboards, a mini-disc backing track and little else. They proceeded to murder various songs.

We left after a short time, as I was coughing in the smoke and outside I was delighted to see real, large capacity motorcycles parked up, belonging to some of the "cool dudes" who had smoked me out of the bar. Big bikes are a rare sight in this city, and I was looking at a Honda Fireblade, a stupendously fast 900cc machine capable of hurtling to 60mph in about 4 seconds. One would have thought that its rarity and therefore status would have ensured it was kept in tip-top condition, but this is China, where one does see car-washes and the occasionally clean vehicle, but most transport is left to decay. Such was the case with this classic of the two-wheeled world. What a tragedy to see such neglect. None of the bikes outside were in anything like good order. Back home, many owners spend as much time polishing as riding.

Saturday, 17th September 2005

It is another fine day on this Moon Festival weekend, where it is traditional for families to be together; I wish that were so for me. My family here is a fat bloke called Winston. Still, he is good company and we organised to meet in the evening, but first my day-time arrangement was to be with one of the young Chinese engineers-in-training (by the name of Hooray). We agreed to meet at a neutral spot, closer to his domicile than mine. He called me twice to make sure I was able to decide for myself on the mode of transport and that I was to be in the agreed meeting place. They do worry about us, whenever we travel. I do not know why, I am quite capable of moving around this world alone. (Friends will note that I frequently go the wrong way, however).

We passed a comfortable time in the air-con luxury of a café drinking tea and orange juice, discussing politics, family, economics and future plans. He was excellent, talking about some fairly deep subjects. I learned something of his parents and home, which I would love to see; it sounds very poor and basic. He describes them as peasants and he will not return other than for Spring Festival. He saw the job in Shanghai on the Internet and was lucky enough to have been educated at one of the country's premier engineering faculties in Xi'an. It seems rather sad, not to see one's family more often, but money is tight and the distances huge. He telephones them each week and they must be very proud of him, but he describes them as very simple folk, his mother always having been a peasant and never having seen a city. His father volunteered for the military, but is now retired. Hooray and his brother plan to drag Mother to Beijing for the Games in 2008.

I learned something of the politics according to my friend, who had read widely about his country and its subjection under Communist rule, as well as taking an objective view as it is seen by other nations. He had a good grasp of his nation's history and of my own homeland. He was a fascinating companion and we talked freely about a wide range of issues. I admired his stamina, talking and listening for a total of about five hours in a foreign language.

He finally allowed me to take him for "dinner", which I did not want to be a lavish affair, so something cheap was called for. Therefore there could only be one option from where we were – Megabite in Carrefour. We ordered a mix of noodles, which appears to be his staple diet in the evening. Naturally I did not see much of him during the meal, except the top of his black head. I did not hear anything from him except for what seemed like a constant slurping sound. The noodles were gone in a jiffy. I was still wading through mine, eating like a true Englishman.

I was intrigued to be described, along with my other English colleagues, by my dinner partner as "simple". This was lost in translation as I explained to Hooray that simple was something of an insult. Following a moment's search through his growing English dictionary, he came out with "pure". I think I know what he was trying to say. So many Chinese colleagues are envious of our apparent wealth and worldliness; the fact that we have visited many places in China and across the world. Hooray is no exception.

We then took a walk around the complex that is Green City, with its bars and restaurants, shops and landscaping, the swimming pool and outside lake. We wandered through the Decathlon sports shop, his eyes wide at the prices and array of kit on show, kids whizzing by trying on roller blades, blokes playing ping-pong and tents on show. The latter were something he has never experienced. I tried to explain how I have been all over the UK and Europe with a tent on my back, but he has never had that opportunity.

We parted after a quick stroll around the local B&Q (yes, they have reached China and the prices are low!). It was good to go into a DIY shop and not have to buy anything.

Sunday, 18th September 2005

It was into the 30s; not a day for being outside for long. Winston and I decided to visit the Cybermart in Hong Kong Plaza, so he could avail himself of a combined computer hard drive and card reader. What we did not expect was a comedy shopping experience.

We found the recommended stand which many of us have visited independently. In his best sign-language Winston ordered a device and they offered to format the drive for him. Fortunately he accepted the offer, but this was the start. Buying a combined drive and reader necessitates opening up the reader box, inserting the drive from its sealed bag and screwing the top back on and firing it up. It sounds simple when you say it like that. Suffice to say that we were there for about an hour whilst the assembled experts (at one time there were six heads looking at the screen, excluding ours!) went through three drives, five reader boxes and three leads, and played on two different computers at three counters in the market.

We were not in a hurry and it was so amusing to watch so many heads being scratched, so many different hands moving mice and keypads. Also amusing was the blatant disregard for the "Don't eat over a computer" law. It was lunch-time when we started, and the bags of KFC and McDonalds had turned up so they weren't going to let them go cold. "Some grease with your hard drive, Sir? How about a few bits of bread-crumbs with that USB port?" So amusing, all these things going on as you stand helplessly by, not understanding any of the chit-chat. Winston was not as amused as I, for he had already paid for his hard drive and could not see much progress towards its functioning for some time. He maintained his composure really well, but finally cracked and said that if they did not hurry up, he would ask for his money back. The thought seemed to spur them on and soon we had a success. We had computer hardware and comedy, all for a good price.

Exhausted and hot after our "hard driving", we sought out somewhere to eat in the Plaza and found the "Bankers Café". We thought that this was quite appropriate, so we settled down to peruse the menu, which was all in "Welsh". We called for an English menu, which when it arrived was clad in a luminous plastic folder. The prices were OK and the choice huge. I had not enjoyed a cold Ovaltine for ages, so that was for me, with a fruit selection, which was the usual work of art on a plate.

Suitably refreshed, we sallied forth to the Ka-De Club, CD and DVD emporium. It is only yards from busy well-known roads, such as Maoming Lu, home of many a sleazy bar, but it is down a really quiet thoroughfare and the shop itself is behind two large wooden doors, which used to open onto a restaurant. Then you disappear through a door, into the hallway of a house and into the main room. It is literally wall-to-wall discs, as I may have described before. This time the delights were the box-set of Monty Python TV programmes and all the "Pink Panther" films. Really, one could fill one's bags with just these things and vegetate in front of the box for weeks. The selection of music videos is the most tantalising for me and I selected a Neil Young live set and Bon Jovi on tour for Sharon. Rather cruelly, I called her up to announce that I had secured front row seats for a Bon Jovi concert, with free beer. She was whooping with delight when I slipped in that she should enjoy the DVD. One slightly deflated wife, but her sense of humour remained intact.

A visit to Ka-De and a short walk around the streets demanded another refreshment stop, this time in a shopping mall on the Huahai Rd. A couple of fresh orange juices were enjoyed for RMB22/£1.57 each and the people-watching began. There was a glass partition between us and the shop-floor of the mall, with the perfume counters in full view. This meant an army of pretty little things sporting all the latest Max Factor, Maybelline and other manufacturers' products. The sales girls had obviously raided the demonstration boxes and were made up to the nines, but the customers were, as usual with most Chinese girls, bare of cosmetics. How do they do business? Someone must be buying it, but it is rare to smell even a whiff of perfume. (Photo p.XI).

We sat there in an Italian-inspired café, surrounded by Chinese, with a girl and her mother to one side and a pair of couples on the other two. Mother and daughter never let their phones leave their hands – calls were received, made and texts sent. They did not say much to each other. In front of me, one couple was most amusing; he was smoking, or trying to smoke a pipe, which is very unusual for a young lad. He also typically had his trousers rolled up to his knees (fortunately his beautiful partner could not see them). She was a tall, elegant girl with lovely long legs, but as ever with things Chinese, the finish was marred. A shaving device had never been close to her armpits and wiry black hairs fought their way out of her yellow summer dress.

She barely touched her drink, and it was not long before her mobile came out and The Pipe was lost behind the phone screen and his cloud of smoke.

I present therefore some rules for dating in China. These have been gathered mostly from actual observation, reading and listening to the young lads here talk about the subject. So I could be wide of the mark, but what the heck, this is just meant to be fun.

- Always check with the girl's parents – are you allowed to take her out? Have you a bright future and do you own your own property?
- Does she know how to get to the date? This must be pursued vigorously. Full directions, checked and written in triplicate must be given. These must be followed up on the day or night in question by regular mobile phone calls to check upon imminent arrival.
- The guy must smoke. He must blow smoke right into her eyes and not even notice the discomfort.
- The girl must not complain at this. A small amount of hand-waving the smoke away is permitted.

- Mobile phones must be used all the time, as soon as any hint of nervousness shows itself. Call or text someone at any time.
- It is perfectly acceptable not to talk to your date at all during the time together; there may be many more interesting people on the other end of the 'phone. This may help to avoid any unseemly intimacy that her mother or the government would not approve of.
- Not talking to your partner is a normal piece of inactivity for a Chinese date. If the mobile 'phone does not go off, or you cannot think of any people to call, then it is time for the ultimate contact-avoidance device – the lap-top. Don't worry, she will go to the magazine rack and pick out some glossies which show blokes who are much better looking than you and just as communicative.
- Guys must slurp their drinks as noisily as possible. Drink tea with floating leaves so this becomes almost unavoidable.
- Any eating must be done, fellows, with the mouth open, revealing masticated food and allowing maximum noise to escape.
- During the meal, please keep the head low, thus showing the lady the top of one's head. Remember to slurp and eat as quickly as possible.
- The only interruptions to eating are for answering the mobile and texting.
- Boys, as soon as eating is finished, either light up a cigarette, or take the opportunity to sniff heartily, looking around for somewhere to use as a spittoon. If all else fails, use the floor. Marble floors are especially recommended.
- Ladies, any make-up is frowned upon on this date. You will spend much of the date cowering behind hands held up to the face anyway. This reaction is in response to any funny or stupid comment the boy makes.
- Don't even think about staying out late, otherwise you have to answer to parents and grandparents. Weapons may be employed to discourage lateness. 9.00pm is late, this is time to put her on the bus and go in the opposite direction.
- Any form of sexual contact is prohibited by the government. You will be informed by e-mail when you are old enough for this step by the local Party official.

A slight over-exaggeration in some aspects, but most of it is based on actual fact/observation. A leaf through some of the English publications here shows similar glimpses of this dating scene. Hooray told me that when he was at school, he and his mates were forbidden to look at the girls and he is only one year out of college!

Monday, 19th September 2005
Always something to look forward to on a Monday with our regular team meeting at 8.30am. Gary always ensures that there is plenty to hear of relevance to our business and personal lives on this assignment. Some of it is good news, some bad. Often there is a comedy speech from Let, which is cringefully bad. There are barely suppressed groans to greet this interjection.

I decided to leave work 30 minutes early, in order to catch a taxi into Puxi to go and collect my plane tickets to Hong Kong and to discuss what may be available for a holiday in the first week of October when our office closes.

On the way I spotted the best non-job for ages. As it would have been so busy in the tunnels, my driver asked if I minded his using the Nanpu bridge – longer but probably quicker and a decent view. At the end of the main bridge section there is a glass guard's hut facing the road. Inside and to attention was Jimmy Wang, in his Nanpu Bridge guard uniform. How long had he been there? Would there be his mate Johnny Ping at the other end? Yes, there he was too, again at attention. The cars were whizzing by, no-one bar me took any notice. Why? What is the point? Do they ever ask themselves?

We made it in good time to the office of Bestrip, a tiny room probably 2m x 3m with Frank and his chum inside, booking holidays for people. Before I could pay I had to find a "hole in the wall" for some cash, as the one at work was dead. The first machine I tried after a foray down the Nanjing Xi Lu rejected my card, so I ventured into one of the most exclusive shopping centres on that auspicious road. A nice HSBC machine, giving out cash lurked within. Suitably armed, I could return through the beautiful Phoenix gardens, opposite the concrete Jing'An Temple and into the Apollo Business Centre for my tickets. (Photo p.XI).

Tuesday, 20th September 2005
In the evening, Rolf and I decided to patronise the new buffet-style restaurant just down the road from the Pent-Ox. It looked clean, bright and inviting. As we approached the door, you could see the scramble from the welcoming

party to open the doors, so much so that we were almost sucked off the pavement and into the place.

As we stood there blinking in the bright lights, it was a case of, "Right, what do we do now?" No-one spoke English and we were keen to show we knew not how to work the system. We were ushered to a booth out at the back, so we gweilos (foreigners) could not be seen from the road, perhaps. A Chinese menu was stuck in front of us; we tried to point at the inviting looking picture of a meal, but no go. We managed to order drinks and then the only chap in the place with any English, which was good enough to say that he did not speak any, showed us how to order food.

This was achieved by picking up the order sheet on the table and walking around to the front counter, filling in what was required and handing it in. We just pointed at that which looked good and he filled in the boxes. Most dishes were about RMB5 each. In the end, we chose badly, or it was not good food. Most was stodgy and cold, even with the help of an English-speaking fellow customer. We had enough food to feed four, but could not manage it.

Many of the waiting staff came around the back to look at us eating. We shunned the offer of forks, preferring to impress them with our alacrity with the sticks. This increased the spectacle for all to see.

Every restaurant and most bars have the cleaner, who mops around your feet, sweeps the floor and ensures that standards of hygiene are maintained (local standards), but at least they do clean up. The lad in the Paulaner mops around your feet whilst you are at the urinal; on other occasions I have been dancing away seductively (or not!) and Mrs Mop has been sweeping around the crowded dancefloor at 2.00am! The mop-girl at this establishment was a real dish – a bit like the dishes we were eating; somewhat stodgy and cold. She sported a five o'clock shadow around her upper lip and moved so slowly as to be almost stopped. She dallied for a long time by our table, leaning heavily on the tool of her trade, gazing at the two white guys struggling with unfamiliar food.

She was desperate for someone to talk to her, dallying over by the drinks counter, listening to the banter, but all the waiting staff just ignored her completely, stepping on her and her mop, nudging her out of the way. It is an interesting phenomenon that these people seem to treat those of a lower social or professional standing with disdain, or even pretend they are not there.

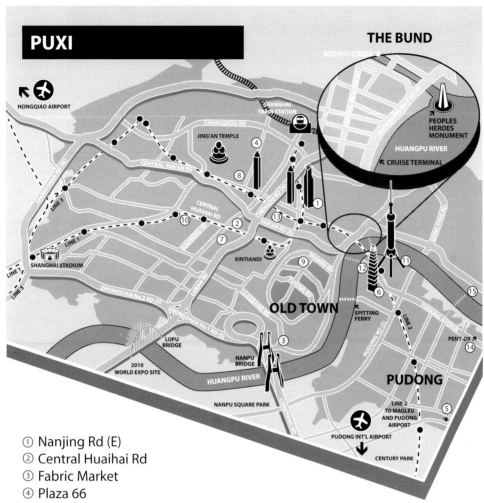

1. Nanjing Rd (E)
2. Central Huaihai Rd
3. Fabric Market
4. Plaza 66
5. To Carrefour-Pudong, Diamond Court on Biyun Lu
6. Jinmao Tower
7. Taikang Rd, Art Street
8. Shanghai Centre
9. Shanghai Old Street – Yu Yuan
10. Shanxi Rd, Xiang Yang
11. Oriental Pearl Tower
12. Super Brand Mall
13. People's Square
14. Pent-Ox
15. Taidong Lu Ferry

"I want my Mummy!" A typical Chinese scene with a crouching child, arm protectors, a bike, the ubiquitous stool and lunch-time litter. (Photographer, M. Allen).

The view from my room in the Pent-Ox, of Pudong Da Dao, the Novotel and on down to the Financial District. (Photographer, I. Pogson).

The two main towers of the "Citic Pent-Ox Metropolis", showing the lower admin block, on top of which was the swimming pool. (Photographer, I. Pogson).

The view towards the river showing the noisy yard and piles of cement bags. These are the alley-ways the trucks would crash up and down. (Photographer, I. Pogson).

The more up-market Diamond Court showing the huge "Tai Sheng Yua" restaurant complex on the corner of Biyun and Huangyang Lu. (Photographer, I. Pogson).

The line of cafés and bars such as the Original Taste (or Mawdesley) to the left, the Coffee Beanary, Japanese Ren and the East-West to the right. (Photographer, I. Pogson).

Some of the buildings around Lujiazui Park, made famous by the film "Mission Impossible III". This is the HSBC building among others. (Photographer, I. Pogson).

The typically styled "New Asia Glory Hotel", which was our lunch venue for many a day. All our local colleagues ate here when their numbers grew. (Photographer, I. Pogson).

Super Brand Mall; 8 floors of shopping and eating frenzy.
Am I in the States or China? (Photographer, I. Pogson).

The Yan'An Road Park or Square Park on the corner of People's Square which used
to be home to 4,837 families. (Photographer, I. Pogson).

The one and only 420m, 88-storey Jinmao Tower, with offices up to floor 50 and the Grand Hyatt hotel upwards thereafter. (Photographer, I. Pogson).

The famous skyline, showing the Oriental Pearl Tower and the globes of the Exposition Hall. (Photographer, M. Allen).

The amazing night sights along the river. (Photographer, A. Roy).

The Bund from river level. (Photographer, E. Harris).

The Bund in all its night-time lights from the Pearl Tower. (Photographer, A. Roy).

Just one of many crazily illuminated shops on the Nanjing Road.
(Photographer, S. Pogson).

The old Xiangyang market, a haggle-till-you-drop paradise for shoppers.
(Photographer, S. Pogson).

The Cybermart on the Huahai Lu. Four floors of everything PC.
(Photographer, I. Pogson).

The Ka-De Club 1, off Maoming Lu and a typical Shanghai street scene.
(Photographer, I. Pogson).

The concrete and brass Jing'An temple, mixed in with top-flight shops on
Nanjing Lu. (Photographer, I. Pogson).

The homely but damp "Spitting Ferry" on Donchang Lu plies across the Huangpu River. (Photographer, I. Pogson).

The cruise ship "Princess Jeannie" which took the 3 Georges and Claude up the Yangtze. (Photographer, M. Billington).

"Looks like a sixties caravan" was how the cabins were described. Cosy.
(Photographer, M. Billington).

The model of the 3 Gorges dam site. The lock up-and-down-flights can be seen, as
well as the ship-lift and electricity generators. (Photographer, M. Billington).

Five 80m stepped locks ascend and descend the 3 Gorges Dam.
(Photographer, M. Billington).

Water is forced out of the lock to attempt to remove silt at the same time and so
prevent damage to the turbines below. (Photographer, M. Billington).

Away from the main channel of the Yangtze river on the Shennong Stream, the water and surrounding became greener. (Photographer, M. Billington).

As everywhere, these local children were ready to pose on the mountain of rubble which had recently been their neighbours' houses. (Photographer, I. Pogson).

A typical Old City Shanghai street, where nothing was more than three stories high. (Photographer, I. Pogson).

This butcher, surrounded by demolition, was still selling uncovered meat in the dusty air. (Photographer, I. Pogson).

Wednesday, 21st September 2005

Today was another hot one and sure enough at 2.30pm around came our lady cleaner, Mrs Mop-Ping with the ice-cream! This employee service was explained to us as "welfare".

The evening was spent in the apartment, as it had rained heavily at the end of the day. We were catching the tail-end of a typhoon out in South China, and about 4.00pm darkness set in and the sky was a very threatening grey, with very low cloud and poor visibility.

Thursday, 22nd September 2005

Being driven around here and watching the way people just do not look where they are going, seeming to trust to destiny, gives one an expectation of accidents. Today was no exception. Two-wheelers regularly have apparent right of way over right-turning cars across them and most never even look left to see if there is anything coming. For their part, right-turning drivers rarely seem to look right, back up the bike lane and so it seems to come as something of a shock when there is one of the many near-misses. Today was our first sight of blood at an incident. She had been knocked off her scooter and was lying on the ground, high heel shoe off her foot, lying on her bare arm on the concrete, but she was still able to use her mobile 'phone. Highly likely she was on this at the point of contact. Her leg seemed to be straight, but we whizzed by in the taxi as a crowd gathered. No-one seemed to be helping, just staring.

Was she calling her Mum, her own ambulance, or just finishing off the call she was already on about who was at the top of the music charts or who was going out with whom?

Another frustrating day in the office. We are here for our advice and support as experts in our fields, but time after time we are actively excluded, or just ignored. One almost wants the project to experience failure to teach these people that it is a serious game we are playing and cheapness does not guarantee success or quality, often the opposite.

It was good to see one of the team's wives turn up from the UK at the start of her planned 2-year residence here. I spent a pleasant time talking with her (on her third day here) about where to go and the ways of these people around us. There is so much to tell a new-comer to this city about where to find information and where to go. I have started a tourist information folder on the shared area at work, for the same reason.

The view from the 18th floor "B" window across the cement yard and over to Puxi was impressive, with clear views of the Lujiazui area, the Pearl Tower and all the massive buildings of the Financial District. Apart from the noise from the yard, it is quite amazing at night, with millions of lights and the river winding away as it forms a swan-neck shape into the distance.

Friday, 23rd September 2005

Today was my long-planned first training session for the locals. I had set the time, 9.00am to suit my team leader and his team. He had agreed the details and e-mailed his team and copied me, with no translation. I struggled to use the PC translator and roped in Hooray to help. I had caught the gist of his message, but he had obviously not caught the meaning of mine, despite it being in English and Chinese, printed out for him and sent as a document.

However, come this morning, he was nowhere to be seen and when I enquired, he was at an "emergent *(sic)* meeting" so could we postpone to later at 10.00?

I then had to shuffle things with the vehicle workshop that were supporting me, with cars and drivers. 10.00 approached and an e-mail appeared on my screen, *from the lad behind me,* Dizzy, informing me that we needed to postpone to 1.00. This was getting silly. I drew on my massive reserves of patience and settled in for a wait. Finally at 1.00 we sat down. I expected four people. I was surrounded by eight, which was fine, interest at least. I started to wade through my short presentation. You could see that was not really of interest to them.

All they wanted to do was cut to the quick – the visit to the hallowed mansions of the workshop and to look at the cars. When this moment arrived, we gathered some more interested bodies along the way and by the time we had been in the shop for a few minutes the crowd had grown to about fifteen. There were people I had never seen before, listening. I had picked a 4-cylinder turbo petrol car to show. There was much interest in the car on the ramp, so I went through underbonnet layout, really unaware of what was sinking in about packaging, pipe runs, system interaction and all sorts. I ran up the engine to about 5,000rpm to show them what it sounded like. Their faces were a picture, so I explained that if we were to build cars for sale to Europe, then those sorts of engine speeds would be common. The car was then raised so they could view the underside.

We then looked at a V6 car, a packed engine bay, with many opportunities for poor quality engineering to scupper the whole car, so I was keen to stress the need for attention to detail and keeping the parts to drawing, as that worked. There was much interest in this, as it should be the first car built by the Chinese.

The next exercise was to take people out in cars, but because the times had changed twice, the drivers were now in a meeting and we had to wait or return at 15.30. This we did, with a very much smaller crew, some claiming they were too busy (yet they find time to sleep in the office; there can be as many as four away with the birds at any one time). 15.30 came and went, still no drivers, so we waited again, me trying to flannel and fill in the time with another run-up of the engine and a look around the boot area. After fifteen minutes the drivers appeared and I could despatch six people out in the cars. I then left my thanks with the supervisor and returned to the office to do some work. The passengers came back with big smiles on their faces and full of praise for the cars. A demonstration always works wonders. Now they know what we are chasing as a standard.

Other tasks for the day included my being asked to "pronounce" as to its suitability on a tub of grease set down on my desk, two castings with big problems and a meeting with the new oil filter supplier, fronted yet again by a bi-lingual, smart lady. Engineering in China is full of these beauties and they just leave their male colleagues in the shadows for ability, character and drive.

Shopping after work, fashion disaster of the day was a rather chunky girl in a brown trouser suit, but sporting shiny red wellies on her feet!

A discipline debacle was yet again another single child, yet again over-weight and over-noisy. He had been a pain in the aisles, screaming "Papa" at his poor, mis-guided father and he continued to be irritating at the check-outs, guzzling back his colour-laden fizzy drink, which may well have heightened his already hyper state. Whatever happened to well-ordered Confucian society where obedience to parents was a bed-rock principle of Chinese life? I see an increasing number of these children. His father made no attempt to calm his charge, grinning inanely at him.

I watched some of the excellent CCTV, an English-speaking Chinese National station, which featured an interesting piece on Chinese students abroad. The paradox is that as there are so many Chinese, competition for jobs is intense, so many parents ship their kids abroad. Then they return and there is still intense competition and their perceived advantage in having been abroad is not quite seen that way by employers.

Some are sent as young 14 years old to Britain, a favourite destination (there can be 60,000 Chinese students in Blighty at any time). Imagine that, 14 years of age and 6,000 miles from your family, facing expensive, foreign food, expensive public transport and all the other things we are famous for in the UK. Some of the interviews with a student in Bournemouth and his parents in Beijing illuminated the earlier observation I had made in Carrefour about ill-disciplined children. He admitted to being a "rebel" and being stupid with his money, unable to look after himself and used to being spoon-fed. He was obviously from a wealthy background and admitted wasting plenty.

Another girl was sent abroad against her wishes, as her parents wanted to kick-start her career and she was obviously bright and slipped into Oxford, growing and having a good time, eventually. She returned, unsure of whether she was Chinese or English, as so much of her formative years had been spent abroad. She did not walk into a highly-paid job and since had to adjust her aspirations to meet new Chinese working life.

This reality does not stop the educational institutions from across the Western world coming to China, recruiting students nor from parents encouraging their off-spring to seek the advantages they believe exist for their loved ones in studying abroad. It is good income for the universities and it does all look very tempting in the brochures and presentations.

When I finally rested my eyes from the box, I took a taxi to the Pearl Tower and walked up to the promenade by the river towards the cafés and the Paulaner bar. The river traffic was busy and as ever fascinating to watch; boats of all shapes and sizes rumbling down-river towards the sea. The lights from the Bund and from my side of the river reflected on their dirty sides. Only three days earlier the high tide would have prevented my walking along the promenade here. Tonight the much-reduced moon was in company with that most rare of sights in the Shanghai sky – stars. I could see three. As usual, the sky was also bereft of birds. It is more usual to see bats than their feathered flying counterparts.

Saturday, 24th September 2005
Nothing was pressing so I lazed about and was planning my ride on the streets of Shanghai to visit a gallery showing photographs of local family residences

across the social spectrum, when Rolf turned up. He had just flown in and was catching up on the latest. He was intrigued with my offer of a place on the Yangtze cruise we had booked (for the October holiday) and just needed to check on Monday with his team at work to ensure that nothing required his attention during the shut-down.

For entertainment, I chose to ride down the road which follows Suzhou Creek and is marked on the map as there. I have been along some of it before with my wife, but had forgotten just how bad some of the roads were. A repair to one of the over-bridges and underpasses meant that there was a diversion and directions were naturally in Chinese, but it meant riding down backstreets, past people's front doors and sinks, then through a tunnel back onto the road. It is a good job that the bike is well suspended at the front, which absorbed some of the pot-holes and roughness.

This is China, so there are always people everywhere; they have no gardens, so they meet and play, eat and gossip in the road. Children run amock in the dust and scrap as kids do, with mothers looking on from their perches atop tiny wooden or plastic stools. On the other side of the Creek, new apartment blocks stood amongst manicured lawns and foliage. The rich and the poor exist side by side again.

At one point, a man was loading some flattened wet cardboard boxes onto a trailer. He was picking them up from the floor, raising them above his head and onto the trailer. I could see from some distance away that this was causing a wide arc of dirty water to be sprayed about, so I timed my arrival at the spot to be when he was stooping down. It came as a complete surprise to those in front of me that they were soaked! Chinese expletives ensued and he just carried on, wetting them some more as they sat there and argued!

Rolf and I walked down to the SB Mall, but we had not ventured very far when our nostrils were assailed by a pungent smell. A group of women had parked their bicycles in typical Chinese fashion across the pavement (sorry, but from my observation, women are really bad at this). They were stooped down, some wearing the blue overalls of the street-cleaners, some in ordinary clothes and some with a bin-bag over the top. They were engaged in a painting session of the small railings, about 400mm high, which surround the small bushes separating the cycle-lane from the pavement. There was one major problem, in that it was dark. Now it is not unknown to see railings painted in the UK and for drips of paint to end up on the floor, but these girls were splashing black paint on some fine, granite blocks which form the edge of the flower-bed, so that it looked terrible. They were also painting the soil, where it covered the lower portion of the railings. No attempt at all was made to keep the stones clean.

Amused by this, we continued our amble, waving at the girls in the "hair-dresser" shops, who vainly tried to beckon us in. It must be a boring life, stuck in the same shop all day and into the night, week-in, week-out, with just the TV for company, as so few clients ever seem to be in there.

The walk to Lujiazui always creates a sensation of wonder at the architecture in the financial district. Each visit brings more detail into view.

Before we made it to that point, however, we passed by the massive advertising hoardings at Eton Place, the new development on the Da Dao. In front of this brightly-lit edifice was a group of locals engaged in some community music – it seems a regular concert is a feature of life thereabouts. Everyone has his or her tiny wooden stool and as we turned up we were recognised by a lady who works at the Pent-Ox. I was wearing my Chairman Mao shirt and we were instant celebrities, particularly as we applauded loudly once the piece had finished. There was a resident singing, accompanied by a sax player, and several traditional instruments as well as a keyboard and a late arrival that was on percussion. For this role, he produced a precision-shaped piece of wood, a plastic water carrier with some string through the handle and a tambourine! The plank bridged the carrier to his stool and he sat thereon, banging his tambourine.

They tried to encourage us to stay for more, but we were on the trail of food, so I rubbed my stomach and tried the best sign-language.

The free entertainment had not finished, for up-river was a synchronised fireworks display, from four different locations. One thing the Chinese do well is make noise. The pyrotechnics were quite superb, and lit up the sky, reflecting upon all the buildings in the area.

Our meal over, we took a walk along the prom towards the Paulaner bar. The Bund was as vibrant and bright as ever; I never tire of the sight and the constant flow of river traffic which makes for an interesting walk, along with the essential people-watching.

It is a magnet for courting couples, who display many of the traits already noted and there are the usual groups of friends taking innumerable shots of each other in true Oriental style. They still manage to drop rubbish everywhere, but the litter-picker was not far away.

Sunday, 25th September 2005

Rolf's day began early with a ride out to Century Park, where he made a lap of the place, but on his return suffered a puncture. Later examination revealed a valve torn at its junction with the tube in his front tyre. This set him looking for the tell-tale bowl of water. This would indicate the presence of a "Bicycle Repair Man" in the vicinity. A bowl of water and a pump are the only signs one needs of immediate support when stricken thus.

He appeared to have his stores in the bushes when Rolf turned up and the damage was investigated, and so a new tube was procured. With sign-language and pointing he convinced our intrepid cyclist that it was of superior quality and worth every penny of the RMB60/£4.29 he wanted to charge. Rolf hacked him down to RMB40/£2.86. This was a difficult haggle with no calculator.

Half-way through his repair, a damsel in distress turned up with a flat and "Bicycle Repair Man" instructed his first customer to pump up the lady's tyre. Sub-contracting on the streets of Shanghai, I hope Rolf declares that to the Tax Man.

Later on, we decided upon a cultural day of Art and Design. Our first stop was the Shanghai Art Museum in the old Racecourse Building. This was RMB30 entrance fee – which was worth it for Wu Zhoudong's painting of the Yangtze River course, with interpretation provided for us by a passing local girl. Other paintings stood out, such as "Two swallows" and "Music on the wire", both of which were notable for their lack of colour and paint, being little more than line drawings.

The displays were of a high standard and featured works from the year-long Franco-Chinese cultural exchange, which included art from the Sun King's collection – Louis XIV exquisite palace at Versailles. I even recognised some of the places shown on the drawings from our visit there some years ago.

A drink at Starbuck's next door followed, as after all that art we needed a sit-down to contemplate all the wonders we had seen. We were greeted by a lovely girl at the counter, with a big smile and welcoming attitude. It makes life so much better and it is free. We spent a pleasant time discussing the works we had just seen and left with another big smile from the little girl. Just that one person made a big difference to our day.

Next on the list was the Shanghai Development Corp exhibition with what must be the world's most ambitious projects and models. This was on another corner of the People's Park and is an incredible piece of architecture in its own right; with plenty of glass and stainless steel and four strange inverted square cones on the roof. The Square is populated with amazing buildings, each wildly different and surrounded by others of equal quality. It is said that sadly the styles are all Western and employed Western architects, but the effect is dazzling and there is plenty of space to view each one. Most are under 20 years old, but there is the odd survivor from an earlier age, although the oldest of them is under one hundred.

Top of the pops has to be, Jinmao Tower, whose sheer strength and majesty is best seen against a dark sky with a hint of cloud, when the exterior is illuminated after the offices on the lower floors have turned off their lights. Then the crown on top is lit white and the orange glow of the Hyatt hotel lobby stands out on floor 50-something. The stepped shape of the building casts shadows up its height, adding to the look of strength. (Photo p.VII).

The Development Exhibition was ours for only RMB30, with an option to take in a Russian impressionists art show for another ten. Time was against us, so we saved the massive extra expenditure. Each of the six floors show something different, with the entrance ground floor exhibiting work from the Architecture Department of Tianjin University, which was of a very high standard. Next floor up was a show of the old face of Shanghai, from the opening of it as a Treaty Port by the Western powers. This was mainly sepia print photographic slides, which conveyed a feeling of age and a couple of dioramas with noisy soundtracks showing the growth of the city from a fishing village to the massive metropolis it is today.

The next floor was the art, so we scooted up to the principal exhibit we had come to see – the model of Shanghai. I had worked for Rover these 24 years, so I am used to grandiose plans dreamed up by marketing bods seemingly off another planet, but nothing prepared me for the dream that was on display in there. Rolf and I stood, stunned by the sheer size of the exhibit, showing a vast part of the city centre, from way past Century Park in the east to Zhongshan Park west and a stretch of the river between Nanpu and Yanpu bridges. All buildings were shown, as they are or planned to be and the Pent-Ox was there in all its glory, but no sign was seen of the docks along the whole length of the river in the model. Everywhere was landscaped into submission and most of the Lilongs (traditional Shanghai alley-ways and courtyard residences) were gone, replaced by faceless high-rise blocks.

We could recognise much that had already been achieved, (this being a plan for the city up to 2015) and the new World Financial Centre, which is currently under construction, was shown next to Jinmao.

The whole effect was most impressive, with one of the aims seeming to be to eradicate all evidence of shipping and docks. Virtually the whole of the Huangpu River banks were landscaped.

The final presentation upstairs showed, amongst other things, the quadrupling of Pudong airport and a container base on an island. These are massively ambitious, mega-million projects.

We adjourned for a meal in a Brazilian restaurant inside Raffles City, another of the city's monster shopping palaces. The sign said "all you can eat for RMB68", if we read it correctly, which was a good price. The scheme was that one was shown to a table, and then it was away to the buffet to feast on the hot and cold dishes, which included mashed potato! Then one struggled back to one's seat with an over-flowing plate and awaited the constant attentions of the 24 staff, and 6 "Chefs" wandering round with barbecued duck, shrimps, mushrooms, squid, sausage, beef, pork, pineapple and hot banana on huge skewers. I ate too much again; how does Rolf eat so much?

Monday, 26th September 2005

Another Monday, another week begins with the usual level of frustration at the office.

Rolf and I decided to do the walk down to the ferry, cross over to Yu Gardens and have a late meal in the "78" restaurant. This is a really funny place, but the food is good and cheap, RMB136 for two. Whilst sitting there, a lady appeared as she did last time, pressing her watch/DVD/handbag catalogue against the window as we dined. Go away, we don't want to buy from you!

We wandered through the colourful backstreets with more pyjama-people and folk selling well into the night. It is as ever funny to imagine what they are saying to each other – "Come on, darling, I'll take you out for some new pyjamas, those are really too frumpy. While we are out we can stop for a bowl of noodles in the street outside Wang's shop, then we can weigh ourselves on the mobile scales, treat ourselves to a RMB4 DVD and squeeze up on the sofa back home under the strip light with Grandma and Grandpa".

Tuesday, 27th September 2005

This evening Native had promised to take out one of the Chinese engineers. It was just a gesture to a really great colleague, not a show of how much money we had and we hope he took it that way. The meal was taken in the restaurant at the side of Diamond Court, which always provides good food and we took the usual interminable time to choose our fare. This perhaps explains why one person normally selects the menu and there is only one provided. We had a good social time with Native, Frau, Marvin, Rolf, myself and Joe. The whole deal for several courses (one each shared) was RMB160.

Wednesday, 28th September 2005

Conundrum of the day was the fruit-seller, who cannot make much money on selling his wares from the back of a tricycle, who was on his mobile. A recent article by a Hong Kong film director remarked that when he arrived in Shanghai only eight years ago, he was looked at as if he were an alien with his mobile to his ear. Now everyone sports such a device and would be socially excluded without. I saw a stupid girl on hers shouting at the caller and then saying "Ah, Ah, Ah", which I believe is a sort of "Pardon, I can't hear you". She was stood a couple of metres from the Da Dao, with buses, trucks and cars really thundering by at high speed. Why didn't she go inside?

Today we discovered that in order for the season to be officially autumn; there has to be five days in a row with temperatures below 22°C. Then it is on with the heavy coats until Spring.

Saturday, 1st October 2005

Today was the day for Lisa to wed our very own Prop. The civil ceremonies had already happened some time before, so they had been married in the eyes of the Chinese law already. Prop wanted to show his new bride what a good British "knees-up" was like. The reception was to be a truly International event – a beautiful Chinese Bride, a Scots Groom and Best Man, a Welsh MC, an Irish visitor, even Brummies were welcome and it was all to be held in a Turkish restaurant in JinQiao. Special guests came, including Ray and Mrs Philips all the way back from the UK and Steve King and Helen.

Other guests included some of the Chinese team from work, who were pleased to be there. We think.

The event was announced to the whole of the locality in Chinese style by having fireworks in the bright sunshine outside the restaurant complex. This resulted in a noisy welcome, but also for us all to be showered with debris from the massive pyrotechnics. Little children were scooped up by tut-tutting mothers and play equipment was hastily put under cover.

As this was a marriage to a Scot, both Prop and the Best Man were in kilts, resulting in some characteristically stupid comments from some Americans who should have taken more notice of other cultures from which they could even have descended. Stunned locals also watched in amazement.

Lisa was dressed in traditional White, which later would change to blue, then red, as Chinese brides have three dresses.

Once inside the restaurant, it took a while to notice the big photo on the wall, flanked by a St Andrews Cross and the Red Flag of China. The picture showed bride and groom looking very slim in Prop's case and unusually dapper. Naturally Lisa looked superb, in all three dresses.

The waiting staff were clad in Turkish football strip, which added to the colour – balloons crowned the entrance doors and a large coloured poster announced that this was the site of the reception for our two friends.

Lilly, the restaurant manageress was on top form, fussing around and organising her staff. She had added another international dimension by employing a new manager to run things in her absence who is Philippino!

There was food for 70 or so and it was gratifying to see the bride's parents smiling and not too phased by the events. At great expense, the specially imported Welsh MC Gary called the proceedings to order and explained how it would all pan out. Precisely 18 minutes into the event, some Chinese guests arrived, characteristically late. The MC commented that we were all previously under the impression that we were 7 hours adrift of Chinese time in the UK, but that this was wrong and we were now 7 hours 18 minutes ahead!

Also, whilst the speeches were on, the familiar cheesy ring of a Chinese mobile phone could be heard. The culprit was suitably glared at.

The food included fare suitable for Chinese and Western tastes, with some Turkish overtones. There was something for everybody and plenty of it. Time passed very agreeably with a very emotive address by the groom, who was simply overjoyed to see everyone and a star performance from the MC. Rachel (ex-HR) translated and then launched herself into a song for the happy couple. She was very brave stood in front of all of us and sang as sweet as a bird. A good deal of socialising was done, which we are now very good at, and after the tables were cleared somewhat, the skinny belly-dancer came out. She enjoyed a short fling with Clegg who is a lovely mover and gave her a twirl. She then came looking for a second victim and came chasing me but I was not interested and went into hiding. I was finally dragged onto the dance-floor trying to complain of a leg injury and hopping along. She was having none of it, that waif-like dancer. At that moment, like a man on a white charger, Steve came in and rescued me from her clutches and pink scarf. I cowered back to my seat, sweating but relieved.

Amusingly, Donk escaped when the free drinks finished, as the groom had kindly put some money behind the bar, but we had drunk too much of it. We are British, after all. The Tiddlies also ran away when the first round of food had been consumed, which just left us hardened party-goers. The Bride and Groom announced they were going three times so we just carried on regardless. More food came out, so round two began. Rolf tipped his plate into his lap and tried to look cool about it.

Chapter 4

FORMULA ONE RACING AND A YANGTZE

CRUISE IN GOLDEN WEEK

Sunday, 2nd October 2005
The Three Georges (and Claude) in the Three Gorges –
a cruise on the Chang Jiang

Following an excellent time at Prop and Lisa's wedding, Sunday dawned and it was time to become "cruisers". We had booked via the Bestrip travel agency (frank@bestrip.com.cn) a five-day cruise upriver on the Yangtze, or Chang Jiang (Great River). The plan was to fly out of Shanghai Hongqiao airport (the original, old one) to Wuhan, cruise up to Chongqing and return via Pudong airport, Shanghai.

The old airport was reached in about half an hour as the traffic was unexpectedly light for the second day of the Chinese "Golden Week" holiday and we checked in the few bags we had, then passed through Security to find refreshment in the 60s-styled airport restaurant. The décor is straight out of an early James Bond film and has certainly seen better days. The food is good enough and not outrageously priced.

Wuhan airport is very small, with two baggage carousels and we stood by the wrong one. Outside, we followed the taxi signs and with our boat ticket were able to convince the driver of our destination. The taxi was a locally made Citroen ZX, which makes a pleasant change from the usual VWs of Shanghai and we endured a tortuous journey through Wuhan city centre. The driving was of the usual low standard, with many close shaves on the way and the place looking like any other Chinese city we have visited. Dusty and teeming with life, Wuhan was not a place I would be desperate to see again. The driver was unsure of the ship's berth and managed to stop at the correct place, then when we showed him the ticket again, he told us to get back in and we drove in a big loop down the dock road, eventually returning to almost the same spot, following some angry exchange by 'phone with the cruise operator. The bill was increased by RMB10/70p, but hard-nosed Winston refused to pay as we had just done a loop.

As it was a National Holiday, the promenade was bustling with visitors as we fought our way to the ship's berth at terminal 23. The dirty, brown river did not look too inviting; neither did the walkways leading down to the ships. We spotted our ship and were impressed with its size and tidy appearance. The welcome once on board was as polite as ever and keys were issued for rooms on the top deck, at the front of the vessel. "It's like a 1960s caravan" said Brummie upon opening his cabin door. It is true, they were small, but as we were to realise, little time was spent in the cabin, with plenty to see outside and a bar waiting. (Photos p.XII, p.XIII).

We arrived quite early on board the "Princess Jeannie", and whilst settling in to our rooms, I became aware of a brass band playing. There, down on the floating pontoon to which the ship was tied, had been rolled out a "red carpet" made of plastic and a beautifully turned out ten-piece brass band of female musicians. For the record, and purely as an observation, they were wearing above the knee red tunics, split up to the nethers, with black high-heeled boots and a cheeky little hat. My glasses steamed up, so any further fashion points were lost. They were welcoming people aboard as they arrived. Most passengers came via organised coach trips, so they arrived together. The musicians turned out to be part of the ship's crew with other functions on board and would pop up at various junctures as waitresses and maids.

We left port with a ceremonial sounding of the big horn and slipped out into the dirty, brown river, which was rushing by in a strong current.

The cabins, although small, featured heaters and air-con, and a combined wet room with toilet, shower and sink. There was a daily supply of hot drinking water in a flask and cold water in a jug, with teabags and cups. A fridge, TV and telephone provided ample opportunity to mess about with electrical devices. Two small wardrobes, some wall-cupboards and a table between the beds completed the fittings. (We noted that the Chinese accommodation was distinguished by having bunk-beds). Unoccupied suites were made available at reduced cost once we were under way, though we decided to suffer in our small spaces.

We had paid for all meals up front, except for the first evening meal, which was advertised at $8 a head; so we booked in and it turned out to be the same set-up as we would have at every meal, namely a buffet-style eat-all-you-like job. The best bit was that you could drink as much as you liked, including beer, which suited the average Brit rather well. There was wine on every table, but the one on ours was RMB350, or £23!

Most of our fellow passengers were wrinklies from SAGA in the UK and Canadian OAPs, as well as a bunch of Americans, some Australians, Costa Ricans and Germans. There were some Chinese and very few younger than us. Brummie cooked up a scheme whereby we would try and convince the Americans on the ship that we were actors, called the three Georges, with our director, Claude Van Dam and we were making a homo-erotic film on board. The SAGA crew found this most amusing, but being British, none of them were taken in.

The vessel was clean and well-organised, with a "ballroom" and bar on our deck level (5), a bar at a lower level (4) and library on 3. Deck 5 also featured a large flat open area forward of the funnel with deck-chairs and tables. This was where, throughout the voyage, the Chinese would be playing cards or mah-jong. Also during the cruise, the guides would stand at the bow on a small deck area narrating about the scenery. One guide, we'll call him Howard, as that was his name, spoke English with an irritating American accent and was full of flannel, talking constantly. Our preferred guide was the novice Becky, who turned out to be Hong Kong born and had spent some time in Vancouver, Canada. She was as thin as a rake and had only stood in to the position as her sister had previously occupied it, but had just moved on.

The Safety briefing that evening covered the usual "there aren't enough life-boats" point (which appeared to be true) and was an aquatic form of the one you see on the aeroplanes. Once over, we ventured outside and the scenery, which had been the same for miles and was not to change for many hours and miles, was spread out either side and consisted of concrete, tiles or rocks along the banks, topped by long grass and a few trees.

Also in the briefing was an explanation of the itinerary we would be experiencing for the next four days. This was to include an excursion up a smaller gorge, with a transfer to a local ferry, then again into "pea-pod" boats, or traditional small boats propelled by oarsmen, who would then re-enact "tracking" or towing the boats on bamboo ropes. These trackers used to be naked for their work and the prospect of seeing naked buttocks seemed to set one OAP Antipodean female on fire, as she could barely (pun intended) contain her excitement. Happily in 2005 these boys would be clothed. Her disappointment was palpable. She was to become one of the star irritants of the cruise.

Little could be seen beyond the river-side vegetation; occasionally there were a few goats foraging among the sticks. These were the first live goats I had seen in the country, although I had probably eaten plenty. Occasional water buffalo were spotted. Very occasional birds were spotted – I can still not believe how few feathered friends this country can turn up, except those barbecued on sticks. Also along the banks could be seen the odd ferry landing, usually situated by a pile of gravel of some sort or other. Meagre shelters and other dwellings, and people living on sampans or barges were also evident. Our ship plotted a wide berth on some bends in the river to avoid sand banks and shoals. We were very clearly one of the fastest ships on the river and made good headway.

Our first night on board was spent in the bar sampling the wares and upon turning in, we found that the NVH (Noise, Vibration and Harshness) Dept. had not visited our cabin. At certain times there were severe vibrations through the hull, which set off many cabin fittings. Therefore, at 3.00am, my cabin-mate, Rolf, was seen clambering around the small room, posting "NVH pads" behind the vibrating mirror. These pads were the freebie white hotel slippers which were supplied. They did a sterling job and remained in place for the entire voyage; even left alone by the maid. At other times the wardrobe doors vibrated, but leaving these open or sticking a plastic bag in the joint sorted them out. Another slipper stopped the toilet door from wobbling. Engineers at work!

Day 1, Monday, 3rd October 2005

Day 1 began with an early morning wake-up call – we expected this to be a bit like "Hi-de-Hi" in a holiday camp; "Hello, campers" in a Sino-Welsh accent, perhaps. The cabin had been issued with an itinerary sheet, so we expected this noisy intrusion to our sleeping, which turned out to be pleasant Chinese music (not always an oxymoron – "Butterfly Lovers" music!) and a gentle Chinese female voice inviting us to partake in breakfast, then an "orientation" as they described it in irritating American English.

We were then treated to a "Yangtze River briefing". River facts:

- The Chang Jiang is over 6,380km long, depending upon where one picks as the source.
- The Yangtze is actually the bit of the river north of Shanghai, which empties into the East China Sea, hence the Chinese call the river Great River, Chang Jiang.
- 1.2 million are to be relocated by the flooding for the Dam project.
- The river floods about every 10 years and catastrophically so every 100.
- It last flooded in 1998, with the effect felt by 300 million people.
- Most of the country's cotton and rice comes down the river and a large portion of the fish is caught along its length (although we saw little evidence of either). We saw plenty of coal and building materials moving, however.
- The river drops 5,500m in a length of 6,380km.

After a massive buffet lunch, the terrain outside started to rise a little and the first sign of major river-side habitation was seen, but still the river itself was populated by endless freighters and small sampans with people living on board. "What's for tea, Mum?" "Fish." "Aw, not fish again, Mum." That's how it looked; a life on the water, if no-one caught anything that was it. No dinner. How did they find clean drinking water?

Dam facts from briefing:

- China claims the oldest extant dam in the world, at 2,200 years old and also has more dams than the rest of the world put together.
  This country is sounding a bit like Texas with its boasts of bigger and better!
- The 3 Gorges Dam will produce 18,200 Megawatts of power, planned to be about 15% of China's needs at conception. However, the country's needs have risen so much that when completed it may serve about 5%.
- It measures 185m high, 2,335m wide and 115m deep at its base. It is straight in section, rather than a normal curve.
- The project cost is about $25bn, with China stumping up 85% of it, with the balance contributed from other nations.
- 13 cities, 150 towns, several hundred villages and countless factories have been cleared before being submerged.

- The dam is built in San Dou Ping as there was a small island in the river to use as a bridging piece and there was a large plain and some granite base to build upon and lock into.
- It is a 17 year construction plan and was first mooted in 1919 by the amazing Dr Sun Yat Sen. It was not until 1944 that John Savage, a dam-builder with experience on the Hoover Project in the US picked the site for the reasons above.
- The earlier Gezhou dam, which we were also to negotiate later, was wholly Chinese built and funded, opening in 1981. The dam improves navigability, gives some flood control and makes power.

Pros and cons of the 3 Gorges Dam:

- It will produce clean power (75% of Chinese electricity comes from coal).
- Summer flooding will be controlled between 145 and 155m high.
- Navigability far beyond Chongqing will be improved, allowing bigger boats further up-river.
- Chongqing's 30 million people may even benefit!
- Conversely, the relocation of 1.2 million people was started in 1992. As land is all owned by the government, no-one has an argument about losing land. Half of the project's budget is absorbed by relocation costs.
- The effect on the wildlife is unknown, but can be imagined. Chinese sturgeon fish will no longer be able to swim upstream to spawn as they will not be able to negotiate the locks. However, they have done so on the single lock in Gezhou. Nature is adaptable.
- 600square kilometres of land will be flooded; including many ancient temples; Ming and Qing artefacts will be lost.
- Pollutants from the flooded areas, e.g. sewage, and factory waste have affected the water.
- Sedimentation and erosion is the biggest problem for the dam, with about 5 million tonnes being moved down river in one year.

The evening's entertainment started with a "Cocktail Party" with the Captain on the after sun-deck. Out came the posh frocks and sparkly shoes (and that was just Brummie). Punch, champagne, wine and nibbles were presented for us and a chance to mingle with fellow passengers. The Captain, resplendent in his white dress uniform, had been sailing the River for 30 years, so we were in good hands (when he was awake). If one was so minded, a photo with the officer could be posed and taken by "Roger" the ship's happy snapper.

This was a relaxed occasion, apart from a short speech in Chinese by El Capitano along with essential details of his credentials and his family history. The night closed in and the wind picked up, so we finished up and went inside. To quote a Saga Brit – "It's not a cold wind; it's a windy wind". Harrumph to that.

Dinner was another good troughing, with plenty of choice and quantity. I did wonder if we were the only ones having fun with the waitresses. Our girl was called "Lansing" and we wondered if her real name is Lan Sing. It transpired not, but to many older UK engineers the name Lansing is always followed by the names Bagnall, as in the steam engine maker or, Linde, as in the material handling company.

We tried and tried throughout the voyage to break the Chinese waiters' habit of using one bottle and pouring everyone's drinks from it, by convincing the lovely Lansing to just leave the requisite amount of bottles for each diner on the table. Even hiding one under the table failed.

As is natural for a cruise ship, the ship's company felt it necessary to entertain, a prospect which did not appeal to me as I run a mile from any mention of a "variety show". We decided to go and see the "Welcome show" put on for our "benefit" and hid at the back, close to the bar. It turned out to be typically Chinese and funny in a rather amateur fashion. Highlights from this hot-bed of internationally infamous talent were such delights as:

"A washing song with help from the military".

A "Mongolian happy dance" (how you can be happy in felt tents and a country which is a sub-zero desert most of the year is beyond me).

A girl with a glass-shattering voice (and beautiful dress).

Some "chefs" dancing (one of whom dropped his ladle and was out of synch with the rest).

Some boys from Hunan Province with sticks.

A man with a multiple bulb flute from Hubei.

Naturally, the Tiddlies (our affectionate name for our host people) were late for the performance. How do they ever make it on time for their own funerals? Overall the event was funnier than anything and it passed an hour or so with yet another view on this crazy culture. The crew were obviously multi-talented and keen to show it. Levels of talent varied as did enthusiasm.

River-guide-turned-MC Howard became a "magician" for the evening, with his beautiful assistant, Debbie, who turned a ladies' shoe into an NVH pad (cabin slipper).

After this cultural event, it was off to the bar downstairs and the wrinklies hit the sack. Some of us went for a few laps of the boat deck, keen to see how this huge ship was piloted down such a busy water-way, with smaller vessels showing no lights and wandering around the shipping lanes much the same as Chinese drivers wander about lanes on the roads. The answer, apart from huge lights trained on the banks and ahead, plus sharp-eyed lookouts was a GPS scanning system, which tracked the ship's progress and showed up any land mass either side and all vessels longer than 3m.

We had passed our first town of any size about 4.00pm. There was the odd mud island in the river plus many freighters, such as four barges lashed together carrying steel containers, railway wagons, trucks and vans. This is a busy waterway for the industrial cities either side.

Day 2, Tuesday, 4th October 2005

The following morning, after a 6.00am wake-up call, we were stirred into a frenzy of excitement for the passage through the Gezhou Dam at 7.30am which was most impressive. Once through the gorge, the scenery really opened up and we crowded around the bow to listen to our two guides, (one on each deck), give their different narrations. We were now faced with mountains proper, tree-lined slopes and the odd temple built into the side of the gorge. Black-eared kites wheeled overhead; one of the few times in the whole voyage we were to see large birds in any numbers.

Simple habitations were scattered about the mountain sides and we started to see the terracing of the slopes which was to continue for the rest of the trip. Some attempt was made at tourism, with a few cable-car rides up slopes and the positioning of a replica junk vessel by a pagoda, and a large drum which was banged as we passed. This was just for the tourists, as they seem to have destroyed so much history here, as across the whole country.

Further on, where the river widened and there was some "beach" we began to see the first of many shipyards along the banks. At all of them, a multiple of keels were being laid and built upon. These were not shipyards as we know them, i.e. organised, concrete dry docks, but temporary pitches on barely flat land at the water's edge. The vessels under construction were mostly ferries; big ones capable of carrying probably 50 articulated lorries. We assume that they will be floated and launched once the river rises. A staggering amount of business must be envisaged by the builders. Hulls were propped up on scaffolding and dozens of flares from arc-welders could be seen. At one yard, I counted 10 hulls in a row.

The scenery changed back to mountains and the kites were more numerous. Some old temples and pagodas were built on prominent rocks. A white statue of a famous concubine to the Emperor was a tourist honey-pot. Friendly people waved from the banks and from other vessels, which were starting to thin out. Very few tributaries came into the gorge at this point and in one town, we saw ex-military bright orange barracks which may be turned into homes for the displaced.

We cruised into San Dou Ping and moored alongside a brace of other cruise ships for our excursion to the 3 Gorges Dam site. A sailor from one of the moored vessels was stood on the bow playing a huge flute, which was a very good free concert in amongst all the noise.

Due to a trip to the thunder room, I missed the announcement telling me where to go, and was split from the other chaps, so I hooked up with the Brit SAGA crowd. This proved most amusing; I could now try my legendary ability to send women to sleep with my conversation on a group who were easy prey. In fact, they were keen to learn why a group of four guys were travelling together on the cruise. I spun the yarn about the "Three Georges", but being Brits, they just found it amusing and were not taken in.

Our first stop on the coach tour with "Kevin Blah-blah", our ace guide, politely gave us the facts, and some of his own opinion, but then allowed plenty of time for us to view the civil engineering marvel. We were driven over the new suspension bridge to the north side of the river, and then along to a view-point at the foot of the massive concrete wall. From here, we were not far from the plume of water, gushing out from the foot of the dam, attempting to suck out some of the sediment that is the main enemy to the continued smooth operation of the dam as a power generator. The noise from such a spout of water and the vapour cloud was amazing. We could also see the partially completed "shiplift". The flight of five locks is operational, with the top lock secured open until the final rise in water level.

We then returned to the bus to travel up to the vantage point on top of the site, from where we could see the whole enormity of this facility. It was very busy, being the Holiday Week and it is a major tourist attraction anyway. The view was spectacular; at last we could really make sense of the vastness of the vision and reality of the world's biggest Dam. Words are insufficient to convey the true scope of the concrete acres below. We could see the river disappearing into the mist where we had been and snaking off from the raised water of the dam area. (Photos p.XIII, p.XIV).

We returned to the boat, stunned, and ready for some lunch, which was again superb. We cast off and entered the first of the five locks about 1.00pm. Each lock has a lift of about 20m and a depth of about 30m. Our ship seemed to use a draft of about 7m. We surveyed the scene from the after deck, and the sun beat down on us, burning my rapidly thinning scalp. It was supposed to take about three hours to negotiate all the locks, which we did in company with several other craft; a bulk sand or gravel carrier, complete with elevator belt stuck out like a crane jib at the bow, another cruise ship and a large freighter. There is sufficient room in each lock for four vessels of the same size as ours.

The cruise ship containing only Chinese tourists was alongside and aft of us. They were all, typically, crowded around the bow deck. Stood at the back was the ever-present old salt with a huge pot noodle in hand, wearing the top fashion garment of a rolled-up white vest. He was the picture of sartorial elegance.

We finally cleared the last lock at about 4.00pm, three hours after we entered. We did fall asleep for the passage through the third lock, as the chairs were comfortable and the sun warm. All this time, the old Chinese guys on our ship were in their usual position, which they occupied for most of the voyage on the after sun-deck playing mah-jong. Our passage through the locks was perfectly smooth, with no banging against the lock walls and another example of our crew's precision steering. In order to steady the vessels in the lock, we were tied up to bollards which slid up and down in huge grooves in the lock walls.

We then sailed out into the first of the three Gorges, the Xiling Gorge, which is the longest. We passed by the Temple of Huangling and the Junan

Stream, which has a distinct line between the brown, sediment-laden main river course and the lime-stone bed of the tributary, which gives rise to greener, clearer water.

We arrived at our overnight stop, Bandon, which was heralded by a bright light in the sky, reflecting the glow from a million lights on either side of the river and another new suspension bridge. A hotel fired laser beams into the sky from its roof. We tied up to a pontoon for the night at the confluence of two gorges. Some of the staff took the opportunity to escape from the ship for some time in the city, as we would be away for the morning of the next day.

Day 3, Wednesday, 5th October 2005

Strange things happen in small confined spaces in the dark; ask any chicken which has been in a fridge overnight. In my cabin, it was Rolf and his NVH work at 3.00am, but goings on in the opposite room with Brummie and Winston were somewhat hotter. The temperature aberration was noted by the latter, so obligingly he raised his tired body and not wishing to wake his cabin-boy mate, used his mobile phone screen as a torch and adjusted the controls to activate the air-con. Little did he know, but he was cranking up the heat. Symbols never meant much to this Integration Engineer; he claimed that he saw a "star" sign and took that to be air-con. In the morning, a fried Brummie could be seen facially glowing throughout the ship!

From Princess Jeannie, we transferred in the morning to a local ferry and sailed 30km up the smaller gorge, Shennong Stream, and the water became clearer. We were promised a sighting of a monkey or two. In the end it was a singular creature, which appeared to have been lured to the spot where we saw it by the provision of food. He or she hardly moved at all, so little in fact that we Brit-cynics suspected a device activated by the boat to move the arm of what we thought could be a stuffed monkey.

The scenery around was beautiful, a real rural retreat with just a few dwellings scattered around, the usual terraced fields and friendly people waving; miles away from bustling Shanghai. This is what I had come for – some real Chinese countryside. Footpaths snaked down to the water, and then disappeared up into the trees. The scenery opened up into a confluence of several valleys in a sheltered area with slightly more imposing buildings, some of which had satellite dishes on the roof! We passed a "famous ancient temple" which appeared to be built of breeze blocks and concrete, which will be moved as the river rises.

Our attention was also drawn to one of the few remaining historical wonders, the so-called "hanging coffins". Legend has it that these 300kg wooden coffins, hewn out of solid trunks were somehow inserted into fissures, caves and clefts in the sand-stone rock face, or placed on natural ledges. The mystery is just how they came to be there. In Chongqing we were later to see a model depicting this activity and a real coffin. It is proposed that they were placed there, high up in the rock face (before the river rose) by three possible methods:

Lowered from the top on strong ropes.

A series of scaffolding stages were built, then removed.

Strong cantilever supports were fixed into holes drilled into the face, and then a sloping walkway was laid.

It was hard to believe, the more so when one was pointed out above us in a cave. It appeared to be very like an RSJ (rolled steel joist), especially on the photographs.

We then cruised on and came to a stop at a new-looking concrete wharf. Lined up alongside was a fleet of the small pea-pod boats we had seen local fishermen using along the gorge. The boatmen awaited their charges and we took up positions on folding benches set out across the craft. Buoyancy aids were passed out; an amazing concession to Western Heath & Safety! Once under way, it was impressive the headway we made with one older guy steering on a long thin rudder and five others who pushed row-locks or long wooden pegs into the hull with loops of rope at the top, through which was laid the oar. This was a two-piece affair, with a thin, flat blade from a simple plank, wired to a long pole. (Photo p.XV).

It was quite "close" down there at water level, with the gorge squeezing in around the small boats. We saw many more fantastic shapes in the limestone rock, not just simple stalactites. The water became clearer still and yet there was little evidence of any wildlife, be it fish, bird or land animal, although I did see some finches. Soon the water level fell and we were in the shallows, so it was time to ship oars and roll out the bamboo rope for a bit of token boat-pulling by our "Trackers". This was just for the benefit of the cameras and old Australian women. We then turned and headed for home. All the while, though, the American bloke behind me kept up a barrage of inane comments to his Oriental partner. I hope she wasn't impressed. (See the "Americanisms" piece).

On the return to Concrete Wharf, we were given the opportunity to tip the boatmen, who to be fair had worked hard and none of whom were particularly young. Once we were under way on the small ferry again, we passed them paddling for home. A barrage of smiling faces, waves and whistles sent us on our way. What an excellent trip.

Having transferred back on board the Princess, we got under way for more gorging in fine style, while lunch was consumed. We sailed from Hubei Province into Sichuan and into the second, or Wu (Witches') Gorge, which would take three hours to negotiate, then into the final of the three, Qutang Gorge. Wu Gorge was where the really big mountains were to be seen, or imagined above the cloud which enveloped them. We were quite lucky with the weather, and although our photographs do show it to be mostly grey and overcast, it was quite warm and dry. It was easy to imagine the old artists seeing these heights for the first time, becoming completely captivated by them and then painting the works as they did. The mountains do seem to come out of the sky and hang there, with others marching off into the distance. There must be great swathes of land upon which human foot has never trod, even in this country of 1.4 billion. I hope the photographs show just how insignificant a 6,000 tonne vessel is beside these monsters.

Wu Gorge featured only two towns, as the gorge sides are so steep. The sides appear suitable for pouring coal down, which is a regular feature of the trip, with many such coal dumps, connected to the water by pipes. It was noticeable that the rock formations changed from brown sandstone to flat "plates" of rock, some of which was formed into very square blocks.

The Qutang Gorge was different again, with one part featured on the RMB10 note, as it is such a famous formation, a massive bluff reaching straight down into the murky water. At this point, the gorge then began to give way to more rolling hills and some settlements, then back again to steep walls and back to hills.

Day 4, Thursday, 6th October 2005
It was interesting to look at old (i.e. pre-2003) photos to see how the gorges have lost a lot of the shoals, beaches and sandbanks as the water level has risen. We would have liked to have seen some "ghost towns" prior to flooding,

but instead we were dropped off in Wanxian, a dirty, dismal place of 1.3 million people, where we were to experience a street market (seen loads before), an acrobat show (very good) and a dusty dead museum about the river and its hanging coffins. This city is not a place for the genteel, it reaches temperatures of 42°C!

Once back on board, we enjoyed another excellent repast and then awaited the "Tour of the Captain's Bridge". This was very good, although we would have also enjoyed a quick dip into the engine room. The bridge had three sets of controls, with the central main bank replicated on either side, so when docking, control could be combined with visibility of the dock or mooring. The ship uses GPS plus the skill and knowledge of the crew to navigate the River. The "Pilot" stands in the centre with binoculars and relays his direction changes to the helmsman with hand signals. He does this for a two-hour stretch, swaps jobs with another and continues this for his 8-hour watch period. The vessel was built in Germany for service on the Volga River in Russia, but after political changes (and probably bought as a bargain bunch – "Buy one, get two free") was brought on carrier ships to the Yangtze, along with two sister ships. They are reputed to be the best cruisers on the River and certainly felt impressive.

On our last night on board, we were to be "treated" to a talent show by fellow cruisers and the ships crew. Fortunately we were not in the same group as the Americans and we managed to avoid being faced with an American doing a rendition of "Old man river". There were, however, two small children, who provided some of the best entertainment on a normal flute and a Chinese bulb flute. The young lad was introduced by Howard as "This little guy is going to play a traditional Chinese song". He gave a short rendition of Beethoven's 9th!

Although no-one believed the "Three Georges" story, we managed to convince Becky, our guide, that we were employed in a broken biscuit factory. One of us broke the biscuits, one put the chocolate chips in the box, one crushed some bits to powder and the last one was in Quality Control. She said that she thought we were in the automotive game, but we explained, pointing at Mike, the PWC (Price Waterhouse Cooper) Aussie, that his company had closed us down, so we had to change jobs. She swallowed this, hook, line and choccy chips. Even Mike, who was listening, said that if he did not know us better, he would have been taken in as well. One really should not admit things like that, but he had already confessed to being a PWC employee.

Special mention must be made here of the efforts of the British to keep China Regal Cruises afloat. Apparently, we spend more in the bar than any other nationality!

Certain members of our party were found to be in need of an afternoon nap, whilst other, more energetic passengers read in the library or stomped around the deck in search of exercise and a constantly changing view. Certain words, whispered into the ear of the "napper" caused him to stop sucking his thumb or comfort blanket and arise quite quickly. These were "It's Happy Hour in the bar!" It is rare to see a man change from infant-like slumber to fully active drinker in such a short time, but this was demonstrated on several occasions.

Day 5, Friday, 7th October 2005

Today was the end of the cruise and it was a case of wake up, eat breakfast and be ready for the enormous conurbation that is Chongqing. Millions of people live here, in this Special Autonomous Region (SAR), which gives it the same status as Shanghai.

The guide book told us that there is little to see in the city, but as we had time to kill before our flight we struck off for the throbbing city centre. We did not get very far as we seemed to be a magnet for hawkers and Chinese who had not seen a Westerner before. We had been informed that the girls in this city were "clear of skin and eye", so we did some on-street research. The results were not convincing, so we took photographs as evidence for Pan, our colleague in Shanghai who had made the assertion, as he is looking for a girlfriend and quite barmy. We retired to a local tea-house and took root in a room with a panoramic view of the confluence of the two rivers, Chang Jiang and Jialing.

The tea was good and we found an English-speaking local who kindly wrote "Please take these four reprobates to the airport" in Chinese for the taxi-driver. When he and his vehicle turned up, we shoe-horned ourselves into the small locally-built Suzuki. He revved that little 1.3L engine for all it was worth along the rough, rolling roads of the city. A monorail had been built along the river at above-road level, but it seemed to go from nowhere to a bridge. Cable-cars also provided links across the two rivers.

The trip to the airport was in places worrying, in others terrifying and the driver had a habit of turning the engine off when coasting downhill. The airport was very new and modern, with few passengers and as a consequence we had time to kill. What was bemusing was the preponderance of flat-screen TVs at every gate, showing old clips of UK football matches.

The flight back to Pudong airport was uneventful, with yet again good Chinese food and the only excitement was being involved in an incident in the taxi when we were shunted from behind by some myopic impatient local in another dented VW Santana.

All in all, a thoroughly brilliant holiday of a life-time.

Cruise data:

- Cruise length – 750 miles
- Fuel used – 35 tonnes
- Speed – approx 20 km/hour
- Three 3,000hp diesel engines

- Displacement – 6,000 tonnes
- Passengers – 250
- Crew – 150

Things said by Americans...

There follows a list of stupid things said by Americans on our five-day cruise up the Yangtze from Wuhan to Chongching. I shall attempt to put them in context for those who were not there, but I apologise if they are not quite so funny – you really had to be there. It is sad to reflect that one or two comments came from Commonwealth cousins, but one of them redeemed himself by supplying material he had heard.

The following must be read in a broad American drawl and would not disgrace the lips of their country's leader, as he leads from the front.

- Bearing in mind we are all on a cruise ship – *"Are you guys sight-seeing?"*
- In the bar before a Safety briefing on day one with four days ahead relaxing – *"Four Bloody Marys and hurry up; we haven't much time"*.
- At dinner, picking up the soy sauce – *"Is this pancake syrup?"*
- Referring to the first part of the cruise, where the scenery on *either* side was mile after mile of identical flat, featureless grass, with the odd tree – *"The other bank is more interesting!"*
- Whilst moored up below the 3 Gorges Dam project site, having sailed up stream for hours, as we would do all five days – *"Are we still going upstream?"*
- Whilst on board a Yangtze River Cruise ship, with reminders of the Great River on every deck – *"Are we on the Yellow or Yangtze River?"*

- Whilst stood on Deck 3, with labels as to the level all around – *"So this is Deck 3. What floor are we on?"*
- Whilst in the first lock of the series of five up the dam – *"Are we in the first lock?"*
- Having been bussed to the foot of the dam, seen the massive water-flume bursting from its base, issuing water and sediment skywards and then been driven higher up to gain a panoramic view of the whole site – *"Is there any water in the dam on the other side?"*
- At the dam site – *"Where does all the water come from?"*
- Later, in a deep gorge, miles from anywhere – *"Where does that road go to?"* (*How would the guide know?*)
- Looking at a landslide which had been turned into a makeshift quarry – *"Looks like they are making a bunch of sand and gravel there, Dave."*
- Looking at yet another massive mountain peak shrouded in mist – *"These mountains sure are beautiful, when you can see them".*
- Looking out on scattered hamlets of simple houses – *"Where are the supermarkets?"* and *"Do all these houses have a fresh water supply?"*
- Discussing the mass evacuation and re-settling of 1.3 million people and looking at yet another small hovel of a farmhouse – *"Do they all move to luxurious homes?"*
- Seeing a white rag floating in amongst the flotsam and jetsam and jumping up with excitement – *"Look! There's a swan or some other kind of animal!"*
- Whilst passing another ferry "dock", where the rough track ended at the water's edge (as they do) – *"Look! There's a highway going into the river!"*
- We passed innumerable types of river vessels, many going upstream working hard against the strong current – *"Hey, why is that tug with two barges going so slowly?"* It had *seven* laden barges in its care.
- Each of the barges had some pot plants eking out an existence on the rusty decks – *"Look! All those barges have got gardens!"*
- This one from an Australian, as I was quietly leaning on the side watching the world go by – *"Are you British?"* I replied in the affirmative. Deflated, she asked *"Have you got a fiddle?"* I was so stunned by the question I was actually stuck for a riposte. She wanted to borrow mine for the talent show. Being British, I normally carry an assortment of string instruments with me, but sadly Madam, not on this cruise.

- There was a line of wall-lights in the restaurant at shoulder height. Said an American of some size – *"I must stop walking into these wall-lights with my shoulder!"*
- Every meal was presented in its dish or large tureen with a label in English and Chinese in 20 font capitals or so. After many meals one woman asked of her friend about a clearly marked dish – *"What's this?"* Even her friend was embarrassed when I looked stunned.
- Whilst in the pea-pod boats on the Shenong Stream trip, we were sat in front of Johnny Know-all from Wisconsin, who made the following declarations to his wife – *"I don't think they had female trackers." "This is just like where we live, except without the water!" "They've got ferns like we have at home."*
- As we were passing big clumps of bamboo, some of which was being harvested by non-naked locals in boats and it was being pointed out by the local guides Johnny Wisconsin added – *"I haven't seen any bamboo yet."*
- All along the river, in order to farm on the steep slopes, terraces had been built by generations unknown, many of which are now below the water, but some were still visible – *"Are those terraces man-made or natural?"*
- The cooking was aimed squarely at Westerners, with some concessions to the few Chinese passengers – *"I can tell the folks back home that I had real Chinese food."* No dear, you can't and haven't.
- We had an explanation of ancient burial rites, where a man was buried with a woman who was about 10 years his senior and who had apparently been killed just to accompany him into the afterlife. This was an ancient custom, at a time when women did not quite have the vote. The question was asked by the guide what we thought the relationship between the two people was thought to be. The stunning American reply winged its way across the dusty museum room – *"Mother and son".*

I apologise to any sensitive readers who may be American, but this is a corroborated record of things actually said in all seriousness by your fellow country-men and women. If the speakers were not so characteristically loud, we may have missed some of the conversation, so short of a nation-wide course for all travellers on the art of polite, quiet conversation and a more accurate, contemplative use of the senses, US tourists will continue to provide amusement for all. We thank you for your selfless and enthusiastic giving of humour to us all.

Mention must be made of a classical comment from (ashamedly) a fellow Commonwealth resident whilst using his digital camera – *"It looks smaller when you zoom in!"*

A Brit describing the meteorological situation – *"It's not a cold wind; it's a windy wind."* These were the only entries from Europe!

Saturday, 8th October 2005

We worked a normal day on this Saturday, in order to "buy back" holiday in the previous week when we had been on the cruise. I was surprised how alive the place was, with suppliers milling and people busier than on a normal day.

In the evening I stayed in after a meal at East-West, which is always a pleasure, watching people interact, especially Brummie with the waitresses, he always seems to bring out a smile, regularly repeating the same comments or tricks.

Sunday, 9th October 2005

We worked a normal day again. Sunday supplier meetings seemed to be happening all over, but I received no invitation.

On the fashion side, it seems as if someone has thrown a switch and people have started wearing jackets and coats. I even saw a girl last night with a scarf on. It is not cold. We are all still dressed as we have been for the past several months, in shirt sleeves. It is still in the high 20s! Men wearing vests have been seen infiltrating the fashion world of Shanghai – what a let-down for stylish men everywhere.

Every day is still an experience in the various taxis we take; it just now feels like normality. It is said by many Oriental observers that some Westerners simply cannot take the suicidal roads and the antics thereon; even crossing the road is fraught with danger. The Oriental way of combating this appears to be to not look from side to side and expect the oncoming drivers to sound the horn and warn others of their imminent arrival.

Monday, 10th October 2005

As usual for a Monday, we had a Team brief, but there was little change or news. Still debates rage on over the tax situation, contracts, flights and our assignment length.

A major cultural difference is the perception of assertiveness here. It is an essential quality for Westerners at home to progress, but in Chinese circles it is seen as very rude to face up to leaders or more experienced colleagues, even if they are wrong.

Tuesday, 11th October 2005

This sudden change in dress-code continues to be noticeable; women in thick black tights, men have lost the striped polo-shirts with odd collars, which are so frumpy, and long-sleeved shirts (often creased) have taken over. I suppose it will not be long before they are into their long johns again. They were still wearing those in June when we arrived back here. As a consequence of this massive dip in temperature, one or two offices are now putting the heating on. Thankfully mine has a "fresh-air" freak sat by the window and she can be relied upon to keep it open, even in really cold weather. Sadly she also keeps it open when we were in over 30° temperatures. This would be OK if it was not for the fact that the window in question is right over the air-con unit, so the hot exhaust air used to just come right in, while our air-con unit was trying to air-condition the whole of Shanghai. They just do not understand the basic principles.

Hero of the day was a guy who walked across a busy street, without looking to right or left and made it to the other side. We believe that the consequences of hitting a pedestrian or cyclist are so severe and it is always assumed that the motorist is to blame, that the former two categories of road users trade on this and just "go for it", without a care.

We decided to eat at the Turkish restaurant, *Antalya*, scene of the recent wedding reception, and so we were treated to the personal attentions of Sheila the Philippino manageress; and as she had nothing else to do walked around looking pretty, which was OK with us. She floated the idea of a buffet for Hallowe'en and we helped stoke the concept as it seemed a good excuse for another visit.

Alarmingly for me, the (thin, with no stomach) belly-dancer was on the premises and determined to strut her stuff. The music swelled, and she popped out from the back in her scanty gear and scarf. As there were only three parties in for the night and one lot were locals, there could only be a limited target audience for the skinny gyrator. I groaned audibly as the girl came our way, but there was nothing for it but to attempt to gyrate appallingly, so maybe one would not be asked again. Scooter, Winston and Brummie were up in a flash, with Scooter being particularly adept at bending over backwards to match her moves. She loved his smooth head and even smoother dance steps. My attempt was as usual rubbish, but I managed to put a smile on her face and not send her to sleep.

Wednesday, 12th October 2005

Today's fashion victim spotted in the Lobby of the Pent-Ox wore a vest and the most awful sea-weed green tartan woolly waist-coat under a similarly-coloured cardigan. It was enough to make a dozen stylish Italians reach for their Ray-Bans in disgust. He looked a right Charlie, but he certainly did not look male to me.

In the evening we went karting with a supplier. There were 15 bodies who eventually arrived at the track, though despite pointing directly at it, our taxi driver could not see it and drove past and away. Drivers included Rolf, Marvin and girlfriend, Native, Frau, Ewe, the supplier crowd and some of our favourite locals.

In the slow karts we selected in deference to our Chinese friends' appalling driving skills, it was a case of pedal to the metal all the way for me. To be fair, Marvin's girlfriend, a true Shanghai girl, was a very good driver, proving again that women here are smarter. Her mode of dress, though, was fashion disaster of the day. She held the Shanghai girl flag aloft, for she came dressed for a drive in dirty smelly karts wearing a knee-length thin skirt and high-heeled sandals. Classic wear for the catwalk, but not ideal for the occasion, as she tried to protect her modesty by attempting to hold down her billowing skirt as she passed us in the pits. We thought she was posing by holding the wheel with one hand. The other Shanghai girl who came was with Bank and she at least wore her designer jeans, but naturally the four-inch heels were on her feet.

We followed the racing with a meal in the Tibetan soup-restaurant, which we had visited before. We attracted plenty of stares as we all walked in together and a sharp-eyed manager realised that he had to organise his staff to create a table for 15. Yet again we were bemused by the insistence upon serving us free beer. Another variety could be bought at RMB5 a bottle, but all other drinks appeared to be free!

For those who had not been there before, it was a real experience and we had to explain the limited bit we knew about the way the cooking worked and how to arrange one's consumption of it. The clever bit is to stick what you want to cook in the sieve or ladle one is provided with, plunge it into the hot liquid and wait until you feel it is cooked, then raise it from the bubbling broth and consume. For me, the trickiest bits were sort of meat balls, with a loose centre of fish meat, surrounded by fat. This changed to oil as the cooking process heated it up and then as it was just too big to put in one's mouth whole, I unwisely bit into one. This sent a spray of almost boiling liquid high into the air and somehow managed to hit Rolf in the ear on his left side, although he was sat to my left! I reckon someone else did the same but would not admit to the crime.

All in all, we enjoyed an interesting dining experience again. We took a couple of taxis home and considered the evening a great success.

Thursday, 13th October 2005
On the way to work, we were almost squeezed between two buses in pincer movement; yet another example of lane-wandering and poor driving. The driving style seems to be to "chop" the indicator on and move at the same time; presumably indicating makes the move legitimate in some way.

Conundrum of the day, and many other days: How can a nation of people with such a vaunted "Working together for the benefit of all" level of co-operation, not want to help each other on the road? So many times they block junctions when there is no advantage to being there, they do not let people out when they can, and drivers and pedestrians *must* be at the front of the queue or line. I know we do this in the UK, but even in London I have seen more give and take on the road.

For a change, I was given loads of work at last and launched myself into it with verve. It is not difficult; as usual the hardest thing is the translation and communication. The most trying issue here is convincing the client to take our advice, when they want to go their own way.

We had a useful offer to visit Phoenix Mansions, as alternative accommodation, which was then rescinded as all apartments were full!

Tonight I put my skates on and set off in search of a hard drive in "Cyber-mart" at Hong Kong Plaza, with its three floors of electronic gadgets. I managed to barter the assistant down from RMB650/£46.43 to RMB560/£40 for a 40 GB one. I had started at RMB300/£21.43, but they fell about laughing.

I managed to park my bike in the approved area, as bicycles are discouraged, even banned from the posh Huahai Rd., upon which stands the Mart. It was RMB1 for attended parking – when I returned to my barely used steed, the parking attendant had just knocked it over along with several other bikes; she was slightly embarrassed. Up to that point, it had been safe in her hands.

As I was pedalling along, the same thought occurred to me as it does regularly here – why do people drive with no lights? It seems crazy not to want to be seen. Rolf has invested in a front light for his bike and he has had repeated flashes from other two-wheelers who ride towards him and do not show any lights! What is going on? Most mopeds, except the "silent death" electric ones, have a generator on board and can run lights. Do they think that running with lights on drains the battery?

Friday, 14th October 2005

Today's hero was as ever, on a bike, but this time the load was several 56lb bags of spuds, piled high across the back. Small vans are few and far between here, so the ubiquitous bicycle or tricycle has to do all the lugging of goods. So we have seen fridges, multiple televisions, heavy gas bottles, water cooler bottles, wardrobes and now potatoes.

For evening entertainment, we trundled off to Super Brand Mall for a meal at Zoë's, a place of good food and Sixties décor. As ever there were a few couples lounging around eating and drinking, as well as a group of four girls, although one person could have been of either sex. They could not have sat closer and were almost touching mobile phones as they communicated across the table. I will not say "talked" as this level of intercourse may have only been to someone who was not there, but on the end of the phone line. I do not know how men can become close enough to the women in this country as they spend so much time on their mobiles. I suspect with a 1.4 billion population, there are a fair few to talk with.

Later on there was time for a quickie at the Paulaner, where we positioned ourselves on a lower table than normal and closer to the other side (our left) of the stage, but on the corner of the dance-floor. This was to be a prime location for watching locals at play. Joy, one of the singers in the band attempted to get some of the "dancers", or people on the dance-floor, to clap in time to the beat. Within three claps, they had lost the rhythm! There was one girl who danced at twice the speed of the others, several who just could not catch a simple beat and others who had been slurping down the beer in a contest with a bloke, whom we were sure were bound to make a run for the Ladies. This they did not do, appearing surprisingly robust for women of such slight frames. One man, the usual older, greasy smoothie, who could dance a little, was obviously Mr. Popular with the girls, for he was seen later on to be doing a very animated, suggestive dance involving bending over each other. He must be cool as well, for he was wearing a T-shirt under his normal shirt; I was hot enough in my shorts and single T. The "cold" seems to have got to these fellers here. I still feel quite warm in summer gear.

Further amusing sights were there on the floor, with so many girls dancing in the same way as one expects 13-year old boys in the UK – badly and with no sense of a beat. Now I know that I dance like "a Corn-Flake packet on legs", according to a qualified observer, but even I can do better than these people. Sad but true. At one point Brummie was crying into his beer at the state of some of the dance-floor gyrations, particularly when they tried to clap to a beat, as they would fall out of time so easily, whilst looking at each other. As ever, the band played on, watching it all pass by. A group of Japanese businessmen, wrapped up in their suits and ties kept respectfully quiet in the corner. They had a couple of token ladies with them, possibly interpreters, and Janet from the band pointed out that that is all they would do all night, just sit quietly. The Japanese in China are well aware of the simmering tensions betwixt the two countries, which are seemingly becoming worse, especially amongst the young.

Without our wives being present, we made up for them in some small part by being quite catty about the attire as well as the dancing amongst the crowd, even the girls. Many young Chinese girls have a hankering for being frumpily dressed in clothes that their mothers would wear. There were two girls sporting cream trousers that hung like wet tracksuit bottoms around their skinny midriffs as neither had the shape to fill out the pants.

Saturday, 15th October 2005

Today was a highlight of the week – Shopping with Brummie & Winston. We had our plans of exactly what we wanted to buy, namely a tie-pin for the lovely Ruby at the Mawdesley, a replacement North Face jacket for Brummie and some socks for me. It was a travesty, really, for we were shopping in a place which is a Mecca for international visitors and a place of retail therapy to satisfy the keenest of shoppers. Coach trips are run to this bartering paradise, and we came out in minutes, with one item each.

One jacket was exchanged (he found the stall!) with no hassle, five pairs of trainer socks and one tie-pin. Blokes shopping: Are we done? Yes! Right, let's go to the bar! Then we decided to visit "Electric City" and have a look, which is four floors of electric white goods, bulbs, wire, hi-fi (new and second hand with some top-end British kit, as well as valve amps). I elected to buy a decent set of speakers similar to Rolf to enjoy music more. I chose a pair plus a sub-woofer for RMB200/£14.29. Brummie decided to have the same and while it was being packed looked at another with a fetching blue light in the bass port and chose to have that instead. Winston decided not to be left out and picked up Brummie's cast-offs. So for a grand total of RMB650/£46.43, we all had some decent hi-fi.

Then we set off to Jenny's bar with our loads, enjoyed discount for our first visit and dined on cheap food and drink. The cleaner came in with joss-sticks, prayed to the North, South, East and West in front of the shrine, made an offering of fruit and started moving pot plants. Once she had done, she wobbled off on her bicycle.

Sunday, 16th October 2005

I cycled to meet the others at Shimao Lakeside apartments in JinQiao for 10.30am to be collected at 11.00am by friends and taken to the new Formula 1 circuit in Baoshan for the Chinese Grand Prix. We had a quick drive, with some traffic delays, but not much; followed by a short walk, then picked up by a free bus into the circuit, another short walk and we were into the impressive stands, with seats at the top and a view of the turn three hairpin.

A stand on the way in had sold soft ear-plugs for RMB1 a pair, so I stocked up for use on the bike back home. We had a grand view of the rather bumpy braking area to the hairpin and then the astonishingly noisy power out.

Different traction control strategies demonstrated differing levels of grip and slip. Even plugged up as we were, they claim noise levels rise to 150dB.

Great seats, free tubes of beer for those who could drink and a supply of crisps kept us going for the race. The Safety Car was in danger of needing a service it was out so much and even on the warm-up lap the hapless Schumacher ran into another car just to our right for no reason at all – very Shanghai taxi-driver standard. Other incidents with debris on the track and some peculiar lines being taken by Schumacher added to the interest. Sadly, there was no "Radio Shanghai F1 English service" to keep us updated on the goings on across the track where we could not see, although we did have a view of a big screen. For the first part of the race it was Renault domination, followed by the McLarens. As the 54 laps wound on, things changed as people pitted and attrition took its toll. All in all a good day and a certain privilege to be there in style, with a dreary two and a half hour drive home. We were lucky, others took nearly twice that.

Non-jobbers were in abundance at the track, with those selling anything vaguely connected with racing and hot days, but again, star prize goes to Wang and Peng, stood to attention when we passed over the Yangpu Bridge, and were still erect when we returned later. One assumes it was not the same guys, but still, why do they stand there? Who would notice if they did not?

Monday, 17th October 2005
A quiet day with the only excitement being a meal at East-West with the boys and I spent the evening typing, trying to keep tabs on this journal. This is quite an onerous task I have given myself, so I'm not going to write any more about an ordinary day. No heroes, no fashion victims to be seen. That or they are becoming so much the common sights for me and I have turned native.

Annoying thing of the day is the pair of screens either side of the lifts which for a change were synchronised, but churn out adverts on a continual loop. I heard that advertising is the biggest business in China, although I would have thought concrete pumping or food was bigger. You can never seem to hide away from the insidious needle of jingles and images promoting this and that.

Tuesday, 18th October 2005
Today I booked flights home via the General Office – they wanted payment, which was another shock to the system care of the Chinese! Native and I

argued vehemently with HR and a Finance jobsworth over the issue. We were not happy at all; so out of the blue we had an edict that we must pay for our airline tickets home via a Bank of China Credit Card. To be fair to the hosts, we had been asked to order these some time ago, but very few of us trusted the system here and many of us did not want the associated Chinese bank account. It is hard enough keeping tabs on a UK credit card and reading the small print. We can't even read Chinese characters, except for a few, if they are in 48 font, never mind 6.

One thing Native said rang very true; "I get home at night drained from trying to live here and make myself understood, even if my Chinese was better, I still could not understand the bank letters". We were however, talking to a granite slab; the Company had decided and we were stuck with it, yet again. So we are facing another issue which is not clear to add to the tax situation, the accommodation and holidays. All these things have been hanging around unresolved for weeks.

We dined at the Mawdesley, which is now on its 3rd anniversary, with an immense banner, featuring some non-sensical English words (why did they not ask us to check it?) and a new menu. We endured Chicken curry, boiled rice, soup and salad for RMB35/£2.50. It was OK for the money, but as usual too many bones in the meat.

With us being sad forty-somethings, we watched the new Wallace & Grommit film, "Wererabbit" in Brummie's room. This is only just out, so our copy that we found on the streets was taken by some criminal in a cinema with a camera. How disgraceful. We laughed ourselves silly as a result.

Wednesday, 19th October 2005

This was going to be a good day, despite a thoroughly dangerous taxi ride in to work; today I was flying to meet the family (or three out of four of them) in Hong Kong. I was like a little child, I was so excited, but had to temper this in the cab, as Winston's family were unsure as to whether they would be travelling as one of his daughters was ill. His wife had called at 4.00am our time to tell him. What he did not know was that he then had only three hours to decide to delay their flight or suffer a crushing £1,150 penalty to change on the same day of the flight. He could think of little else and I felt bad bounding away happily to see my lot, although I did not know for sure if they had arrived at the airport, I just assumed they would be fine.

The day wore on until my set time to depart and I left in a flurry and hailed an unusually decent taxi for the fast ride to Pudong International Airport. All papers filled in and barriers scaled, I settled down to wait. Even in the internationally clinical surroundings of the airport terminal, China leaks in; there were three screens within easy vision of my seat, two were playing the same irritating Chinese TV programme and one was a loop of intrusive adverts. All were noisy and one was horribly distorted. The guy next to me was chewing gum loudly and with his mouth open. Opposite, a huge extended Chinese family babbled excitedly about miserable *gweilos* or something and the announcer's voice chimed over the PA. Peace in our time, or not?

The flight was boring as ever, but a chance to read in reasonable peace, or so I thought, until that wretched woman started "singing" on the China Eastern Airline's screens, which swung out from above. Not content with just letting the visuals appear on the screen and for people to be able to choose to listen or not via headphones; they pipe it over the PA system. She has a voice typical of Chinese female singers, which to me all sound the same, with a piercing shrill quality, capable of cutting glass at ten paces. If you look along a shelf full of Chinese music the covers all look the same and the popular music is glossy, squelchy smooching "muzak" with no real substance, and I don't like it. I saw a "hot" local rock band on the TV the other day. They were inoffensive, glossy, well-coiffeured young men who would not upset anyone. That's not rock and roll.

Arriving on time in Hong Kong I was in the middle of the aircraft so had little chance to see the famous sky-line. We had a good in-flight meal, as is often the case on China Eastern, and I was ready to meet the team. I landed some time ahead of them so I could search out their baggage carousel and wait to hold them in my arms at last. The minutes dragged by and then English-looking people started to filter through. There they were, my two youngest and the woman who had given them to me, looking as lovely as ever. The kids raced up for the first cuddle, with red faces aglow. Sharon held off saying that she would "wait my turn!" Then it was time to hold her tight; a dream come true, to meet in Hong Kong with *my* team. (Photos p.XXX, p.XXXI).

Chapter 5

A PRE-CHRISTMAS MASSAGE IN CHENGDU

Monday, 28th November 2005

I left the UK in fine sunshine and landed in the same at Pudong. I also left behind my lovely family – it had been brilliant to be with them since 19th October, when we had met by baggage carousel no.9 in Hong Kong airport. Apparently I cut a lonesome figure stood by the passing suitcases, waiting for the love of my life and our two youngest to appear through Passport Control. We have seen and done so much in all that time with our sojourn in HK, a flight on to Shanghai, a quick dash to Beijing, a drive out to the Wall, back to Shanghai and onwards to the UK.

Sarah was presented her Duke of Edinburgh Gold Award the day after I flew home, so I had been back in London, this time with my eldest, for a great occasion.

Amusingly, when I arrived at the Pent-Ox, I was not expected. It was not until later when in a jet-lagged haze, that I finally found my Chinese mobile in one of those "easy to find" places where I had placed it.

Then I picked up a text from Winston which informed me that I was actually booked into the Phoenix. No wonder they looked through me at the Pent-Ox. Quickly recovering her composure, the receptionist had found a "hotel-style" room on the eighth floor, 801 and booked me in. I began the "nesting" procedure, unpacking and finding homes for things then decided to shave and shower and travel in to work.

When I returned from work and dinner, and had collected my bike and belongings from Winston's room, it was about 9.00pm. Reception then rang to tell me that they had changed my room for one of the regular long-stay places and could I move? This meant undoing all the nesting I had started, re-packing and moving up twelve floors. Somehow in the process, I managed to lose a bag which contained my kettle, toaster and top-quality washing-up liquid; or did I lose that when I left last time?

Tuesday, 29th November 2005

I managed to ignore one Chinese mobile phone alarm and set the second UK phone as back-up, but forgot it was still on (later) UK time, so when Winston called me at 7.50am I was still in bed! It had been a bad night, with the expected 2.00am to 2.30am sudden wake-up, (which seems to affect most of us coming out here) so I had sat up in bed to read. I was frozen, so on went the room heater for the first time and as often when one is cold, one harks back to Shanghai times when the sun shone warmly (too warmly sometimes).

As it is useless to fight the early-morning wake-up, a good read was followed by welcome sleep, but as usual, I had just managed about 5 hours maximum of slumber. I had not slept well on the plane, unlike some of my fellow passengers, who like all good Chinese, can sleep at the drop of a boarding pass, especially as some were very quick to commandeer the empty seats and lie down.

The taxi ride in to work, although only one hour later than normal, was quick and easy. It was good again to learn more from Gasket who was only here until Wednesday. It is always interesting to realise how much one knows – and even more, do not know – about automotive engineering. He is a grand teacher and a thoroughly gentle man. We need him here longer.

The evening was spent very pleasantly with Rolf, as we met at Carrefour and enjoyed sweet-and-sour pork with rice, washed down with a drink: just over £1.50 for a great dinner. We strolled upstairs to pick up a few things and enjoyed the games at the 5-items-in-a-basket tills with local after local trying it on with a laden trolley. It is quite amusing watching the Chinese deal out discipline to each other. We walked to his new apartment in Phoenix Mansions and he gave me the tour, as I had not been there before. This is the place many of us in the noisy old Pent-Ox aspire to live in.

Wednesday, 30th November 2005

Today finished off with a thoroughly tedious teleconference with people in the UK, one local on a mobile, us in China and people in Japan. It was hard to hear, you cannot see people's faces to read the actual meaning and pick up body language, and added to this I listened most of the time to irrelevancies. I was lucky; I had to exit after only 50 minutes for Chinese lessons.

Wednesday meant Paulaner night with the boys, but also those Chinese lessons, where I fought waves of sleep to try and maintain interest. Why does most of what I learn go in one ear and out of the other? This is such a difficult language, compared with my experience of picking up French, German or even Latin. It is also often imprecise. We will ask our teacher what a certain word means and he is often stumped, as it seems to depend on the context and there are many words which are similar, but depending upon the inflexion or accent, mean wildly different things. For example, the word "tang" can mean too hot, sugar, soup or to lie down, depending upon whether one uses a falling, rising, flat or fall-and-rise inflection, respectively. So we have not just four meanings, but according to our teacher an adjective with superlative, two nouns and a verb. This is some language, but English also has many words with the same spelling but different meanings.

There were few of us tonight in the Welsh lesson, but it was good to see Ewe again, on her tod as husband (Tup) is out doing CET (Cold Environment Testing). Native, Frau and Let joined me in the room as the faithful few.

I heard Winston and Brummie pass by outside in the corridor, having finished being bored to bits teleconferencing. I had intended meeting them at the East-West café, but had to attend to some urgent e-mails before leaving and was too late, so I carried on to Carrefour to buy some passport photos to extend the old visa. As I was walking into the place, I was hailed by Frau, who was going for a meal in the new Mexican restaurant, Coyote, in the Green City complex. I gladly joined Frau, Ewe and Native to make a foursome and thoroughly enjoyed the food, drink and company. Ewe was bemoaning the fact that Tup seemed stuck up north until nearly Christmas and their girls were coming out to visit. I'm not much of a stand-in for Tup; I am severely challenged in the facial hair department, my glasses are not thick enough and I haven't his dress sense, or lack of it.

Thursday, 1st December 2005

This place, this country, always succeeds to surprise and is currently running at 9.48% economic growth, with industrial output up 16.6% over last year, whatever that means. On CCTV there was a piece about a mountain in Anhui province where Zen Buddhism was really cultivated early on and a place famous for its stone carved inscriptions and calligraphic delights. So way back in the Tang dynasty, some Zen chap spent ages cutting beautiful characters into the mountain and some time later the whole thing was stolen! A whole piece of the rock face was missing! How do you steal a slab of rock?

The next article covered the fact that the steel industry has 1.2 million tonnes over-capacity and that out of 150 automakers only 37 are indigenous Chinese companies. I am full of boring facts today.

As Bling-Bling and Post had just flown in today, the former being my boss from the UK, and Post being an acquaintance from the old Rover days, and a really solid bloke, we dined together in the Mawdesley. It was a bit like the old days when the place was full of MG Rover people, as it soon filled up with many of the current contingent.

Friday, 2nd December 2005
It is amazing how many locals have declined the offer of a free night out next weekend for our Christmas Shindig, saying that it is too late (a 7.30pm start!!) and it is a long way from where they live in Puxi. This will be our ex-Pats Christmas Party.

I had to scoot quickly from work as it was time to collect my tickets home from Frank at Bestrip at his office near Jing'An temple. I managed to learn the Chinese for the station I wanted and the taxi driver took me to another! At least it was closer to my destination than the one I wanted.

I enjoy going to Jing'An, it is an interesting district, full of the usual contrasts of West and East, rich and poor. The park by the temple has a decked area around the lake in front of the Bali Laguna restaurant where I stood enjoying the view and could not help notice a nutter singing to the plants in the water! Perhaps it is an ancient Chinese growing song.

I took a walk along Nanjing Lu, witnessing the varied sights of penniless beggars, then the massive Shanghai TV station screen, the pavement restaurant tables in tents with their heaters, the Ferrari showroom and then finally, the usual "offers" along the pedestrian part. I have walked along there loads of times and each occasion is amusing and amazing.

I continued my walk with a leisurely promenade along the Bund with other strollers and the usual lovers. I walked as far as I could along the Bund and then across the ring road and around a closed park with yet more lovers craving privacy from family, but cuddling away on the pavement. There was also a group of middle-aged ladies with fans trying to follow their choreographer, but getting it horribly wrong. Still, it was colourful with the fans they carried and good exercise and fun.

Once close to the Yu Gardens, I came upon another group of ladies of a certain age, this time doing step aerobics to European disco music with another unfortunate trying to choreograph movement. So while the men play mah-jong, the young girls are kissed beside darkened parks or on the Bund and the ladies "of a certain age" dance to keep fit. Not a bad society.

Whilst in the Gardens I tried to buy painted bottles, but could not haggle down as low as last time – it must have been the presence of my beautiful, blond-haired daughter; she was such a popular figure!

At the appointed time, I met the boys by the restaurant chain "78" and Rolf and I guided the visitors through the menu to enjoy a truly massive meal, ensuring all were well-fed.

We walked back along the Bund, to the People's Heroes Monument and back down to Nanjing Lu, where we decided to catch the lights and although they were going out, as it was 10.30pm, they were still impressive. In the middle of the pedestrianised bit there was a film crew with numbered extras hanging round! The set was roped off with a press of nosey public waiting for the chance to see their favourite top Chinese actors and actresses perform in the cold night air. We did not hang around, so to assuage our disappointment, Rolf stumped up for a hot custard each – lovely!

It is the first time Bling has been here long enough to cover a weekend and even Post said it is rare for business travellers to see much more of a place than a factory and the airport, so they really appreciated the Shanghai tour – we walked miles. And all I spent was RMB10/70p on two DVDs!!!

This had been a real "Rolf and Ian" tour of Shanghai. Rolf was my cabin-boy mate on the Yangtze. No jokes, please; the sight of him in his briefs every night and morn was enough to put one off food for the day! He is a great engineer and a real gentle man. (Photos p.VIII, p.IX).

It is great being with Rolf; he is arty and different to Winston and Brummie, love them as I do. We rarely go to a bar, him and me, being much happier to walk and soak up the atmosphere. It is much healthier being with him, but he leaves for the UK next week, then two days later he flies to Turin before returning to the UK for Christmas. He is so excited to be going home.

Saturday, 3rd December 2005

Today was a beautiful day; I walked down to Lujiazui Park, which was very quiet, bathed in winter sunshine.

We all met at 10.00am at Lujiazui underground station, where the Diamond Court shuttle stops, then down to take a train to Shanxi Nan Lu (Nan means south and Lu of course is road).

Rolf took us on a tour to the art and craft market off Taikang Lu. When trying to find this place he had originally gone by mistake to Taicang Lu. One letter and you are 2 miles off course, in the wrong district!

It is a great place; in one shop, some pearls for my girls were strung by the oyster fisherman's daughter, who placed the necklaces in silk bags and all for a very reasonable price. Bling was on hand to advise on jewellery, which was useful of him.

Lunch was taken in a "protest café", where old Communist posters from Korea and Russia plastered the walls.

We then walked to the Cyber mart for a hard drive and HD card for Bling's computer. There was much haggling and the usual stony-faced woman was not giving much! We could not find any cheap cameras for Post, though. Some items from time to time have a "World price".

To keep out of the rain, we descended onto the underground from Huangpi Lu to Shanxi Lu and then for the short walk to Xiangyang Gift Market, past the "Welcome to Shanghai" sign on the Huahai Lu.

We went on for watches where Bling bought fifteen, Post nine and Rolf, in a bid to wind up Bling, bought a fake Rolex like the real one on his colleague's wrist for several thousand pounds less than Bling had paid! This all took about forty minutes, during which time I slipped next door to haggle for a Chinese jacket and used all the theatrics I knew to secure a good price, but still paid a bit over the odds!

Just when we thought it was all over, Rolf decided to buy a glasses case, then seeing the locals swoop in and run away with reading glasses at RMB25 a pair, decided he had to have some of these, but he wanted black frames, of course, so much rooting about later he handed his money over. We were just about to leave when his eyes fell on the Calvin Klein boxers on the stand, so he had to have some of those. As he is such a big bloke, this necessitated sending out a runner to another stall! In the end both Rolf and I had two pairs of pants, with my order involving a second run out in the rain by the girl to another stand!

On the way back to the Pent-Ox, we had a very near-miss in our taxi with wandering truck lane-waving – he seemed surprised to receive severe abuse from four Brits and one Chinese taxi-driver. He was probably completely unaware of his trailer's wandering behaviour. It scared the willies out of us and generated a scratch on the taxi's door mirror against the central fence barrier.

Sunday, 4th December 2005
It was a beautiful sunny day, 2°–4° but bright sun. I went out on the bike via a new route – went horribly wrong, finally made it to the ferry where it was quite windy and cold on the river; the spray was lashing over the boat, so people huddled inside.

I cycled off to Electric City for the stocking-fillers; it was so cold, and I was worried about the security of my bike, so I shopped and hurried back to the Pent-Ox for warmth. As I became so wrapped up in this writing, I did not remember that I had set a pan to boil on the stove. The hapless pan boiled dry and the room filled with the smell of burnt plastic!

In the apartment lobby there is a life-sized Father Christmas figure, a flashing cone with green "fur" as a tree and two curtains of lights outside; it is like a grotto here. It is strange, and all this in a Buddhist country.

I am making some progress at work, and have been asked to do some more training "because you are good at it". Oh, to be noticed! We have invited all our local friends to our Christmas bash on 10th, which should be good, although we are missing Winston. He has now been made Senior Manager in the Chinese structure; he deserves it – he's good. The rest of us await developments, although about five of us have positions, including one who is a Director. Amazing how these people do it, even to fool the locals.

Using the lobby PC to access the Internet and write some e-mails home, from which some of this writing is extracted today, I noticed that mails to and from my wife were lost in translation, as some of the characters were mixed up. I have set my lap-top and work PC keyboard up with English characters, as I did not know that a US keyboard and an English one have 102 and 101 keys, or the other way round!

The trouble is, my password to access my UK-work mails uses a Pound Sterling key, (which is also unobtainable on the key-pad in the Pent-Ox lobby), and so for a while I could not understand why I could not connect, as of course the password keys do not show up on the screen!

Time for bed now; I think of all my children of whom I am so proud; everyone who has met them whilst over here remembers three well-balanced, well-mannered out-going young people. My kids really impressed – Sarah dancing on the bar at Zapata's and strolling round when she was here on her own, Jessica dancing with the "Stick" and Ashley Stick-dancing too, both joining in the adult conversation.

Monday, 5th December 2005

We had the usual Team Meeting; our tax situation is still not sorted. Sat in the room were the "regulars" with coats on, the visitors in shirt sleeves – have we gone native?

I left work today slightly late, the wind was very cold, like a knife through butter, and few taxis were evident. We met up with Ewe and Frau at the Mawdesley.

Rolf only arrived at 9.00pm following a late session with Italians and Chinese – his comment of "why do they have to go into so much detail on a turn-key project?" caused some amusement. The point of a turn-key project is that the job is handled from beginning to end by a supplier to one's own spec. If there is a problem, they are not paid until it runs properly.

Ewe was talking about the life in CET (Cold Environment Testing) country up north in Xianfan, as she had visited her husband who is working up there. They stayed in the "Ruby Hotel", which has a paper-thin façade, rats in the walls and rats in the restaurant, which is a glass conservatory and a keep-your-coat-on job. Waiting staff are trained to ignore rodents. Rabbit could not sleep due to the rats, and this in the town's only five-star establishment.

Ewe's husband reported via e-mail that he had ordered Bull's penis for tea! The other Chinese managers were also in the Ruby, but the bulk of Chinese were billeted in dorms by the test-track, with dirty carpets ingrained with cigarette ash, more rats and cold.

It was another great night with real friends who help and support each other.

It is night-time and I write sat by my draughty apartment window, (very little seals well in China – I have just draught-excluded my fifth window), overlooking the Huangpu River with some opera playing in the background. Ships of all sorts ply the dirty river; I can sometimes count over 40 vessels in my view.

From here I can see that the downtown area of the financial district is warming up with lights, but the temperature was 3°C today – on the river ferry it felt less. Apart from the spitting (hence we call it the "Spitting Ferry"), and despite signs prohibiting this practice, it was a case of dodging the spitters, avoiding the tramp selling bent cigarettes he had picked up from the floor and also the wicked spray kicked up by the wind. Shanghai is not a healthy place sometimes.

It was International Aids Day yesterday and the TV interview on the news had an HIV specialist claiming that the dreadful issue had been around in China for 20 years, with the government ignoring it for ten (probably because it had not authorised the disease in the first place), then floundering about for five years whilst it decided what to do and then only actually DOING something for the last five. It was a sad view and he seemed informed.

Sex education is very patchy here. We continue to ask our Chinese friends and colleagues for information on how relationships form between the two sexes. Our latest informant, an attractive, fairly worldly, self-supporting translator, tells us that the age of consent would appear to be 14, but most Chinese are brought up to believe that sex before marriage is wrong. Sounds very plausible and laudable, but what education are they given for when the moment comes along? We will investigate further.

It is clear from our UK young unmarried mothers' statistics, that we do not ride the moral high ground here.

Moralising over now, the lights continue to increase in number and the draught through these stupid patio doors is unrelenting. Even with the heater on I can still feel it, but I will suffer to enjoy the stunning view, as I have said before, the sort of thing often depicted in US films to show Johnny Bachelor in his high-rise apartment looking down over the ordinary people below. I can just about see the Oriental Pearl Tower pinnacle and most of the majestic Jinmao tower from here.

Daily we see sights funny and startling and none more so than the recent space mission, which has resulted in the astronauts being feted around the country as real heroes. The mission was for the first time shown on Chinese

TV, as normally military hardware is well out of bounds to cameras. There were even screens up in the capital showing the usual progress reports we normally see from NASA as well as TV bulletins.

I caught one and saw the usual sequence of shots, the launch, followed by the stage separation, a view from the cabin port-hole of the distant Earth and China, the Motherland below. The classic, which had me howling with laughter out loud, was the shot of Mission Control – the usual big screen tracking the course of the vessel, the serried ranks of computer screens and controllers talking on head-sets, but the crazy bit was that typically for Chinese people, several of these controllers had their heads on their folded arms asleep!!! I see this every day at work, in shops, receptions, all over. It is normal for these seemingly perpetually tired people; it is their regular reply to "How are you?" – "Tired"!! As a Westerner, one does not expect it in Mission Control; anyone from NASA must have been horrified, but not knowing these people even as little I do, the average Yank would have had their gast flabbered.

Tuesday, 6th December 2005
The laughs started today before we stepped in a taxi. We were waiting to cross the Da Dao when a woman ran across the junction. The Traffic Assistant blew his whistle, but she ignored him. The policeman blew up too, but she kept on running, so the former gave chase and she threw him a couple of dummies managing to avoid him. The copper then decided to take on this streaking lady, disrupting his junction. The crowd looked on in amazement and then got bored at this Benny Hill-like chase. It continued for some time up Yuanshen Lu opposite the Pent-Ox. We looked on as she tried the old swerves again, but Plod was a very determined official and he gave chase in a most impressive fashion. He actually chased her into the path of a speeding Buick, so when she turned to avoid doing a pedestrian impact test, he caught her in his arms and took her to the side of the road, where she was given the right to remain silent, which she ignored. We watched from our taxi as they continued to discuss the merits or otherwise of re-enacting classic British seventies comedy chases.

Has the heat picked up in the office? There is a different feel. There are still silly things, such as there was a meeting in room 403 before lunch, then we came back to resume and most of the furniture was being moved! How many Chinese women does it take to move some tables? – answer seven!

We have been asked to move our lunch-time venue to a separate room away from the main office after complaints about the food smell – how do sandwiches smell? This was probably a back-lash against our complaints about their hawking in the toilets and smoking in the offices. That or we disturbed the power-napping at lunch-time. Sadly, now, as there are so many people in the building, they are obliged to walk a short distance to the local hotel for lunch.

Wednesday, 7th December 2005

Today was to be a mass of contrasts; in the morning our visit to the SGM (Shanghai General Motors) plant, with its very Western feel, perhaps Japanese, whereby everything had a place and was in it; the plant moved at a steady, measured rate; details were as they should be; the right machine tool names were in evidence and much money had been spent. The plant makes cars – the Rover 75-sized Buick Regal car and smaller Excelle. The afternoon at SICERI was right at the other end of the scale.

It started with a set of road-works on the Yanpu Bridge, slowing progress to a snail's pace (the usual guards were there in the glass guard-rooms on the bridge supports – what do they think? "100,000 cars, 100,001, 100,002........"). Then the trip, once off the elevated highway, became more and more "local" Shanghai, away from the glamour of Pudong and the clean-swept roads, and pristine cycle-lanes, and became dusty, tatty and earthy. Once over a railway level crossing after the train had passed (followed by pedestrians walking down the track – it must be deemed "safe" after the train has gone!) we were onto the worst-maintained tarmac road I have been on in my Chinese tour. "It is the road to the docks, used by heavy, over-loaded trucks" ran the excuse, but it would have made a good test-track for a shock-absorber manufacturer. Even our driver in the minibus drove slowly. I nearly wrote safely then, but his tailgating of a lorry carrying tonnes of steel re-enforcing bars stuck out without a flag over the end of the already-lengthened trailer was worrying. His cutting up of the same was in stark contrast to his earlier calm behaviour in the roadworks.

SICERI is modelled on the UK's old BICERI, which apart from the S standing for this city and the B for British, is an acronym for "Internal Combustion Engine Research Institute" and feels like a quiet, leafy university campus in France, with tall planar trees, harbouring twittering birds and sunlight streaming through from a deep blue sky. A boulevard-style avenue with a sward of grass lay between two brightly-painted office blocks. This was just to lure one into a false sense of order. The test-beds were apparently much improved since we Brits started going there, mainly due to the input of money and specifically to the efforts of DIY and Turk, who are gradually turning a sow's ear into a Chinese silk purse.

There were builders everywhere, and new kit was arriving and being set up. The test-bed buildings looked like prison blocks inside and out – dark, satanic places, with many doors and windows open so they were as cold as possible. This country should be a massive market for self-closing door mechanisms. Do they like being cold?

That evening, dinner was partaken at Ewe's, where I sat by the window, which was draughty, so even though I kept my shoes on (should have taken the slippers) my feet were like blocks of ice. It was one of those occasions where when the first person says "Oh, is that the time?" you realise it is quite late. We all enjoyed a good laugh and Ewe's excellent food. It was so amusing to see how in the short time she has been here, there we were in her apartment, eating Chinese home-cooked food with chopsticks, drinking Shanghai "sherry" and finishing off the meal with French-inspired, locally made pastries and "lashings" of Jasmine tea; the pot being re-filled many times – very Oriental.

Thursday, 8th December 2005
We left work on a supplier visit almost on time, waiting for the PQ (Parts Quality) engineer to stop faffing about in the office. There was more indecision on the road to the airport – I watched amazed as one wandering "Jinbei" people-carrier swept across our path in a last-minute three-lane change, when blow me, due to arguing amongst the boyos we too executed a last-second two-lane change and selected the correct road (the one marked "Pudong International Airport", in Chinese and English......)

We flew (three Chinese engineers and I, after more faffing about in Pudong airport – do they really know what they are doing?) to Chengdu in Sichuan Province, home of the Giant Pandas, the bamboo upon which they feed and hot Sichuan food. This province, if viewed on a relief map of China, is directly west of Shanghai and is a deep depression, surrounded by mountains. It is not too far from Chongqing, where we disembarked after our

Yangtze trip. The airport was much less grand than Shanghai and smaller, but clean and airy. Our party was met by the usual smiling supplier team, as in this country a supplier will often collect customers by road or pay one way rail travel. We faffed again at the airport, in order to ensure we were booked via our E-tickets on the next day's return flight – they asked at three different desks before finding the right one marked "ET Check-in" (at least in English). I know Chinese is hard for me to understand, but do they not listen to their own language when instruction is given? I have witnessed this before.

A welcome Buick people-carrier lay outside and we set off for the city. "Lost in translation" delights began before we left the airport surroundings, as pointed out by one of my colleagues was a large sign over the exit toll-booths, which said "Export", not "Exit"! He thought it funny, anyway.

The driver was typical, trained by a monkey or worse. I regularly wondered what lane we were meant to be in. He nonetheless sounded his horn at anyone who offended him in the slightest and was one of those irritating Eastern drivers who honked to warn a car as he over or under-took. One never knew which it was going to be until the last moment. Dusk was gathering and as the good old engineers at Buick had fitted light meters to the van, the dash display helpfully showed "Headlamps suggested". Sadly, the suggestion remained resolutely ignored. He only turned off the left (overtaking) indicator when we were in the outside lane after the same display told him it was still on and peeped. He responded to that one. Despite having spent some hard-earned RMB on a lumpy brown steering-wheel cover, bearing the curious moniker of "Frangle Snoopy", he was a "spoke-steerer", resting his hands on the wheel spokes, causing more wandering. Safe we were not.

He delivered us through a fairly tidy and low-rise but foggy Chengdu to our hotel, the "Jinyu Sunshine", where I counted six "helpers" outside pointing us to park! Do even Chinese drivers really need all that assistance? When one of them reverses, people spring up from nowhere to guide and cajole. The hotel was quite cheap and very plush; the floor the usual marble, with glass, brass and leather desk-covers in Reception. A bare polystyrene model of a Western cottage with a fence was awaiting (Christmas decoration?)

I had a massive twin room, with all the accoutrements and some real Chinese flower tea; none of that Western coffee rubbish.

It was quite modern, with a push-button door opening switch and outside the "Do not disturb" sign was no longer a tacky piece of card swinging from a door-knob, as there were none, but a typically Chinese illuminated device, giving the alternative "Please clean me" at the touch of a switch.

After a short freshen-up, the 'phone rang. "Herro, Reception here. You come down now!" Great, the others must be here, and a polite receptionist selected for her command of English to summon me, but better than my Chinese, yes I know. We met the General Manager and his Deputy, plus the Engineering Manager and others when we reached the restaurant selected for our delectation. As I said, Sichuan is famous for its food, and this was to be no empty claim. They really made a fuss of us and me, as the supplier had been trying to strike some business with my colleagues for some time and really rolled out the best food. I estimate we had twenty different dishes and it was without doubt the best Chinese food I have ever tasted. Spicy, yes, so best to avoid chilli-like red things and also the green bits, if possible. My taste-buds were having a ball; they did not know which signal to send to my tiny brain – sweet, sour, hot, cool, soft or crunchy.

I was sat next to the General Manager, in a seat of honour and he asked what I would like to drink. I did not know then, but that decision would be binding for all, so out came the "Pijiou boo-hao" or "Beer no good", patting my stomach and making chucking-up motions. "It makes me ill" I said, in my best Sichuanian accent. So "What would I like?" I responded that Chinese rice wine goes down well; a fine choice as it turns out, for they do not drink it in volume like beer. Sadly, in the smallest glass was some local fire-water which would be used later for the many toasts. If it was anything like the last fire-water I bought, it was about 55% proof. Alongside these two glasses was another for coconut milk – warm – and a cup of excellent flower tea. Four drinks to help one along.

The meal was really quite superb, with the General Manager and his team obviously targeting my Chinese Team Leader as he was the subject of many a "Ganbei" ("Bottoms up") toast. He became quite red-faced early on. The fish was from the Yangtze and the duck still had the head on the plate as usual. I am quite unsure as to what many of the dishes were, but they were so good I just carried on, which appeared to please my hosts. Mushrooms featured quite heavily of all sorts of shapes and sizes, as well as spicy beef, various vegetables and some beautiful sweet doughy buns.

The meal rolled on with the ganbeis coming thick and fast, but I managed to keep my cool and only responded, not proffering any of my own (don't know if that was right). Just after I had declared "Woh je Bao-le" ("I'm really full"), the mushroom soup appeared, followed by the noodles – great I thought, nearly at the end now, only the fruit to go. Sure enough that came and the sweet taste of melon and orange called an end to a true culinary masterpiece.

"Would you like to go for a foot massage?" was the next question. That sounded harmless and a good way of digesting the meal in comfort. Or could it be a code-word for something a little shady? I can always say no, thought I. "Yes, let's go" I replied, so it was into the Buick and off again.

The massage parlour had the usual "Welcome girls" on the steps, shivering in the night's damp wrap of fog. We were shown into a tatty lift and I thought "Oh, no, it's getting seedy". Once on the third floor we were welcomed by more girls, this time with walkie-talkies. "What sort of place is this?" went through my mind, but then I saw the quality awards and brass tourist plaques behind Reception (all Chinese companies collect these, so they could be meaningless) and I was a little re-assured. Before I knew it, we were being escorted down a corridor, flanked on either side by red hardwood Chinese windows, framing frosted glass. A glimpse left showed an open door with a view of a room and a man sat on the edge of a mattress, looking smug. Hmmmm, interesting place. After some debate, I was given to a young lady who drew the short straw and landed the "Ghost-face" foreigner, leading me towards the end room. My colleagues evaporated into other rooms one by one and I entered past a sink and flasks of hot water, through a frosted-glass door into a room with an adjoining shower, toilet and sink and into a small room featuring a mattress on the floor, a glass of tea, a sliced orange, tissues, a monster TV and a coat-stand.

The girl, Lai-Ting (not a play on the illumination in the room) turned on the TV, asked me by grunting if I wanted the big light off, so I declined and then she left me to undress. I took off shoes and socks and she returned with a bowl of water with a tea-bag floating therein. Ah, a foot-washing first, I thought that was a good start. A massage accompanied that and an examination of my injured ankle. I had a good foot-wash for about five minutes, then she towelled me dry and proffered some flip-flops and a T-shirt and shorts. She left so I could slip into something more comfortable. Upon her return, she pointed me to lie down, so I did on my front, but this was out of process, so I was rolled over and the job began. It was to be two hours long, the job. She gave each limb a good pounding, occasionally hurting, but stretching and working bits of me that haven't been exercised since I was last with the physio. She was thorough and kept just the right side of my dodgy bits, which thankfully remained unruffled.

I cannot say that I enjoyed it all, but felt very relaxed. One worrying bit was the part where she lay under me, supporting my head on her feet, knees under my back, pulling down on my shoulders and arching me to stretch bits that did not want to go that far, with me looking at the ceiling. We made pretty good communication by sign-language. The final act was a facial massage, or so I thought – that was really nice and smelly, but she left me to relax and returned with what I thought was a balloon of water. It turned out to be a burning hot bean-bag, which she rolled all over my back until I had to wimp out and cry "Boo". It was very pleasant, but too hot. After these third-degree injuries, it was my stomach's turn to be fried alive. Again after a while I had to cry out, as I did not really want red marks down my front, these may have been difficult to explain away to my lady later. At the conclusion, she shot out pointing at the shower and I took this to be the end of the show. There I found my only disappointment of the whole night; the shower was well down on power and consequently cold.

I attempted to pass her a tip, such as "Avoid the gweilos in future", but she would not have the proffered note, positively jumping away from my outstretched hand. I hope I did not offend, but she had worked hard on a reluctant body for two hours. I took a seat in Reception, tea was brought and I waited for the others, who duly arrived looking relaxed and smiling as I must have done. So ended another amazing night in the Orient.

Friday 9th December 2005
After the best night's sleep yet, I toddled down to breakfast and dined alone until I was just about to go when one of the team appeared. We had to wait for the usual one who was late and faffed again, but then we were transported in the old Buick to the factory which makes wiper, starter and other motors, as well as alternators and motorcycle ignition bits, with the starters and alternators being our interest.

Apart from how unusually tidy it was for a Chinese place, the first thought which occurred was "Why do they not close doors in China?" It is cold outside, so they leave them wide open; the whole office block was cold, with people sat at their desks in coats. We were ushered into a conference room for the obligatory Company presentation. My printed copy was in English, thank you, and the Foreign Business Manager sat by my side translating. He was great and very helpful.

It quickly became obvious that we need not go any further; this company was to be the one we were searching for, as they made under licence all the products of the Japanese supplier we knew and loved when we manufactured in the UK. Why had we not stumbled on them before? I was given a present of a wooden fret-work frame in red lacquered wood, with a pivoting glass etching of two pandas – guanxi time. (Guanxi are relationships, literally).

This was time to give them as much information about our starter motor application as I could to encourage them and hang what my Chinese colleagues said. It became quickly apparent to my new friend that we were the new customer they needed and we made progress. Then it was time for the factory tour. The scenes which met us were tidy versions of what I had seen when I first started in the automotive industry; lots of people on single-purpose machines, with little automation. I asked all the usual questions and squeezed out the answers I was after. I could see and feel that this was a plant run to tight quality standards and I really liked the colour laminated process sheets on each machine, with a colour photo of the current operator clipped to them; a useful touch. The rest areas amused; they were identical throughout the 35,000 square metres of production space and were pine benches lined up to pine tables with green spots upon the table centre line with almost identical flasks in position! It was all so regimented and tidy; everything had a place and was in it. The test cells were clean and new, engineers playing with rigs and components as they should, special German, Italian and American machines pointed out proudly, with an interesting set of front-end car bucks and rigs outside doing wiper-motor tests. I wonder what happens when it freezes.

The wrap-up session enabled me to use my translator to answer my audit questions, which was brought abruptly to a close with the comment "We are wasting time now, it is lunch". Nothing comes between a factory tour and lunch in this country, as feeding your guests is so important and keeps thousands of restaurants in business. This was yet another brilliant showing of provincial cuisine; a little lighter than last night, but still spicy and so very tasty. One of the waitresses was the best-looking girl I have ever seen here and

I could not let the occasion pass without comment, saying that "my guide book talks of the pandas, the bamboo and the great food, but does not mention the beautiful women". The plain waitress will have gone home happy, but the one I meant responded in Chinese that she wanted me to teach her English! Shame I was busy. My observations aroused great mirth around the table and my Chinese Team Leader perked up with a translated comment about there being little better than good food and pretty girls. He's not such a bad old stick after all! I do look forward to taking my wife out for a meal again, though.

All of a sudden, it was over. I have yet to recognise the imminent closing of a Chinese meal, but I could feel something final in the air. We collected our gear and left again in the Buick, with much hand-shaking and requests to return. It had been a thoroughly useful visit, though long overdue as it would have saved a lot of worry and a false start with another supplier; but knowing this lot, they will ignore the people we had just seen and stay with the false starters (pun intended).

The only amusement on the way back to the apartment was the many questions from my colleagues who joined me in a taxi from the airport if I knew my way back. It turned out the taxi driver hadn't a clue and I had to direct him; ho-hum, it's a big city.

Chapter 6

A HUMBLE HOME AND ATTACK OF
THE SHANGHAI COUGH

Saturday, 10th December 2005

The staggering noise level in the cement yard right outside my window reached a crescendo, waking me up at 3.30am. I was livid and cold. I felt like throwing something at the workers. As usual, it was the empty flat trucks crossing over the loose concrete slabs which made an incredible noise. I wish I had a noise meter to hand.

It was another rainy start to the day, with an excellent chance of becoming very much colder. So it would turn out to be, but there was much excitement to be had before then............ shopping! Yes my fellow male-types, a habit much popular with those of the extra chromosome tendency, but not normally with us blokes. It is so much more fun though when you can HAGGLE!

I chose to walk down the Da Dao, dodging the rain drops and soaking up the moisture and Saturday feeling. I was distracted by a crashing and sliding sound and spun round to see a glove-less scooter rider take a toboggan run down the road. He probably braked too hard and slid on the shiny wet road. He looked OK and started to get up immediately, so he may only be slightly injured, but I leapt up once from a spill and was unaware I had punctured a lung coming off my bike. No-one ran to help (including me) and he sorted himself out. A passing ambulance did not stop, either.

The next interesting stop was Lujiazui Park, where a married couple were doing their stroll in the green zone for the camera. She had a white dress on, red high-heeled boots and a pink coat! The picture is most amusing! I ran around for the shot and to leap about wishing them happiness. Marriage has been good for my wife and I, and I'd recommend it. (Photos p.V, p.XXVI).

I had arranged to meet Frau and Native down the market, so we could again enjoy being soaked. Rain in Shanghai just seems to add to the atmosphere, the same way it doesn't in Manchester. They had camped out in

Starbuck's, so I joined them for a drink. The rain did not ease, so out we went to do battle. It was obvious something was wrong on the first stand, as half the shelves were empty. The stall-holder grinned and proffered an explanation, with gestures and face-pulling. It transpired that for the second weekend running, it both rained and the police had raided the place. The authorities have vowed to close the market, or at least that part which sells counterfeit goods, or even the real goods sold cheaply. So we are to lose some great sport and an excellent source of Western needs!

The scheme now was to look innocent and ask for products. These would then be brought to the stand by a runner, and then haggling could begin, but not too much as the police may be back. At the next stand, one we had frequented with Post and Bling last weekend, the story was similar, but as we needed DVDs, it was time to follow one of the girls off the stall back to her "house". It was a fair stroll, trying to dodge the drops of rain, even though brollies were provided free!

We eventually ended up down a side-alley off the main Fuzhou Lu and the world turned darker. Buildings closed in, the courtyard was dirty and the floor broken. There were no lights to brighten the gloom. The girl darted into an open doorway and I followed. Again it was dark, with light bulbs hanging there, not doing what Thomas Edison envisaged. She urged us to be careful as we were about to climb some steep, dark, stairs. Some light fought its way in from a tiny landing window, which turned out to have no glass in one pane. It also had a pair of shoes sat on the ledge, which judging by the dust had been there for years. What would it take to go and buy some glass, and keep the weather out?

The landing brought us to a door, which like the whole staircase, had once been painted. A sharp tap brought a puffy, red "just woken up" face to the door and we could squeeze inside. This "house" was just a room, a bed-sit which was but a bed wide and featured a scruffy chest of drawers with a TV sat on a foam block, and a set of shelves under the window at the other end, supporting a single electric ring on top, whilst below lurked some half-eaten bowls of something. It was unnecessarily grubby and untidy. Paint peeled off walls and the ceiling, the electrics were extension upon extension, the bed upon which we were invited to perch was more like a board it was so hard and covered with the thinnest bedding. Really, with very little money, but an investment of time, it could be quite cosy; but this is China.

It felt almost as if one were depriving the girls of their next meal by accepting the discount they offered us for being good customers! They are so straight, these people. There we were, in absolute squalour haggling about a couple of RMB, when our wallets bulged with 100 notes. Bizarre is a word often used here.

I had missed it, but there had been an exhibition of photographs taken in people's living rooms or bed-sits from the very poor to the very rich here in the city. Frau and Native have the resultant book, which includes interesting comments from the inhabitants in answer to a series of questions from the photographer about contentment and ambition, I think. It revealed how very few of them have any real ambition, just unattainable dreams or goals for which they have no plans to achieve. So his conclusion was that they will stay in their current situations, some of which were quite sorry. This room seemed to be very much a part of that sorry crowd.

We then returned to the market; I bought some gifts for my lovely girls which should earn me a "Great Dad" badge for at least five minutes at Christmas and then we shot off for the nearest taxi, as we needed to pick up some more special purchases at the recently-discovered Taikang Craft Centre. We took refuge in the "Protest café" again (it features lots of old Revolutionary artefacts) and rooted amongst the goods, some of which were priced to suit Westerners. Time ran away and before we knew it, the clock demanded that we make tracks for the evening's entertainment, the Christmas Do.

By special permission of Brummie, the author, I reproduce his account of the night's ex-Pat's Christmas Party, which he sent by way of an e-mail to Winston, who was at the time doing his stint in the UK. I have used it unabridged and unchanged except for the names and it shows that he can write, well at least for an "ex-trackie", as we call him when his back is turned. (Brummie, when I first met him in the mid-80s was a shop-floor Team Leader on the assembly tracks, (hence "trackie") and a good one).

'You missed a brilliant night on Saturday, it was fantastic! Probably the best night I've ever had in China ever!!! Right, now I've made you feel bad for missing it I'll tell you the truth.

It was a good night, about 100 people turned up, the music was loud, the food was good and the beer flowed freely, by 8:30 most of the Tiddlies were tiddly so Gary decided to get the party games going. It was just like being back at junior school with all the squealing and giggling (and that was just the blokes). The first game up was pass the balloon along a line without using you hands (a bit like pass the parcel but without a parcel and you have to stand up and you can't use your hands and you don't rip paper off or get a prize at the end and you use a balloon!!??! Other than that it's identical!). Sonnie was in this and had had rather a lot of red wine so kept bursting the opposition's balloons. Gary gave him a yellow card and warning, but his team still won.

Next up was musical chairs. I got roped into that one and won easily; Tiddlies have no idea about tactics. I was brilliant at it and am thinking of taking it up as a profession when this engineering malarkey all falls apart.

By now there was that much cigarette smoke in the room you could hardly see above chest height, but that was ok there were some lovely chests to look at. Then came musical statues and most of the Tiddlies joined in. This game seemed to last forever until Shifty decided to join in and gyrate with some tiny sexy little ones, but that soon finished.

Then came 10 o'clock and as if someone had blown a whistle in their brains they all started to leave, by 10:15 there was not one local left in the Mawdesley (besides the staff) just 20 Brits standing around wondering where the hell everyone had gone. People soon started to leave then, 'Up Blue Angel' or 'Home' and by 12:30 there was only me and Mr. P. left and as we could see the staff wanted to go home (they had their coats on) we had another couple of drinks and then went home. Naaa! We just went home still feeling quite sober for some reason.

In all a very odd but enjoyable night and judging by the conversations on Monday the Tiddlies thoroughly enjoyed themselves.'

Thanks to Brummie for that colourful account. I wonder if I could persuade him to contribute more as his style is quite engaging.

Cheers, mate.

Sunday, 11th December 2005

I'm writing this at the apartment, trying to keep my feet warm. My personal nurse has informed me that it is vital, due to the special connection between nose and feet that the latter be kept warm, a job not easily accomplished in this room. Cloud base is at coffee-table height, below which it is fairly cold. But why should I worry? There are people out behind this block living in packing cases.

The temperature has only been 0° to -4° today; in Hohot and Harbin in the north of this vast country it is sub-20.

I haven't been out of the place today as my cough is foul and I want to be warm. Bed is very appealing, and I am using the guest room as it is smaller, easier to heat and I had hoped quieter with a smaller (single-glazed) window. I spent ages sealing it up with draught excluder, but because it is China, the turn-buckles on the sides of the window had nowhere to go, as the returns on the window aperture were plastered right up to the edge of the frame. A little scraping with a blade provided some space to turn the latches and it sort of sealed.

Monday, 12th December 2005 – Frustration Day
Office quotes of the day:

"Wang, you decide; you're an effin' engineer not the kitchen staff".

"Even with the test results in front of them, they can't believe it – why do they have to change it?"

"Of all the things to get hung up on, they choose the simplest concept".

"It's the obvious thing to do, so they won't do it, that's too easy".

"Sonnie's used reverse psychology on them, telling them they must do something, knowing they will not and do the thing he really wanted them to do!"

These were the most reasonable. It just seemed to be one of those days when our hosts got under our skin. Our esteemed leader threatened to remove one of the Marketing guys as he is so dangerous to the Company!

The Transmissions group have installed a gearbox in a car. When pulling a tight right turn, the box shifts and clashes with the chassis rails, making a horrendous noise. We did tell them that it would not fit and work properly, but to them it fits. We have differing views on basic quality. It does fit, true, but an engine and gearbox installation moves in operation, when you start and stop it in particular and in response to cornering and gravitational forces.

This represents a frustration for Brummie – he keeps telling them it is unacceptable, but to them the box is in the car and it works.

Tonight was dinner at Frau and Native's palatial apartment in the clouds on floor 30 of Shimao Lakeside Garden, to give the place its full style. I was prepared for the cold, by taking extra socks and my travelling slippers. Taking slippers is a tendency my old friend Will and I used to great effect when we were struggling teenagers on old, noisy motorcycles, trolling around Southport from girlfriend to girlfriend. One sure way of being invited back by at least the Mother, if not the girl herself, was to arrive ready to take off bike boots and dress for the lounge in slippers. Mothers all over the town appeared to enjoy this as much as our repeated mantra "Your cake/s is/are lovely. Thank you." We often went back to the house, even when the girls had dumped us both!

As expected, Frau had gone all out to decorate the flat and make it homely with a seasonal feel. Candles burned all over, nibbles were on the table, Christmas music floated quietly over the airwaves, and various baubles and star things decorated the room and ceiling. Where would we be without our ladies? I reckon Brummie and I felt quite homesick. Ewe (wife to Tup) turned up and the party was complete; she's as mad as a box of frogs.

The food was as good as the anticipation – beef bourguignon and all the trimmings; there was far too much for me. The tastes were superb; Frau is as good a cook as she is top company. The mulled orange juice before-hand was also inspired. After, for dessert came the fruit, which was all I could manage. There was even coconut juice for me to drink!

I was feeling fairly dodgy; the cough which was to fell me the day after was really bothering me; I sat on the settee after the meal chain-sucking Hall's mentholyptus sweets to stop me spreading my germs everywhere. It was hard not to cough, as after the meal Native played a CD by an old friend of ours. It was odd to be there, 30 floors up in the Shanghai sky with the sounds of ex-chassis engineer and all-round Brummie star, Giovanni Esposito (Spoz) coming from the speakers with his renderings from his one-man CD. He had been the inspiration behind the production of "A Brummie Rock Opera", which had featured his maroon red Morris Marina on stage (he still drives it too). A thoroughly decent and genuine bloke and a good chassis engineer. We did have some of those, for sure.

Tuesday, 13th December 2005

This was a write-off for me. I rose at the normal time, but felt quite unlike going to work, but missed having someone there to tell me to go back to bed, which was needed. I should really have taken Monday off back-to-back with Sunday, but I did not want to miss the dinner party. I asked at the desk if the chemist would be open. It was a 24-hour place came the reply, so I waited for

Brummie, grunted a greeting, started coughing and walked for the taxi. "You should be in bed", said he, which is also what the receptionist had offered. I did not need telling twice, but I had been, so I left Brummie to a lonely ride and went in search of the place with the pills and lotions. Why can you not find a shop you have walked past loads of times, but never needed so far? I wandered up and down the Da Dao, with no success, so I shambled off down Yuanshen Lu, to seek my fortune there and then down Yandeng Lu, where Rolf's favourite supermarket lurks. Opposite I saw the sign my eyes craved the most – a green cross. I coughed my way through the door, coughed on the way to the counter and spluttered onto the counter. The pharmacist sort of got the point, but pointed to some capsules. I made glugging liquid motions and he reached for some mixture at the bottom of the cabinet. I handed over the princely sum of RMB23 and left. A bottle of what turned out to be organic medicine for under two quid – stunning. I went back to the Pent-Ox, filled the hot water bottle and knocked back some medicine. I slept for four hours solid and awoke a new man.

I stayed in all day, so nothing happened, except good old Brummie coming around to see if I needed anything. Sleep and warmth were the two necessities, I think. What a decent guy. As today is a bit short on incisive observations, unless you want a blow-by-blow account of the movements of shipping on the river, I have scoured the excellent newspaper "China Daily" for interesting snippets, using their "Chinascene" section for inspiration.

An example of a story from the North:

"A grieving woman has lived alone in a mountain cave for more than 20 years since her baby died in Helin in the Inner Mongolia Autonomous Region. Huang, a native of Sichuan Province in her 50s, married a local man surnamed Sun. When the couple's six-month old son died, Huang became extremely depressed. After a major quarrel with her mother-in-law, she moved into the isolated cave. Sun brings her food every day, but she refuses to return home with him."

From the South:

"Residents of Luozhu Village of Shenzhen, Guangdong, are being forced to take agricultural evening classes. Their residents committee organised three classes of different levels of complexity at the beginning of this year. More than 60 pupils plough the fields by day and hit the books at night. Qiu

Xuiqun usually carries her daughter on her back to the classroom. "Nobody takes care of my kid at home as both my husband and me have evening classes at night". Another villager surnamed Liao said his usual evening entertainment – games of mah-jong with his neighbours – "have been interrupted as his friends must study instead."

You will have to wonder at other gripping tales I read of, such as "Veteran police officer keeps traffic moving", "Seafood price war turns violent", "Cold cells may replace dreams of wedding bells" and the glorious "Duck's diet of snails finally pays off". You have missed some real crackers there.

Wednesday, 14th December 2005

Much refreshed I returned to work a new, but still coughing man. These Shanghai coughs are really tenacious, if that is a word for a cough. I certainly cannot say it when I am coughing. Few interesting things happened at work that comes into the amusing cultural bracket, although I was invited to a hastily-convened session, referring to my comments after the Chengdu visit. At least I added my ten penn'orth to something that was going to take place anyway. It is good news, at least someone is listening.

Brummie left today, lucky geezer, and I stopped off in Carrefour on the way home, and had a "Billy-no-mates" or "Lonely Joe" meal in Megabite. As usual, the food was cheap and excellent. I then wandered upstairs to buy some Scotch to take home to my dear Papa, who is an avid collector of Malts and connoisseur of the gold liquid. The Chinese market is a really open one for expensive Western drink and is packaged garishly to suit the local tastes. It amazes even me what some of the classic drinks cost out here, when one considers how little the local beer costs and the local wine, too, which is probably the equal of many a Western brand; it just does not have that cachet, I suppose. Spirits and liqueurs are the ones which really seem to appeal, or at least are being pushed. The Chinese do have their own spirits, but delights such as "Blue Bols" or "Crème de Cacao" do not appear to have been emulated. The local liquor is mainly clear "fire-water". The best use I found for some of it was gargling when I last had a sore throat!

Today was the last Chinese lesson of this series. It is amazing, but not surprising how the numbers have dropped off – at the end there were but three hardy souls. It is a stupendously hard language to learn, and I am a lover of language, but as usual, one needs to practise and I do far too little. It does not seem to sink in even with constant repetition, and only the very basics have stayed with me. My vocabulary has not really grown very much over the time we have been here. Brummie and Winston seem to get to grips with it and do not generally attend the classes, not enjoying the teaching methods. They just drink beer in the Mawdesley and pick it up! Some of the others that intend being here long term are taking personal lessons, but most are willing to be English about it and just shout to ensure they are understood.

Thursday, 15th December 2005
Today I was asked to run a course for some of the local engineers in the Concepts Section. I wonder what on earth they are working on. I was pleased to receive their spontaneous applause, but saddened to see that none had heard of the famous quality guru, Dr W Edwards Deming. I suppose we have not heard of many of their famous characters either, the country is so big and full of its own heroes. I do wonder, if like Edwards, do they have similar "quality gurus"?

Any notion of quality here is submerged below a question which sounds like "Can we do it cheaper?" That is no way to build up a car brand. At least it is not the way the last market entrant did it and here I refer to Toyota with its Lexus brand. No, they bought market share with immaculately built, but expensive to manufacture cars that almost never went wrong and were bullet-proof.

Today was also time for our regular conference call with our colleagues in the UK. It is always a hassle trying to connect either end, with the "engaged" tone being the familiar noise on the line from either side of the globe. Quite what we would do without mobiles to hurdle the gap, I do not know. The addition of trying to locate Chinese managers who are then whipped away by their own bosses is also wearing. To be fair, if you ask most of them to be there, they turn up, even though conversation in another language without being able to see the other must be really hard for them.

Friday, 16th December 2005
I knew I would have trouble with today. It is our first-born, Sarah's 20th birthday. I cannot help but feel older. I well remember that day in 1985 when

I stood in the bright sun of a new December day as a father for the first time. I still get the goose-pimples whenever I hear "Sarah" by either Thin Lizzy or Fleetwood Mac. We had a good chat on the phone and she was looking forward to her party.

Saturday, 17th December 2005

Amazing, I made it down to breakfast, which turned out to be a disco affair. Every time I go down there, some disco music is blaring out of the adjoining function or games room. It was quite loud today, and made the noise from the slurping, snorting Chinese guy to my right a little less noticeable. Nothing barring a face-mask and breathing apparatus could mask his smoking. At breakfast! These people seem to smoke industrial strength tobacco which is awful.

I quite enjoyed shopping for a while, then I became bored with no-one to share the fun, but steeled myself to make some brave purchases, which may even turn out to be inspired, but I shall have to wait until the family see what I have bought.

One of Brummie's pet hates is people shopping in their slippers. The Chinese have taken this type of footwear to new levels. Added to this fashion statement, I saw a couple out in their quilted jim-jams, showing incredible style for this time of year. (Photo p.XVII).

Next year, according to the Chinese Lunar calendar, is the year of the Dog. My friend Stuart says that he hopes that the dog in question is not the car he is busy engineering. He hears so often from the other UK guys he is with about quality not being felt, understood or even spoken of. In the engines section, he has several failed components on one of the test units, but they still regard the test as passed, merely because the engine was still running at the end. Sadly, even his local colleague who runs the whole engines section has only been driving for two years, so the "feel" for a car does not extend to many.

Sunday, 18th December 2005

I am sat on my settee, with the grand vista of the Huangpu River in front of me, one of my favourite bands playing away on the DVD and the heating is OFF! I am drinking my usual tot of J&B, some honey and hot water for my abused throat.

There are two large passenger vessels at the Passenger terminal away up river, one of which I photographed as it sailed in earlier, as it looks like it has a mosque in the stern!

A huge freighter lies tied up opposite the apartment block, and is being filled with who knows what. The usual circus of small local boats ply the brown waves, although somewhat reduced, as even locals seem to take it a little easier at the weekend. There is a massive freighter, tied up mid-stream, where only a couple of days ago there was the biggest floating crane you have ever seen. I do not know why it does not submerge when under tow.

It is now 3.45 and the sun is starting to run away for the night, its beams have left my balcony in shadow and I felt the heat escape from my feet, so they are now covered and the heating is on. In the distance, two long, low barges have made a spectacular stereo turn, the dying rays glinting on the wash as this Eastern side of the river settles into the coming gloom.

I have been out on my bike today in the glorious sunshine, where it managed to struggle through the smog. I really love hacking through this city on my own two wheels; there is so much to see and so many really pleasant places to go; myriad parks and tree-lined avenues. At this time of year, a very rare and endangered species comes to life in the trees – the Shanghai tree-surgeon. Many have climbed and many have fallen; it being a real problem for the City to attract employees to this particular branch (ha!) of horticulture. They seem to be quite brutal with the trees, but the effect come spring is impressive.

Today's foray was to the Xiangyang market. Yesterday when I was there I forgot to buy the old mother-in-law a handbag, and as she is such a good woman to me, I was only too happy to oblige. A quick dash to stand A41 and there was Lu Yun Qing, who knows many of us ex-Pat guys and the low prices we are prepared to pay! I selected a bag and legged it. I was a little concerned at leaving my trusty steed some distance away, but there it was, just as I had left it.

Then there are the many invincible riders on powered bikes who feel adequate protection for their heads is provided by the hood of their anorak (they are fur-lined, after all). For some it is just a woolly hat. I suppose for the speeds at which some of them travel, they consider this sufficient. All are graduates of the school of "It will never happen to me" and the Chinese branch, "If it happens, that is Destiny". I prefer to consider that God gave me brains and it is my responsibility to look after them. Hence I am one of very few cyclists who wear a helmet and gloves. I also fasten the old seat-belt in the car – how many kids have we seen rolling around here, stood in the front foot-well? I suppose I have seen too many vehicle crash-test videos to consider that I am protected in a car.

Upon my return to the Pent-Ox, I was stood waiting for the lifts and wondered at the noise in the games room. It was two middle-aged women sat in front of a TV singing along! I have found Karaoke in my own building! How I was tempted to join in, especially as the words were in Ying-tong. There are some real music-lovers here in this building, as breakfast was punctuated again by loud disco music. I suppose anything is better than slurping noises.

Well, the sun has finally bid farewell and the land is succumbing to a veil of darkness. Fingers of cold are reaching out to those still shopping or working. I am quite happy here in my heated room, but I'd be much happier if I were home.

Monday, 19th December 2005
One day to go before I fly home. The morning taxi-ride was fraught with the usual worries. It was apparent as soon as I stepped into the car and it set off that this car may well have been on its way to the scrapyard, but I merely interrupted its journey. The clutch and throttle were of the "digital" variety, with two positions; in and out or on and off. The clutch came in with such a bang that I am amazed that there are any gearbox bearings left at all. Maybe there are not and it is best I do not know any details of their fate. The driver was a classic "Mad cow" wanderer; she had no idea what those white lines on the road were for. I tried to guess which lane we were due in next, but as usual, the slide into another lane is made coincidentally with the indication, so it might as well not be made. For many Shanghai drivers, the flashing of a bulb merely shows that the lamp and the relay are working.

At the Team Meeting this morning it was good to see old Tup is back in town. His reports from the frozen north have been relayed through his wife until now. He reported on the outrageously long hours the test drivers are expected to work and that any interruption is not welcome, as that means extra hours have to be put in by the team to catch up. We always thought that one result of testing was to show up problems, which could then be sorted. Testing is there to confirm that the product is as intended, but there will always be issues. Our job as Engineers is to sort those issues out and close them down properly.

He was repeatedly told by the drivers to not rev the engine hard and that most Shanghai drivers do not extend their engines above 2,000rpm. However, the engine is designed and able to stretch right up to 7,000rpm, a figure that would have your average Shanghai driver reaching for the ear-plugs or kill-switch. What they fail to understand is that Shanghai can be driven around at low revs, as there are little in the way of hills, but if you take our little excursion up to Chongqing, then those little 1.3L Suzukis were thrashed within an inch of their lives.

Tuesday, 20th December 2005

Today was Leaving China Day. I was looking forward to breathing in some clean air, seeing more than a mile in any direction, hearing the birds and gazing at stars high above. Simple pleasures these may be, but when you cannot enjoy them, they take on a new, precious meaning.

Those nice people in HR had laid on a shuttle bus from Shimao Lakeside to take us up to the airport, but had not asked when we wanted to leave, which would have been useful, as in order to reserve long leg-room seats, one needs to check in fairly early. Therefore, Native and Frau were leaving at 9.00am and the bus picked us up at 10.00. There was Lucky and his lady, Visa, Donk and myself on the roster. We always worry when being driven about Shanghai, as most of us know where we should be going to hit a certain destination, and regularly have to direct taxi drivers around their own city.

The bus driver was no exception and none of us had been that way to the airport before. He was slow, a real lane-wanderer, and either had no clutch left or did not press the pedal down at gear-change time. He fairly crunched his way through that transmission, but the sad thing is that one knows that he would not realise anything was wrong.

Nonetheless, despite his slow driving, crazy route and repeated dabs of the air brakes for no reason at all, we arrived at the airport in Pudong within forty minutes.

Chapter 7

ART ON THE CREEK AND ROLF'S BIRTHDAY

Tuesday, 3rd January 2006

It is a funny series of emotions, leaving again, but normal life has to go on; people cannot sit around moping because Dad has to go away, I would not want them to. On the other hand, one feels as if one needs to make the most of every minute with them, but then it could become too intense. It is a hard balance and if one has made the best use of the preceding days, then the last day should be like any other. We prefer a quick exit in our family and so it was when taxi-man Bernard came at 4.30pm.

The flight was typically Chinese; there were people up and down like Jack-in-the-boxes and what sounded like stiff arguments at regular periods during the flight, people changing seats and two women who whittered the whole of the way through an 11 hour 50 minute flight. How did they have the material to talk for so long? Sleep was not possible near them.

Wednesday, 4th January 2006

Shanghai was reached pretty well on time and the usual long wait at Customs from the people who invented bureaucracy, meant that when I found the baggage carousel, my bag was there doing the rounds and I was away. The taxi rank wait was not too long, but the wind was very fresh and I was ready with the scarf and hood. At the Citic Pent-Ox Metropolis, I wisely checked my room card would guarantee me access to the room at Reception before rolling my case into the lift. It was good to settle in and I checked with Rolf to wish him Happy New Year, looking forward to seeing him on the following day, if I managed to wake. After the break, the room was freezing cold.

Thursday, 5th January 2006

I had planned to stroll down to breakfast and so set two alarms on two mobiles to ensure I woke. I still managed to slide back to sleep and it became too late to have a Pent-Ox "disco-breakfast" (they do love their loud pop music in the morning. I do not, but it is funny watching the girls jig around). I dined in my room and took a taxi to work. It is amazing how one misses the details of Shanghai life and how they have now become as familiar as sights back home. It was too cold for the ballroom dancers outside the Chevrolet showroom, or that particular venue has moved the "movers" on!

It was good to be back in the fray; I had a few gifts to pass out for favoured and effective colleagues, who seemed to appreciate the thought, if not the strange gift itself (for Nimitz, my Team Leader, I bought a funny book on British Roundabouts for a joke – I hope he got it). There was the odd question and then a lot of catching up with the other guys who had been to various parts of the globe over the Christmas break, such as Rolf to a supplier in Italy, Marvin to Hong Kong and naturally lots of us back to the UK. The Chinese had been busy whilst we were enjoying ourselves and a certain urgency is creeping into the operation.

We had a pre-arranged conference call with the UK in the afternoon, to coincide as usual with 4.00pm here and 8.00am GMT. It gives us an hour to talk before the theoretical end of our day, but as usual, it went on for nearly two hours. Being jet-lagged, Native and I were wilting visibly; my eyes were heavy and closing of their own accord, my head snatching back as I sensed it sagging. It is just so obvious someone is falling asleep, but out here it is viewed entirely differently to back in the UK, as here sleeping on the job is just "napping" and nearly everyone does it. Of course, some of the UK guys thought it was funny to keep us talking beyond our finish time. In the end I said "Going now, bye!" and the line was cut by a Chinese boss!

I needed to visit the shrine that is Carrefour supermarket for the essentials on the way back. It was comforting again to be in a familiar environment so far from home. The New Year Festival decorations were out, they having only just capitalised on the non-Oriental season of Christmas, with most Chinese having no knowledge, I am sure, of the existence or importance historically and religiously of Jesus.

I had decided to eat in Megabite, the cheap fast-Chinese food eatery below, but had left my card in the apartment, so another cold smoked sausage hit the shopping basket for later zapping in the microwave, as Pizza Hut is not for me (I am wheat intolerant) and I could not face a walk in the cold back to the Mawdesley or the other café down the road. I just wanted my own place and the heating on.

I was ready for the night, with the hot water bottle full, ear-plugs at the ready, as I had seen the big ships tied up at the dock-side and men busy loading the bags in the yard, crashing and banging away. The room heaters, especially in the bedroom, struggled to conquer the cold penetrating through the single-glazing. I was also ready for the 2.30 to 3.00am sudden wake-up, (due to jet-lag) which seems to catch everyone. There is no point fighting it or becoming annoyed as I have observed before, just roll with it, read, refill the hot water bottle and ensure one is comfortable. Sleep will come, usually about 5.00am, with barely 90 minutes before the alarm sounds!

Friday, 6th January 2006
What a great, two-day week to break one in to the Chinese ways! I managed to struggle down for breakfast and catch Spit who had not long landed, so we could taxi together to work. It helped that I knew the way, as the driver needed some help; not as much as the clown the day before, but it was good to share a few thoughts with a fellow ex-Powertrain employee.

The day featured a meeting where the Test Engineering Manager was bemoaning the failure of components due to Quality problems and the consequent impact on his Test Programme. Yes, success! The message is getting through and they are feeling the pain. Someone remarked that our Chinese colleagues are experiencing all the emotions that we have been through across many years of engine development in a much accelerated time-scale. They are running out of time for this project and it is beginning to show. The other interesting interplay was that between this same Manager and his old gaffer. They rarely met each others' gaze and talked over each other. This would not have happened six months ago or even less.

Once work was over, it was the usual game to find a taxi on a Friday night. This was not easy or comfortable in such low temperatures. I was so glad to be sporting a vest (not for the first time since I had arrived) as well as a hat and gloves. These precautions were wise as Visa had an uncovered head and hands, whilst stood in the road trying to hail a taxi and he was feeling the effects of Shanghai's wind. We finally beat a local to a cab, which is always satisfying as they are so quick with none of the "After you" graces and manners with which we are sometimes blessed.

This was good for me, as I had walked out of work alone and found Visa, Donk and Fluff all wandering around taxi-hunting. We clambered in, grateful for a VW heater and repaired to the welcoming confines of the Mawdesley, where for some reason I ordered a cold G&T rather than the tea I had planned. The food was good as usual, with me just opting for a soup and a bowl of chips. Donk naturally made life difficult by using long words and ordering something tricky like a glass of red wine. Bottles were brought, including white, but finally an old box of red was proffered and the "nose" on Donk's face set to work. It twitched in a most unsatisfied way and suggested a hint of vinegar. The bemused bar staff left him to it, with head barman Nelson probably wondering where these English people come from to be so particular about red wine. In the end he sent it back and it was duly funnelled into a can and sent to the kitchen for use in the next meal requiring juice of the grape.

Saturday, 7th January 2006
Well, I do remember waking up to fill the hot water bottle again but it was 11.30am before I made it to real awakening activity. Jet-lag is a debilitating feeling – how do flight crews manage? I bet they have warmer digs in which to sleep; it is absolutely freezing in my bedroom – how can I be cold in bed?

Rolf and I had agreed to meet for another trip around the Shanghai Art Gallery and it was bicycle time again. I had missed my bike and the freedom of Shanghai's streets, which are designed around two wheels. He cycled to meet me here and we set off in brilliant sunshine, but well togged-up against the biting wind, with two pairs of gloves on my sensitive hands. We headed for the ferry at Dongchang Lu, the "spitting ferry" and I treated him to the RMB1.3 (10p) fare as I am brimming with generosity and had the right change. It was so good to be on that slab of floating concrete again, seeing the sights from the river and all the nautical activity around us. It is rather like crossing a busy street trying to make it from one bank to the other, except that boats do not have very effective brakes.

We turned north on the other bank and set off up the Ring Road to then turn east just as the Bund proper started. It's a scary bit of road, with trolley-buses, cars, trikes and two-wheelers competing for space on a piece of road which funnels down to one lane from three and turns right. Only the brave cycle where we go. I always enjoy this bit, especially going quicker than the other traffic (which is easy as most are slug-slow) and then hitting a greater mêlée around the corner as traffic joins from the left. It is then a case of avoiding the buses and cars and heading for the relative safety of the short bicycle lane outside the market building. This is always full of pedestrians, tricycles and two-wheelers or every description. There is an obligation to stop at the next traffic lights, but many cyclists ignore this. At this point, one is skirting the outer edge of the Yu Gardens and there are mad shoppers everywhere. The road can then be followed across Hennan Road and the Jaguar/Land Rover dealership which is an oasis of automotive excess (though not as much as the Ferrari or Rolls-Royce palaces) in a city where there is no need for four-wheel-drive or any chance to drive fast.

We next turned down a narrow street to take us north to meet Jinling Lu, which would lead us towards People's Square, in the north-west corner of which stood our target, the Shanghai Art Gallery. This is a place which never disappoints in its quality of displays and the variety therein. Today was to be no exception. We completed our circuit of the southern and western sides of the Square and parked with all the other bicycles. This piece of architecture is itself a sight worth seeing, being housed in the old racecourse building and once out of bounds to Chinese, (as was the whole of the racecourse), which was built for the edification of the colonial powers such as the British. Makes you proud to be one, doesn't it? No? Correct answer, then. I feel quite uncomfortable at some of the things my forebears have done in the name of the Empire. We trampled upon a huge amount of the world, oppressing people across the globe without a care for their welfare in many cases. Perhaps now we are reaping the seeds of earlier humiliations. Having said that, we are still welcome here and apparently much more so than many other nationalities.

The exhibition in the galleries was obviously going to be good, as there was a queue at the ticket desk to part with one's RMB20 (about £1.30). We were treated on the ground floor to a display of modern architecture, featuring work by a Japanese architect and his team who had projects in hand or completed in their native islands as well as the US, Italy and France. Some were striking in their brilliance, others just more concrete and glass boxes. One of the best was in earthquake-devastated Kobe in Japan and Osaka, where a quarry had been landscaped on the coast to return it to nature.

One floor up was a treat for those lovers of Chinese portraiture. The artist seemed to go out into the poorer parts of this country and capture ordinary people at rest, most of whom would not be flattered by the result. In particular he accentuated two features of Chinese anatomy which result from hard work, a lack of care, money and poor diet, i.e. bad teeth and deformed feet. One or two were comedic in their proportions and were more like caricatures, with over-sized heads and other features. He did have a knack of capturing sun and work-hardened skin on faces and hands as well as the facial expressions which told of a life on peasant wages. A complete surprise was a small collection of nudes, which is not what one expects in China.

There were a few which really caused me to stop and read the words by the side of the portrait, with one being a simple head and trunk of a young girl with sights set on the high life, but who was probably destined never to see them. The mixture of emotions on her face was complex and deep, the artist really having captured something there. Another was a collection of peasant or migrant workers sat on their bundles by the side of the road, waiting for employment to drive by. These were sad, care-worn characters, of a type we see regularly, especially out of this city of Shanghai. I saw many like this on the drive with my family up to the Great Wall.

The next floor was completely different again; in fact it could not have been more different. This was a travelling exhibition from Italy of some of that country's finest art. Quite how the average Chinese visitor would relate to a three or four-hundred year old painting of Christian icons was beyond me, but the skills of the various artists was beyond question. Some of the scenes were of parts of old Rome in decay, with once-great, now tumbled-down buildings strewn in the foreground. There were cherubims and seraphims hanging in the skies and near-naked figures lounging around. It was all very arty, but so, so different to the previous displays.

Finally, the top floor was a feast of modern Chinese art, there to show how this genre is progressing and questioning if the country's artists were abandoning traditional art forms and subjects. Naturally with modern art, some of it was a little too far out for me and looked as if a 5-year-old had splashed the canvas whilst tripping up on an errand to the art cupboard in school. Some was staggering in its colour and vivid interpretations of the title. Sadly, though, the gallery P.A. called "Time" and we were obliged to leave; but what a visual treat we had enjoyed. Whoever co-ordinates the exhibitions deserves a medal for the quality and diversity. It never fails to entertain and stun.

The return journey on the ferry was fun for the ride around Shanghai as well as the breathtaking views of the Bund and Pudong on the opposite bank lit up like only a Chinese city can be. We never tire of these sights and they are free, except for the ferry fare. We then cycled straight up Dongchang Lu to Century Avenue where we split to go our separate ways.

Our dinner date later was in the Coffee Beanery, where we spied on the Chinese menu a meal with soup and a drink for RMB25 – less than two pounds. It was lovely – pork strips and gravy with onions and a pile of fried rice with mushrooms and seafood. I am still not keen on cold vegetables as the Chinese seem to enjoy, especially greens, but stuck in the pool of gravy it warmed up sufficiently for my tastes.

We enjoyed a fine repast before sidling next door to the Mawdesley and the excellent company of Mr. and Mrs. Native. There we whiled away the time until about 10.30pm, amused by barman Nelson's choice of music. This was mostly slushy Western rubbish and that most irritating of songs by the feebly titled MLTR – "Michael Likes to Rock". This is a group who do not "rock", more like emulate Chinese "car-sick" music as Frau describes it. There is one particular track that is played to death here in Shanghai and Frau was determined to find out what it was, knowing how much it annoys me. No doubt the next dinner *Chez Native* will feature MLTR as background music! They sound like one of the most girlie of our "boy-bands" at their insipid worst.

Sunday, 8th January 2006

Not bad; I just made it for a disco-breakfast, but what! No disco, just a crummy film on HBO (Home Box Office – American movies).

Rolf came over and we walked down in the sunshine to Lujiazui. It is so rewarding to come from the earthier part of Pudong Avenue to the Financial District. We passed down behind the China Merchant's Tower and Marine Tower to cut across the park at Lujiazui.

From here one is afforded the best view of the Bank of China building, which looks very much like the prow of a massive ocean liner and is most impressive. We slipped down to the underground and discovered that the maps of the system were now really hard to read and not at all logical. Typical Chinese: if it works, fix it. The maps used to be a simple line, with stations written horizontally above and below the line alternately. Now it was a jumbled mess, with much smaller writing and the fare bands added in big digits.

The train was full of the usual characters, many either on phones or plugged in to some electrical gadget, but the stations were unusually patrolled by two policemen at each. The recorded station announcer appeared to have been silenced, too. Some changes are afoot, and not for the better.

Rolf and I emerged at Jing'An into the sunshine and strolled down towards the river and into Malone's (a Canadian bar on a road of bars called Tongren Lu). Mr. and Mrs. Native were already seated, so lunch was enjoyed in good company.

We walked out of the bar into a cruising taxi and headed for the arty quarter in Moganshan Lu, to the north and just short of Suzhou Creek. This is a collection of old factory buildings, given over to art studios and where once wealth was created, now art is created.

The buildings are a rabbit-warren of art studios, some quite gritty, others rather chic. Some sold tatty furniture, rescued from old Shanghai houses by giving the hapless owner a couple of RMB, now priced up to attract the hip, hop and happening crowd. "Feels like my Grandad's house", observed Native.

All the places we visited had one thing in common; they were by any stretch of the imagination, cold. I reckon that the Chinese are really tough, as they work in the cold, shop in places with open or no doors at all and many cannot afford heating, sleeping under thin quilts; so do they ever get warm?

The variety of art we were presented with for free was amazing, unlimited except by the artists' imaginations. There were sculptures made of stones and bronze, all wired together and very clever, but so pricey; and there was a massive display of Cultural Revolution exhortational posters, once common across the Red world, now selling as glossy re-prints for £100 a time! The great thing was that they all had a date and an English translation of the Chinese characters. Some were most amusing and all featured smiling peasants, factory workers and military personnel, with perfect teeth, which does not fit the reality, I am sure. One has to be amazed at the control and power of the nation.

The shops here are now filling up with Chinese New Year trimmings, having just put away the Christmas things for a festival they do not really understand! It's another way of making money, I suppose. I am hoping to persuade a friend to visit when we have our next enforced holiday away from our families, in May for Labour Day week. We missed that last year as we were redundant! I now just have to find something to do in the first week in February. Hibernating sounds good. We will do some cycling and might do some more art galleries which we missed at the weekend, as there are loads in this city and I am improving my appreciation of the arts. It might be a good time to visit the "water village" near here and one of the islands off the coast which is to be turned into a Nature Reserve.

Monday, 9th January 2006
I decided that I would do something I thought I would never do until I was very old, or even on a long-distance ride on my motorcycle in the winter, and that was to wear long johns. It is *so* cold under my desk; there is a micro-climate down there which is different to the one above. The day started with the usual Team Meeting, but in the absence of Gary, Let took over and we were in the dark, literally, as when he began to blather, the lights went out in the block. A torch was proffered (RMB10/70p down the market!) and blathering continued. There was, as expected, little substance, but it was good to see the crowd gather again; we are nearly up to full strength after the Christmas break.

The evening was to be spent alone, with Rolf wanting to go and do some training and everyone else going their own ways. In order to warm up, I briskly walked the two miles to the Coffee Beanery to enjoy a RMB25 session again. I took the opportunity to read the excellent "Shanghai Talk" publication, which featured a great response to a letter from a Westerner, asking about "clingy" Chinese girls. The writer asked why the girls he met seemed to be so highly strung, very intense and after 3 dates considered they had a "relationship" and after 3 months it was wedding bells. They also threatened suicide and other dire events, such as threats of physical violence if they were then spurned.

The reply, from a woman, was most amusing. She pointed out that the sort of girls that the writer was attracted to for quick thrills were not representative of Chinese females and basically "you pay your money……"

My taxi driver back to the Pent-Ox was unusually playing Western music in his cab. Normally passengers are treated to a monotonic monologue, a dry dialogue or a Chinese version of "The Archers" – "The Wangs", or something. The problem was that at every opportunity, particularly when stopped, he would try and tap along with the beat using his feet or hands. Try as he did, it was only by sheer fluke that he managed to match a beat of one of his digits with a drum being struck. He remained hopelessly off the mark all the time. I could not have done it trying hard. A beat-less society surrounds us.

Tuesday, 10th January 2006
It is cold here today, but not as bad as yesterday, when my legs were cold to the touch. Our office is opposite the stair well and lift shafts and because some time ago the Government suggested that it was healthy to have the doors open, the front door to this block and many others stay tied open, so the wind whistles up the stairs and straight in here. No wonder the energy bill is so high. And its not fresh air, either; this is one of the most polluted places on earth after Beijing. I reckon most locals were born in a barn, or a place where the door was tied open. So many of the shops have no doors to shut, except a roller-shutter door at the end of the day (or night). They are cold at work, and cold at home as they cannot afford the heating; either these people are tough or I've gone soft. Having said that, my sporting a short-sleeved shirt (only did the washing late last night) caused a stir today, but it is not my top that is cold – it's my legs. It was so bad yesterday that I had my fleece wrapped around my lower half against the draught.

So why do they leave windows and doors open, and then wander about with coats on? The security guards on the ground floor were shivering behind their desk, facing the tied-open door, so they now have a radiant heater by the desk to keep warm. Surely it would be better to shut the door and save on the heating bills? This would not occur to them, I am sure, to question the status quo.

Conundrum – How can a neighbouring race like the Japanese have a process called the "Five Whys", which basically just asks "Why" five times to reach the core issues and the Chinese rarely use the word? Collectively we reckon that this would mean work for them in the answer, so it is left un-asked.

An illustration of this comes from one of Gary's manufacturing mates, who reported that he took a Chinese guy on to operate a form press. All he had to do was load the sheet of steel, press the button and the press would do its bit, then his opposite number would remove the part. Walking around the facility, the manager heard a fearful row and found it had come from this particular press. The new operator had loaded it, pressed the buttons and when he saw nothing there after the pressing, had put another sheet in and fired the machine again. He did this several more times until there was so much material built up on the press that it virtually pressed itself apart. He did not think to ask "Why has nothing come out", he just carried on with the last order.

An inability to plan is our biggest gripe here; they cannot do it, be it behind the wheel or on a project. So I asked how they had come up with such a grand plan as the Century Park grand boulevard, the Science Museum and all the complementary buildings that now formed the financial district of the city. The answer is that the driving force behind the planning was French. The new, soon to be tallest structure in China, the Japanese Financial Tower, is being built with Nipponese money and the building work planned by Europeans. The tower was to have a circular opening at the top, so the Rising Sun motif would be visible for miles. Much local opposition has changed this for a rectangle!

Winston and I agreed to meet later at the Coffee Beanery for dinner, and then repair next door to the Mawdesley. It was only supposed to be an early do, with time after for some new arrivals (Rumble, Bond and the PM) to go to Carrefour and make it to bed in decent time. Not surprisingly, we ended up having one more followed by one more, etc. Most of us know and appreciate each other's company after many years working together. All of us share a frustration at the low level of engineering knowledge and experience we meet daily, plus the legendary inability to make a decision or plan ahead. We also look back on projects completed and agree that we were not as bad as the Press often made us out to be and we were better than *we* thought we were.

Wednesday, 11th January 2006
Sufficiently rested, the new arrivals looked better this morning and were ready for their pre-arranged agenda of meetings to be high-jacked and/or

shredded. Meetings agreed only two days before were cancelled and plans to conduct training were now not required (although they need all that they can get out here). It is a culture shock for the visitors and their reaction is most amusing, reminding us of the same feelings we had ourselves.

Most people think, as we did, that upon first landing at Pudong airport and being deposited at Diamond Court, in JinQiao that one has landed in downtown USA. Familiar names and signs abound, the place looks tidy and has a veneer of wealth, there is space and wide roads and American accents can be heard all around. This is not real China, as is much of Shanghai; it is a Westerner's idea of what Shanghai should look like, i.e. a reflection of our own cultures. It is only when leaving the city and seeing peasant life or walking around the old part of Shanghai that real China opens up.

We made ourselves available for escorting the new boys, but they had their night planned out for them by others, keen to show particular favourite haunts. It is always the same; every time someone new comes out, there is a queue of us volunteering to steer them to places we rate. We the "residents" are often asked if we become fed-up chaperoning all the visitors. We reply that we do not, and that it is good to see the same places through someone else's eyes and have some different company. There are only about 20 of us full-time "residents", so we spread out to accommodate the visitors.

Wednesday however, was to be just Winston and I dining together. He regaled me with some more of his recently acquired wisdom on relationships, gleaned from conversation with one of the translators. There is a curious pairing in Chinese couples quite often of an ugly bloke with a stunning girl. This is to "balance the power struggle between the sexes" to try and prevent either party, especially the man, "wandering". Another insight was that it is almost expected that the man will have at least one affair, but as long as he still loves and cares for his wife and family, it is tolerated. This is hardly surprising, as in this typically Eastern male-dominated society there are so many girls set up to render services, be they innocent "Welcome girls" in their slashed skirts at the restaurants or those out to provide some deeper pleasure.

We were told by one of the blokes who was here with MG Rover that his ayi (house-keeper) offered herself to him, which is the normal route for a wealthy Chinese man to stray. Naturally he declined, being an English gentleman. His wife would have killed him anyway and he enjoyed life, so the decision was clear.

Thursday, 12th January 2006

Rumble reported that he had been to the engine test facility and the legendary canteen there. He described the meal as "cat-sick" in his own note-book, just to remind himself of how appealing real Chinese food can be.

Today was Rolf's birthday and we had arranged to visit the always excellent Chinese restaurant at the front of Diamond Court in JinQiao. Ewe, Frau, Native, Spit, Winston and I joined him for a really excellent dinner of umpteen dishes. Not one was a disappointment, in fact we enjoyed the mandarin fish so much we ordered an extra after consuming the first. We still cannot understand the idea of the rice arriving at the end of the meal! Also, they always want to serve me beer and look around for some lady to consume my coconut juice or other soft drink. All real men drink beer, obviously.

There are two or three guards outside the restaurant entrance who marshal traffic entering the car park, which is the wide pavement at the front. They wear big coats and berets against the cold. They also have whistles; as I have observed before, any device which makes noise is popular here. They love their whistles and speak through them, with drivers being directed by an out-stretched arm and a series of blasts. You can see they love their job, so much so that a departing coach group of diners who must have been on a works outing were being herded with whistles! It was like watching sheep being penned in.

An observation of these people is that they do little to help each other. At road junctions they stand in the road so turning cars have to swerve out. They stop their bikes or scooters way over the line across the zebra crossing so that pedestrians have to dodge in and out; they block junctions when there is nowhere to go. All this does not happen if there is a Traffic Assistant or Policeman there! At work they often refuse to help each other in different departments. One example of this was an engineer just behind me. She was asked for information by another engineer upstairs, but would not answer or go upstairs. The other was expected to come to her (she is a bit of a prima-donna locally). It took Native to negotiate via an interpreter (Hooray) to suggest that there were several outcomes to the situation and the easiest was to walk up the one flight of stairs and talk. In the end it was easy and the job progressed. Having said all this, are we any different?

Friday, 13th January 2006

We had the weekly conference call last night before the meal, which raised some serious behavioural issues on the UK side towards our Chinese colleagues and I felt so moved that I wrote a "coaching" e-mail to the boss, which was particularly aimed at two individuals on the home side. There is no need to try and belittle these inexperienced engineers; they simply do not have the battle-scars that we have, nor know what to do in this complex automotive world. It is our job to teach them, not make them squirm. They may not wish to learn, or appear that way, but it is our job to coach. Interestingly, the response from the boss thanked me for my coaching and he copied it out to the others. Friday is just another day here in China, whereas in the UK, with its shorter working week (I am paid the same, wherever I am) Friday afternoon would be available to take my lovely wife out, just us two. We used to treasure that time and now I am stuck here.

We have some interesting conversations at work, with us often trying to pass on accepted wisdom or practices to our new colleagues, some of which they do not want to hear. Today's classic was about component changes; in our industry they are traditionally shown in an "issue level" text box on the side of the drawing. This data is backed up by a series of records in a system, usually by the title of "Product Change Request", or similar. Nonetheless, the drawing usually has it all in summary. The local engineer did not want to accept this. He then found one of the very few original drawings where the change was not in the issue level box, citing this as the way forward. Why make life difficult? It is so much easier to look at the issue level box for changes, rather than scour the whole drawing. In the end the UK engineer got bored and said that the Chinese guy could do what he liked. No doubt he will.

Friday is also Test Meeting day, when we review how testing has progressed the last week and how much is to be done in the week and weeks ahead. This is always one of the week's highlights, seeing what parts fail and the reaction. There is not much we have not seen before and we usually know the whys and wherefores of any failure by careful study of the components and data. We like to present data in graphical form, believing that a picture is worth a thousand words. Marvin had presented the graph at the test centre already, but they would not use it, preferring to wade through columns of figures and make deductions. Either they see figures more clearly than we, or they refuse our help.

We pulled our conclusions from the graph and presented a likely scenario. They were looking for every way to prove that a UK or European original part had failed, rather than the new, China-sourced parts. The fact that the original parts have been satisfactory for many years passes them by; they have to be suspect. It is a strange, almost arrogant way of thinking. Rightly they should be proud of their own parts, but they are untried and untested up to now; that is why we are doing the work. The best outcome of the meeting was something we have been saying for some time, but was articulated by the Chinese boss; he said we needed more data on components before testing starts, so we know what we are testing. As he has spoken, there might be some progress on this front, we can but hope. We talk of "birth certificates" for engines, so one knows exactly what has been built in to the unit. They talk of intending to do it next time.

Friday seems like time for conundrum of the day, as I have not recorded one for a while, although they do pop up regularly. This issue of coaching and how that is best done – we discover that we can say things until blue of face, but if the Chinese boss says jump, then they are all in the air jumping.

So the conundrum is a cultural clash issue; we have heard from friends in other companies how hard it is for the German mind to cope here, with their discipline around "the Process" and un-questioning following of it. In this respect, both peoples are similar. How then can neither of them queue, unless there are police around, such as at the airport? I am now becoming less tolerant of their jumping in front of me in a shop, it's tedious.

The evening's entertainment turned out to be just Winston and I again at Zoë's – always a good people-watching spot, be they shoppers trying on the latest styles or couples in the café enjoying some "Private Time". One couple camped in my view and they had not sat down before the chap had his mobile out. It was not to leave his hand the whole meal, except for reading the menu and eating his ice-cream. He was so nervous, but she was pretty, so perhaps he felt in awe; his leg did not stop shaking, bouncing up and down on his toes as people do when nervous, all the time. Fortunately, he did not smoke, but the phone was a "fiddling-stick" substitute. They both had tea, but when she was in the ladies, he scoffed a complete ice-cream and did not offer her any, as far as I could see.

She was not totally cool, as her leg was going as well in sympathy, but not I suspect, because he was good-looking! There is a real atmosphere of tension in so many of these meetings we see, yet there is a conflicting show of child-like abandon. In all the couples I have seen, there is very few signs of attentiveness and often a clearly irritated woman. We have had it from Chinese females that they regard their own men as somewhat inattentive and sometimes offensive, particularly when it comes to the smoking habit.

As it was Friday, we ventured down to our favourite haunt in the Paulaner bar. We had not been there for some time and were warmly received by staff and the band, Blue Heaven. The band were not really on form, there was a huge draught through the door because Chinese people are much worse than even Brits for leaving doors open and so it was not the best night out. However, the welcome and just one song that Joy sang ("Fire", by Chaka Khan) was so good it made the neck hairs stand.

We ended up talking to a Texan and a Brit from Bristol. The American was bemoaning the jobs export from the West to the East, but was part of it and powerless to stop it, similar to ourselves. We all had similar experiences of working with the locals, but all enjoyed the city and our lives here. Their line was semi-conductors, but the business issues are the same and the cultural divide is still being bridged with difficulty.

Saturday, 14th January 2006
At home, I can rarely sleep beyond 6.30 at the weekends. Here, I seem to be able to roll over and take no notice, unless the docks are noisy, or the clown above me is not clip-clopping in her heels around the room and running her 4.00am bath. This activity is starting to get up my nose. Slippers would be cool for a start and a shower preferable in my view, later if possible.

I finally left the apartment about 2.00pm and cycled down to the Ferry at Dongchang Lu. I squeezed the RMB1.30 from my savings and as ever enjoyed the ferry-ride, although it is always a tiresome experience being cooped up with so many smokers. The other side of the river, where once stood rows of tenement blocks of up to three stories, is now looking like a scene from tea-time in Baghdad after a really serious street fight. The houses are falling down, although there is no sign of demolition equipment, it looks as if they are crumbling away on their own. There are, however, still people living within, judging by the washing hanging outside, although this is not an infallible guide. In many ways it is a shame that these old communities are disappearing into faceless high-rise blocks as the community spirit is lost. However, looking at the state of the inside of these old places, they were a real health hazard and very small.

I ventured on to the Market, following familiar routes and enjoying the freedom having one's own transportation brings. I parked my steed in my now normal spot on the leafy Chengle Lu and walked down to the madness that is the Xiangyang market. DIY and Turk were not in Jenny's Bar on the way, so I walked on into the hubbub of the stalls area. I fell upon the team almost at once, laden with goods, the one "fresh" visitor talking excitedly as he had not been before. I had found them in a tightly packed, busy market with no prior arrangement. ·

It was mildly amusing to tag along and see the visitors in action and with Rumble as the new boy to see the place afresh through his eyes. They had already been to the "Cyber-mart" for hard-drives and other electronic gizmos.

We enjoyed the final bit of shopping (yes, dear lady reader, men can enjoy shopping. It is usually based on the principle of going with a definite purchase in mind, haggling to a good price and then retiring to the nearest bar to recover). Our various ladies and families will be pleased with the results. Little is over RMB200/£15 in the market, if one is a skilled negotiator, although many asking prices start at RMB900/£64.30.

We agreed to eat at Jenny's Bar later, and were given the usual warm welcome as we were with regulars DIY and Turk. This is a great, no hassle place where the music is good (controlled by Jenny's son who sat by the amp and deck all night – does he live there?) and the place clean, complete with Buddhist shrine. We ate and drank to our heart's content, with the matronly Jenny being so forward as to stroke our backs and shoulders whilst talking over the future of the Market. Word is that the place has only until March to live in its present form.

Sunday, 15th 2006 and Monday, 16th 2006
Some days nothing new and/or funny happens.

Chapter 8

NEW YEAR GUESTS AND A BIKE RIDE

TO THE SEASIDE

Tuesday, 17th January 2006

We have been offered a New Year Party by HR this week, which is to take place in the "New Asia Glory Hotel", where we used to endure lunch in the summer. We are to be divided into teams, shown how to make Chinese dumplings *(jiaozi)* and then judged on our labours. This will be followed by a Chinese banquet, naturally. I just hope it is not a meal of the dumplings. It sounds a bit like "It's a Knock-out", but "have a big meal" as it states on the invitation. Sounds good.

The cold test events up north show some disparities between the Chinese and Western teams; they want us all to be the same, but the Chinese managers have better treatment than their subordinates and the Brits would not stand for the Chinese conditions, remarking that the accommodation that they were given was not really up to standard, with rats running around inside. They may also have been on the menu!

There is a husband and wife team in this office, but one would not know as they appear not to speak to each other all day, although they arrive together, as he now drives. They do not share the same surname, either, which is a common occurrence here. The offspring can choose to take either parent's names; the boy normally electing to take his father's and the girl her mother. The boy is at liberty to take mother's as well. After all, it is a man's society, despite Chairman Mao's words in his Red Book about women holding up half the world.

Further insights into the Chinese relationships maze were seen tonight in the Mawdesley. As we walked in, Brummie noticed a young couple cuddled together enjoying a meal. "There's a dumping coming tonight", he remarked, "He's brought her here to an expensive restaurant to do the deed and give her the bad news". Astonished at his perception, we (not very subtly) watched proceedings unfold. Sure enough, after the meal the body language took a turn for the cold and they separated, then the tears began and he made an attempt to comfort. It was all sadly as predicted by our cultural attaché. Unsurprisingly, they became aware of our voyeuristic tendencies and hurriedly departed. Poor girl, but that is how it is done here. Better than a curt text such as "You're dumped" I suppose.

Wednesday, 18th January 2006
It rained again all day and night. The chance of catching a taxi in this weather is remote unless you leave work early and jump the queue. Winston and I did not do this as we were going swimming, which we could have done by standing in our trunks in the road. The pool is in a sports centre where we had the badminton competition. The centre showed typical Chinese organisation, as do many public buildings when it rains – a member of staff had non-job of the day here where he stood outside, dispensing plastic bags for accommodating wet umbrellas. This is a great idea in a country where there is much rain this time of year. Many restaurants feature lockable umbrella stands outside, so one is not bothered lumbering a wet shelter around. This is a place prepared for the weather, except for the fact that a little rain sends the taxis scurrying for shelter in case they dissolve.

The foyer of the centre was ideal for a wet day; the floors are mirror-finish large cream tiles, with no grip when wet, which is funny, as there is so much dampness around today.

Conundrum of the day is the odd fact that so many public buildings have a "Security Department" like this place, from whose secret door emerge staff in ill-fitting uniforms and great big coats. So why in a society which does not appear to us to be particularly unruly, with even graffiti noticeably absent, do they need so many security people? Or is it that the presence of so many men in big coats reduces the incidence of trouble?

Frau remarked upon one of those many non-jobbers which we see in the road below their 30-floor penthouse apartment. The security guard sat in the hut in the little-used road, with an expanse of waste-ground to one side and their housing compound on the other, not stopping anyone doing anything for months. Why? What for? We see many lonely guards in lonely huts looking after derelict sites, building plots and now a barely-used street. I suppose it gives employment, but the best ones are still the guys on the bridges, rapt to attention in their glass cubicles.

Earlier in the day we had some fine antics when Rumble gave a presentation on NVH (Noise, Vibration and Harshness). This was presented in response to a Chinese request. What worried me was the level of knowledge within the audience of the fact that NVH is not something one can hold in one's hand, it is an experience. All us engineers can drive or be driven in a vehicle and pick up on a wide variety of noise, some welcome (like a V8 exhaust burble) or otherwise (such as a rattle under the seat). We know about these things, we discuss them at great length and in the old days we engineered a quiet driving environment into our Rover cars and a slightly harsher, sportier note into the MGs. There was a noticeable, designed-in difference.

Most of the audience did not drive and I doubt that very few notice even the rattles on the bus. For a nation who seemingly loves noise (witness the whistle-blowers last week and the fire-crackers), this subject could be off to a tricky start.

Rumble began well and spoke clearly, if a little fast for the 40 minutes he addressed a packed room of 36 people. It was his first slice of mass teaching and we had all the elements of this culture in the session:

- People arriving late.
- People going out and coming in again.
- Leaving the door open.
- No real idea that we had actually started.
- People arriving well into the session with office chairs on castors in tow.
- Mobile phones ringing.
- A gaggle of them stood at the front due to the lack of chairs.
- People in the wrong room.
- Someone sleeping.

Some questions were posed during the presentation, but at the end there was a strangely ordered queue waiting to ask the "expert" his advice. It was refreshing to see his reaction to the event, but in the end he received a spontaneous round of applause and some of them understood a little more about a complex subject.

In the evening we had agreed to meet Pinion, one of the Chinese engineers at Super Brand Mall, to recce for a team-building event the week after. For this activity, the Company gives each employee RMB300 allowance per year, so we were checking upon how this may be spent. We were to find a restaurant and then a place of entertainment afterwards. Winston, Brummie and I waited for him, in the warm and dry of the Mall foyer. We were there early. After a while, a flustered Pinion came in with his umbrella dripping. "I've been waiting for you and looking outside" said he, clearly immensely relieved to find we had not been abducted by aliens or become lost in the city. "We prefer to stand in the warm and dry", said I. He agreed this was very sensible – what sort of people are we dealing with, here? I suppose we were not specific and did not say that we would be inside if it was raining, it just seems so obvious, but he is 24 and can work these things out.

We led him up the escalators to the restaurant floors, where we asked for the impossible – a decision. We gave him a range of options, simple ones, and then had to decide for him. We advised that it may be a good idea to try the "Old Shanghai", where we have enjoyed many a reasonable repast. We were greeted like the long-lost customers that we were by the owner and the head waiter. Some of the waitresses remembered us and giggled into their hands. There then ensued a long period stood outside the entrance, looking at the menu and discussing what, we do not know. Pinion seemed to be intent upon going into minutiae. The owner motioned him many times to enter and in the end we had to push him in and towards a table.

We ordered our usual favourite dishes with some "help" from Pinion, who we had to insist chose something. He would have sat there grinning otherwise. It was rather like having a ten-year-old boy on the table, but he was very polite and easy to please.

The meal was as usual excellent, with every dish arriving more or less together, hot and tasty. The bill came to the usual RMB80/£5.71 per head, but we would not allow Pinion to pay as that was probably the best part of a day's salary. He debated the suggested menu with the owner and he then pointed out for our benefit the pictures thereon. The price was OK and the food passed his inspection.

We have a theory here, that our local friends cannot walk in a straight line and this was proven again in the stroll from the Mall to the Paulaner. Pinion was walking beside Brummie and he was leaning on him; our man had to lean back to achieve a straight trajectory!

Thursday, 19th January 2006
Evening began with another desperate "hunt-the-taxi" game, all the while becoming more and more drenched.

It is getting really fraught hailing a taxi in this weather; we are trying to understand the bus situation, so we can at least clear the JinQiao area around work and get as far as Carrefour at least. No one in HR has thought to tell us how to work the buses.

I bought a gift for tomorrow's gig at the "Asia New Glory" restaurant – Cadbury miniatures for RMB29/£2.07, plus a New Year card (as requested) and a jolly red bag in which to put the chocolates, which saves all that tedious wrapping.

Friday, 20th January 2006
Friday is always good for the Test Meeting, where there was a whole week's course-worth of cultural studies on display by the participants. We had:

- dodging responsibilities.
- passing responsibility on to us, the consultants.
- denial of receiving information, which was passed over 10 months ago.
- waffling.
- summarising.
- older/experienced engineers being revered even though they were wrong.
- exhortation, but little practical help.
- gazing at tables of figures when a graph is superior.
- red herrings.
- a learning opportunity not taken.

Also on this day, we had the unusual experience of a team briefing – even if it was only opening a meeting by reading notes on confidentiality – it's different here as they do not respect IPR (Intellectual Property Rights) and have to be told about confidentiality. It is second nature to most of us with any industry experience.

Part way through the meeting, one of the engineers spoke Shanghainese, with the words "Air/fuel ratio" stuck in the middle and "Training Processes". It sounded really odd. Again, the meeting was full of exhortation, but little practical help.

I accept that I have seen these characteristics in the UK, but here it is every meeting, every time.

Tonight we had a New Year Festival Party, New Year's Day itself being on the 28th, organised by HR. It could have been a disaster, but proved to be the contrary. The theme was making traditional Chinese dumplings *(tang jiao or jiaozi)*, so we were organised into teams, with each ISP (International Support Person, causing some confusion with my initials!) having a "guest" Chinese colleague and the girls from HR & Admin being the coaches. My guest turned out to be better at English than he shows at work (?), but a real chef as he cooks for his family. He is a really decent engineer and therefore passed over in the promotion stakes.

We made *tang jiao* until we had run out of ingredients and then the judging began. I put a one Jiao note (one tenth of an RMB, 0.14p) under the best dish on one of the opposition's plates, which served to ensure he lost a point for attempted bribery and lots of laughs all round. I was never going to win with my attempts, anyway, they were irregular. The following banquet was up to the mark for food variety and quality. I think I have eaten every single bit of a pig. I ate something that looked like jellied eel, without so much eel in it.

We had all been instructed to buy a present and card to share, so these were numbered and by a stunning Chinese process we ended up with two different tickets, one bearing one's own number and the other different, so one knew who had given the present and who received. It worked well and thanks were expressed all round. Amusingly, the chap next to me received my present and I one from a beautiful Chinese lady on my table. It is as ever a small world. After that it was late for the Chinese, (7.30pm) so we trooped down to the waiting coach and it dropped us all off at our various apartments. It was a really good evening with plenty of varied food and great company. No-one got drunk or annoying and we cemented some more Sino-British relations.

Saturday, 21st January 2006
The ride to the ferry was uneventful and only really dangerous on Pudong Da Dao, when some deviant had pulled out in a car without looking. The ferry

was busy as usual, and I attracted the customary stares; either my good looks, foreign appearance or expensive bike attracted attention, though I suspect a combination of all three, except maybe the first.

It was good fun as ever and peppered with the average level of cycling accidents waiting to happen on the journey to the Ka-De Club for the DVD search. I was careful to lock my bike outside to a tree, as I worry about its security, especially so close to Spring Festival, when people are more prone to steal in order to make the money for the ticket home.

I managed to secure what I was after and more, as usual and left into the night.

I deliberated returning to the Pent-Ox, as it was cold and wet, but decided to cycle on to the Xiangyang Market. Somehow, I managed to lose my way in the rain; my excuse is that my glasses were covered in raindrops. I went so far out of my way, but saw a new part of Shanghai I had not visited before, so that was interesting.

One aspect of cycling around here is that when one is (as I was) faced with a whistling policeman who will not allow one to cycle up a road, and it is marked as a no-cycling road, what does one then do? British reserve and road manners fight against the instruction and Chinese custom of reverting to the pavement, (but I do feel 14 again!). The problem for me was that I was very concerned about cycling on the slippery pavement, which was barely wide enough, with people opening doors from shops and trying to squeeze by on foot or other bikes. I decided to try and find a parallel route, which in a city of grid-laid streets should be possible. However, yet again I failed to do so and crept back to the original road, the Huahai Road. At least I managed to reach the target, after only one front wheel slide on a slippery surface (Shanghai is full of these as well as many pot-holes). Remember of course our tested theory: that the Chinese cannot even walk in a straight line, so any on-coming pedestrian is a mobile chicane.

It was becoming cold and I was wet. Riding the bike keeps me warm, but I was keen to head back for a warm shower. The return journey was good fun, jousting with other road-users, out-dragging other two-wheel users. I managed again to cross the ten-lane junction under the North-South Overhead Road at Jinling Xi Lu; I just did not stop, saw all the green lights and went for it. I still have trouble, though, with the Chinese tactic of "I won't look at the danger – therefore it will not hit me". Self-preservation muscles in on the attempt to become a totally two-wheeled native and try this ploy. One sees them all the time; on bikes, in cars, with the best (or worst) being the way they join the bike lane, without looking left at all for on-coming vehicles. They just pull out, and often widely.

It was gone 8 o'clock by the time I hauled my weary frame up to the lift door and rolled my bike inside. I was wet and not too warm. I had amused a few people on the ferry as usual with my helmet, flashing rear light (I do so like to be seen) and generally looking British. I phoned around and found the boys in.......... yes, you guessed it, the Mawdesley. So I showered and made my way over, hungry and ready for a Scotch. Nelson the barman, now smokes at work, so does Dennis his boss (she looks like the cartoon character and has been seen wearing a suitable stripy jumper) and there were other customers puffing away. Still, the food was good and the measures of Scotch very generous from young Bombay, the understudy to Nelson.

Sunday, 22nd January 2006

Today was "Rolf's guided tour" to the seaside. We knew it would be a fair distance, around the 30-mile mark and were ready for a gentle ride. What we were not all ready for, especially those three of us who had not been that way before, were the sights that lay in wait. We have all been here for some time; a year next week since I originally arrived, but even I was to be amazed. That is what is great about this place; once you feel you have the measure of it, the pace picks up and it gets all crazy again. The party included Frau and Ewe as the ladies contingent and Rolf, Native, Fluff and me. All of us were mounted on Taiwanese-made "Giant" bikes.

The basic scheme was to follow the course of a canal which flows east to west through the Pudong side of the Huangpu River.

Now Rolf had spoken of this trip before, but nothing can prepare one for the reality, as I was to find all day. We left the comfort and order of the cycle lane past the posh Dulwich English School, through the wall and onto a concrete pathway. This wound its way into a shanty-town, past local meat sellers (no hygiene standard), stands selling the usual bike locks and other spares, nut and fruit vendors, stagnant pools full of litter, mangy dogs wandering around and cages of squashed up live fowl. The houses were hovels and sheds, many not far off the bulldozer's cruel blade, but it was a Community, living and breathing, albeit polluted air. Just beyond the edge of the shacks bounding the path was a development of newish flats, which were merely empty shells, perhaps built to re-house these poor sods and the developer did not pay off the right official, or was in the wrong Party or maybe ran out of RMB.

There were cries of 'laowi' (lao-wei – "Foreigners!") of course, as we passed through, but no-one really took much notice. We had to make a right turn onto another path through the community and as we were doing so, because I am observant, I noticed a local wobbling towards us on his rusty bike. He was leaning left as if to join the same route as us. Naturally, being Western, we looked out for ourselves. He, being Chinese, looked out for a call coming on his mobile phone and the floor. We had actually broken the local rules and not rung a warning bell. He just saw us before contact was imminent, wobbled even more, and slid off the concrete path, onto the mud and nearly into the village pond. I was in bits with laughter; he was ringing his bell in anger and shock. A real culture clash, just narrowly avoided.

We then wound our way onto the main road beside the canal; a smooth concrete run-way of a road, bounded on the canal side by a neatly tended hedge and/or trees, with a concrete "wood effect" fence (they love that here and do it rather well). The other bank was manicured to death and sported grass, bushes and huge greenhouses beyond, with many new factory buildings and housing developments as we rode along.

The canal was criss-crossed by several bridges, mostly resplendent in blue paint and the whole canal margin was very tidy, with smooth concrete walls much of the way. However, just to the side of the path ran a widely varying collection of houses, shacks, factory units and desolate wasteland. Barges powered by ancient (total-loss evaporating coolant) engines clattered away in banks of three or four, driving belts and pulleys down to the props, passed by slowly. They were, as is usual here, carrying mud and gravel from one hole to another. At various points on the waterway, cranes with grabber buckets dug away at the banks to create more canals, or widen the cut.

We passed some dwellings which I would consider living in; they looked from the outside to be well styled, large and comfortable, but as ever in this society, form usually comes before function and it is often just a façade one is taken by; the reality behind the front is often quite dreary or bare.

Conversely, many of the dwellings were very simple, crude structures. One or two original Shanghai timber-framed hovels remained standing, added to and leaning, but nonetheless there. Of particular note were a couple of new, concrete roofed mansions being built at the canal-side. We were amused by a single-skinned building of almost Tudor proportions (mixed with a little Disney), whereby the upper floor was cantilevered over the narrower ground floor. It was held up around the edge by bamboo props and by rights should not be standing; the walls were bare brick and the whole place was leaning. Around this most peculiar place was a vast expanse of flat, brick-strewn land, where only last summer apparently had stood a complete town of traditional shacks.

Further on, we passed the remains of a factory, whose demolished remains were being picked over by scroungers, looking for steel scrap to prise from the concrete rubble. At the edge a group of elderly people were digging in a hole, for what we did not know, but there were pipes in the mud.

Another surprise and delight was the sight amongst this flat wasteland of a purveyor selling toilet pans and cisterns. Were they second-hand? We did not venture sufficiently close to assess the conditions of the U-bends. There was a range of colours and styles, should anyone be interested. In order to maintain privacy, the "owner" of all this sanitary ware was also selling doors, presumably rescued from the demolition area. It was the first of two places selling this particular piece of furniture. (Photo p.XXI).

There was so much to see on the ride that I could fall asleep at the keyboard typing the details. One amusing point was that our group leader had done a recce of the route and discovered that it was now not possible to continuously follow the canal-side route, due to the demolition area having spread and the concrete path now ended in a bog effectively, so a detour was planned. This took one through an interesting local community, different in character to the previous ones, but still, shall we say, colourful?

We had two main roads to cross on the route, which demanded a certain amount of care, as the first one featured a "central reservation" only as wide as the barrier fence which kept the opposing lanes apart. Therefore, when one rushed across the first lane through a gap in the traffic, both of one's bike's wheels were in both lanes – very tricky – a case of pulling it parallel to the lanes and risking clouting fellow pedestrians. We were tooted at by passing vehicles and stared at by the locals, but we all made it safely. I get really cheesed off being hooted at, although the drivers have to assume that all road users follow Chinese rules and do not look for themselves.

There are always amusing things to see and one bridge had a severe height restriction, with a loading bar ahead of the structure to warn high vehicles. The only issue was that the bar was higher than the bridge – very Chinese!

At one point we came upon a bridge over one of the waterways which joined with a raised road on an embankment, bounded on both sides by trees like poplars. It looked very French, with all the bicycles. There were some very old, traditional Chinese style houses on the banks of the waterway between it and the road, which looked very spartan and not at all immune from flooding.

On the other side of the road, having just passed through another community of shanties, there was a "new" development of pink and cream-tiled block-houses which looked most uninviting and were mostly unfinished and unoccupied, as well as having a moat of stagnant water around them as they were set very low. Another development which ran out of time, but the "best" one was yet to come.

Eventually the canal-side path ended in a sort of park area, with the houses behind us. If we were not mistaken, ahead of the sluice gates which formed the end of the "cut", there was an area where people could swim in the muddy brown water. Indeed, someone was hand-washing clothes at the edge on some steps with a handrail that looked remarkably like swimming pool access.

We stopped for lunch here, having celebrated reaching the coast itself by running down to the water's edge. I dipped a toe in the water (well, the sole of my trainer) so I could claim I had paddled. The sea view was really impressive, with a vista across the Yangtze River estuary to Chongming Island. The sea-lanes were busy with vessels of all sizes sailing back and forth, and the sun shone on the righteous cyclists.

In true British style we had a picnic in the sun, sat on the grass and slapped ourselves on the back for a job well done. Had we known what was in store, we may well have decided to run for home then, rather than follow the guide's invitation for a "3 mile" ride to the sea resort. This turned out to be six miles, making a return total of twelve, rather than six! It was, however, worth it. We followed the concrete road along more embankments and looked down upon pig-sties with the people living next door in the same mud, in rude chalet-like buildings of traditional Chinese design set in

179

terraced rows and one place on its own which was best described as a shack. Estate-agent speak could have bulled the place up no end; riverside bijou residence, with access to beach, surrounded by fields, boat-launching facilities and thatched roof. The reality was somewhat different. The residence was a set of lean-to shacks, the river was undoubtedly polluted, the roof was a mix of straw and plastic sheet and a sewer pipe crossed the property. The boat had a hole in it and the launching facility was a slide in the mud. (Photo p.XXII).

The next treat was a crossroads; this was a meeting of the bizarre. Behind us lay the mix of places I have already described. To the right was a road passing a factory unit and on the actual junction was a small shack labelled "Western food – Mama's Pizza". It was shut and uninviting. Ahead and right was another part-finished development of very elegant houses, with verandas and columns, plenty of room inside and fancy plaster frieze-work. There were tall wrought-iron gates at the entrance to the property and these were surmounted by two "lions rampant" in heraldic terms. The gates were rusty and forlorn-looking and were closed over an access road to the properties, some of which had glass in the windows, gazing emptily across the fields.

Opposite this derelict might-have-been was a newer pair of somewhat smaller gates, but these opened to reveal the usual guard's hut and a green sward of manicured golfing heaven beyond. The fairways were busy; caddies in their bright waistcoats slaved to carry heavy bags for the rich players. There was a large lake to add interest and the whole area was surrounded by a high fence. Beyond the fairways rose copies of large Western houses looking like the set from the film, "Stepford Wives". There was little movement otherwise; perhaps these were weekend homes. The juxtaposition of all these sights at one crossroad was startling. The rich and the very poor in one area, side by side as ever they are.

The road curved around a bend in the river and opened out to a bridge over one of the main rivers through the Pudong land mass. The bridge was also a sluice-gate control tower and beside the river bank was moored a huge floating restaurant. Children played in the dirt and dust and loose dogs and cats managed to avoid the cooking pot for a while. It was a real Chinese pastoral scene, with a small fish market in progress and a few shanties selling all manner of necessities. A small child swung from his parent's arms having a pee through the usual slit in his pants that most children seem to be dressed in. Nappies are not for the masses, obviously. The "toilet" was just outside their own front door.

Another turn once over the bridge took us alongside the sea side of the river. Several derelict sampans lay in the mud and a man was at work smashing concrete to extract the steel re-enforcing bars again. A young couple, thankful for the warm weather and sunshine heightening their passions, snuggled and nuzzled each other awkwardly. They seemed quite oblivious to six Europeans passing by commenting on young Chinese love. Looking to our right, we were able to see where all the scrap polystyrene we see plied up on bikes and trikes disappears to – here. It was collected in a massive hollow in the garden of a house and wrapped in a sort of voile mesh, until it was the size of a bath-tub. The ends were tied off and hey – presto! One had a fishing float. (Photo p.XXII).

At the next corner the road swung right, parallel to the coast and opened out to reveal a harbour or safe haven where a fleet of boats was moored up. A group of women trooped by who had been shopping, one of whom had a couple of packages swinging from a yoke about her shoulders. They climbed up the top sea wall and over, heading down to the lower wall, where a boat was waiting to pick them up. They were rowed out to one of the fishing boats by an old gal stood in the stern. All the boats seemed to have a wind generator spinning above the cabin. A party appeared to be taking place in the stern of one of the boats; perhaps the girls had been sent for more beer.

The "Resort" was in sight now, featuring many sights which one would see at a British equivalent and some unfinished hotel buildings, which managed at a distance to have that seaside look to them and appear bright and fresh. Later examination revealed one to be plastered in eye-straining mosaic of the most garish colours. This would have looked OK on a portico or small area, but to cover a whole façade and a giant fish statue as well was too much.

There were fancy caravans, but covered by aspirational, Western-style activity posters. Small chalets sat at the water's edge, with rows of lesser cabins along the promenade. A lagoon was formed by natural features and was sprouting lifeguard posts or seats on poles with shades over the top. A guard's cabin sat just off the prom, with a huge dog chained up. It looked very much as if the guard slept in his hut, as there was a bed and many personal features therein. It is amazing how many people's lives are determined by very close boundaries.

Inland from the prom in the near distance was a huge, part-finished development, which looked like a modern Chinese interpretation of the Coliseum. It did look like a part-completed sports stadium, but was nothing more than a framework. Again, it looked abandoned.

To the side of the promenade was one of those swinging "Pirate boat" rides, which oscillate back and forth, driven by a rotating wheel below. We stopped to examine the unusual model figures on the ship, one of which was very female-looking, with a much exaggerated right bosom. What was all that for? As we were looking and conjecturing, the owner came out from nowhere and remonstrated with us to have a go on her exciting ride. She was frightening, as was her ride, so we ran away. A short way further on we rolled down a slope to the "beach" of concrete "tank-trap" shaped spikes and watched the locals at play.

There was little else further on down the promenade, so we retraced our steps and our leader took us down off the prom and into a messy car park area, which was bounded by typical seaside resort rides; there were sad-looking donkeys, karts on a straight track and a few fairground style kids' rides. Sadly, it looked very familiar to me, as the fair at the sea front in my home town of Southport, Lancashire looked not too dissimilar for many years until the council re-developed the area. We did not frequent any of the tantalising amusements as we valued our health. We circled up and along the main road which ends abruptly, as many roads do at the sea and passed the part-built hotels along the front.

We returned via the same route as we had come and it was a case of nursing our legs and buttocks to make it to the end, as for several of us, these parts were beginning to complain quietly, but severely. It was with huge relief that we saw the familiar shape of the Ramada hotel becoming sharper and nearer, signifying an end to the torture. The ride had been a real eye-opener, even for those of us who have lived here for a while. We crawled into the welcoming warmth and comfort of the Biyun Lu Coffee Beanery, where the saddles are shaped like comfy chairs and also you don't have to pedal. I had a few miles to ride after to reach the Pent-Ox, but I was very pleased with my total of around 42.

Monday, 23rd January 2006

More details are now emerging of the plight of our engineers on the CET (Cold Environment Testing). To say it was grim is an understatement. We agreed to meet them in the "Blarney Stone", one of the Irish pubs in town, known for its shandies, shanties and quiet behaviour, or not! Guinness was downed and some of their excellent sausages and mash followed it. Over dinner we heard more "stories from the cold north".

The twelve hour "hard sleeper" rail journey was very cold, with frozen toilets, and urine frozen on the floor. Our boys were huddled together on the train for warmth, fully clothed with thick boots on.

The most common description of the place was "like the Wild West, very primitive". Food hygiene standards were not good; they survived on chocolate and crisps, as so little of the food was edible, the local diet being composed of the "waste" products of animals, such as pigs' ears, tails etc. As a result, everybody (including the Chinese) was ill, and two were almost hospitalised. Our stomachs have become used to Shanghai food, but not that.

One practice that contributed to the food problems was the leaving of food defrosting on window-sills, with birds landing on it to feed and doing what they do after; photographs were taken. The hotel maid was seen wiping the toilet bowl with a cloth, then with the same rag, wiping sinks, cupboard tops and then glass tumblers. What do they think of when they are working? Do they know about basic hygiene? Washing clothes in cold water was also hard to comprehend, but was the norm up there.

On the work front a comparison of tool kits was made, with the Chinese sporting a Halford's Imperial/metric socket set, a hammer and pliers, compared to our man's full Mechanical and Electrical kit in separate cases. The difference between us could not be more graphic. The fitters here are again compared to a famous marionette show, being described by the ISP who is trying to teach them as real "Muppet" fitters. Whilst in Shanghai, another of their inabilities was shown by them kerbing several cars and when told to move a car, driving the vehicle into the workshop wall where the smokers normally stand. The driver failed to say to his boss that he could not drive and he was therefore unlicensed as well as incompetent. He just did as he was told.

Their lack of tools caused them to steal wires from our man's lead-light to use for themselves. They managed to break his "guaranteed for life" screwdriver and one socket through brute force and ignorance. His insistence that the correct way to remove a gearbox from a car was quicker than their proposed route ended up with him being ignored and the whole engine, box and sub-frame hanging from the power steering pipes – a weight of about 300kg on two small rubber pipes. Will they learn? We hope so. Working conditions in the workshop were also grim, the temperature being a feeble 3°C and the whole floor and walls being covered by frozen spit. In the town, they burn a sort of brown coal, which gives rise to a thick smog and the inherent effect on the respiratory system. Spitting in the hotel was commonplace, due to the smog conditions.

Other Western companies are trying to raise standards with the civil authorities in the area but it seems like a long slog.

Another interesting activity was driving on a frozen lake, and hearing the ice cracking; although it was many feet thick, this was still disturbing.

Interesting, but only because it was dangerous was the bunch of spaghetti-like wires, just piled up on the back seat of the car, which were not terminated properly and sparked, causing a small fire. This is how not to prepare a car for test.

The guys also complained of the fact that there were government offices next door and partying was carrying on in the hotel, with girls from these parties knocking on the other guests' doors and calling them on the phone. Not a way to ensure the testers wake up refreshed!

Tuesday, 24th January 2006
More taxi ride amusements include a driver who was driving in a steamed-up VW taxi and one of our team leaning over and setting the controls. The windows cleared almost instantly and asked our man "Do you work for VW?"

Someone else described their journey as a "Need for speed 2" ride!

"One-wipe jockeys" also worry me in the rain. Do they believe that their wipers will wear so much that it is worth sacrificing safety by not having the things on permanently? Other wipers just desperately need replacing.

Having been faced with the usual practice of people leaving doors open and freezing one's nuts off, it was suggested by one of the Brits that self-closing doors at the engine test centre might be useful to keep the place warmer. No thanks, was the response; they would make too much noise slamming! Considering the place is a noisy test facility, this was just ridiculous; they just did not want to do it.

Wednesday, 25th January 2006
On TV tonight I saw the presenters on "V", a music magazine programme, interviewing a boy-band. When the one began singing, both presenters were clicking their fingers, but they were out of time with each other and the singer – amazing. Later on in the programme were some soldiers being entertained by musicians; the soldiers were even out of time to the music. How do they march in time, then?

An interesting article on polluting cars appeared in the "Shanghai Daily". Have they woken up now? Watch out, world.

Thursday, 26th January 2006
Thursday comes around again and end of the day entertainment is always guaranteed at the conference call with the UK. Rolf came in for a guest spot and rambled on at length without seemingly coming up for air over a fairly involved subject. Once he had finished his spiel, you could hear nothing on the speaker from the West. Were they all asleep? Had Rolf done "a Poggo" on them and caused mass sleeping? Had they lost the will to breathe? Would they wake up in time before we had to leave? Why am I asking you?

The evening was spent in our apartments (recovering in some cases), from the excesses of the "Team-building Events" the night before, but not my team. The event, for which we had done the recce the week before, was held in the "Old Shanghai" restaurant in Super Brand Mall. Just ensuring that the Chinese engineers made it there safely was apparently a trial, with the UK chaps herding the team down the road outside the office and losing some of them within 50 metres. One group of four were bundled into a taxi by one of our boys and then asked Loch "So where are we going?" Conversely, the Manufacturing mob all had a matrix of who was going with who and where.

Apparently they were all well-lubricated at each event by 7.00pm, with the Chinese really getting into the swing of New Year by ganbei-ing each other to submission. Boxes of beer were stationed by the tables as the waitresses could not keep up bringing single bottles to the table. Even Rolf at the Manufacturing event was over-faced with food and drink; it seems as I have observed before, that a measure of a man is taken by his ability to sink alcohol. However, bonds were strengthened and good times were had. Perhaps it is rare for the engineers to let their hair down as they were reported to be acting like excited children in the Old Shanghai. Following the meal there of "simple food" as Pinion described it, his team went as planned to the Paulaner for, as he explained, "complicated music". A curfew of 11.00pm was set by the departmental head and the drinking continued, though a little slower, but augmented by Chinese dancing to the complex tunes of Blue Heaven, the resident band.

Back in my apartment, I was just returning to bed about 10.30, had my mouth full of toothpaste and the phone rang. It was Reception wanting to know if the various maintenance jobs I had asked to be done were completed to my satisfaction! 10.30pm is an interesting time to check! Perhaps they believe that we retire as late as they retire early, but then the Reception staff are on duty all night, we see them sleeping when we come in late.

Friday, 27th January 2006
Friday's Test Meeting was another cultural master-class. We were delighted to see one of the senior managers spring up at the end of the session to draw an action plan (in English too) on the dry-wipe board. Naturally the Chinese pen did not work, but a runner was sent and the pearls could be recorded. This time, noticeable by their absence were Waldorf and Statler, the two old guys from our office who actively dislike our presence and whisper about us to each other. We were therefore not treated to any of their words of wisdom, commonly known as a "Waldorf Salad".

(Those of you old enough to remember the "Muppets" will recall these two characters, Waldorf and Statler, as the old guys who booed and jeered from a box at the side of the stage in the Muppet Show).

Saturday, 28th January 2006
Although Saturday was a working day, in order to gain a holiday day in the following week, we had left work early at 11.00, after an e-mail instruction from HR that the place would be closing and all the provided works transport would leave at 11.10. So that was it. I was to leave with my colleague, Diva, as I did not know where she lived; so on we went via the works bus. I was the only Brit in six vehicles and attracted stares from other companies' coaches too!

As soon as I arrived, the daughter, Chen Lian Lian (Chen is her father's family name, the second two words together mean beautiful and bright; not far short of the mark there) was waiting in the doorway, slippers facing towards the apartment landing. A clean, modern, bright room beckoned.

Chen Lian Lian and I went out for a stroll in the sunny afternoon to grab some lunch – at KFC! She paid, not allowing me to open my wallet. And so it went on with the hospitality. She was keen to practise her English, which was very good.

Father came home just before we went out and was as gentle a soul as one could ever meet, very gentlemanly towards his wife (not a normal Chinese trait) and obviously the love of his daughter's life so far.

I wish my family could have been part of the night; it was so very gentle, polite and welcoming. Nothing was too much trouble or pressed on me. They are a lovely, balanced family and the daughter is going to make them proud; she was quite mature for a Chinese girl, streets ahead of the other two girls who turned up to look at the weird foreigner. One girl was the daughter of another colleague who sits in front of me sometimes, when he is not asleep or at his other job with Shanghai GM. He is one of the "respected elders".

The afternoon was spent wandering around the apartment complex, chatting about China and the UK, and then we all sat watching "Garfield"! We chatted and then it was time for mother and father (who do not share the same family name in China) to disappear into the kitchen for the meal preparation. What came out was fine fare – jellyfish (usually have a piece to remind me I don't like it), cucumber in soy sauce, cold meats including sheep's stomach, pork ribs, fried pork, and bean sprouts with other animal gizzards. Naturally the rice came out later, after some superb steamed fish and fried shelled prawns. It was a real feast. I was given some Cabernet Sauvignon wine.

After the meal we sat down to watch the biggest live performance in the world, or the one watched by the most people, on CCTV, the end of year gala fling, which features acts from across this vast and varied nation. We talked about politics, the Royal Family, Chairman Mao, all sorts and I had a cultural and geographical tour of China through a book.

Meantime, it was a true battle-zone outside; there were times we could not hear ourselves speak! There was some heavy ordnance at work, each bang vying to outdo the previous explosion. Windows rattled, fireworks became lodged on verandas, spinning and flashing their colours into the night sky. Others on the ground barked and spat their intention to ward off the evil spirits for the New Year. Then there would be a lull and we could discuss Charles and Diana again, or look at more photos of this amazing country. There was never a time that I was left out of the conversation for more than a minute or so. This was hospitality in a foreign land of the highest order.

When it came time for us to set off our arsenal, we descended into the road between the apartment blocks, not more than two and a half cars wide, with many vehicles parked there, large bombs themselves, just waiting for a stray spark to catch a leaking fuel or brake pipe. The Chinese were again to demonstrate graphically to me their complete lack of any danger awareness. Fire-crackers rent the night, mortars lobbed explosive star-shells into the alley-ways of the estate and I was scared, really scared. They set off their fireworks never less than two metres short of the cars and let rip. Spent red cardboard wrappings of gunpowder rained down like autumn leaves dropping all at once; the road was carpeted in red. During this fire-fight, cars amazingly moved up and down between the flaming torches of spent boxes, Roman candles and crackers, whilst taxis dropped off their fares!

My leg was shaking: I was scared of the possibilities, not the fireworks themselves. Images of exploding cars from a hundred films leapt in and out of my mind as I gazed around and skywards for the next star-shell burst. Debris caked my glasses as more devices were ignited by smoking, unprotected men and kids. Just how many injuries would ensue this night, and if there were one in this small road, how would the emergency services make their way through the cacophony? How would one stop the crazed residents from their lust for more noise and fire, sufficient to allow the paramedics through? I sound really paranoid, but that is just my imagination. Chinese market cars must have under floor anti- terrorist shields.

A taxi was called for me soon after 12.30am and there was no extra charge (unlike the UK) for the ride back across the river, so he earned himself a big tip. I had enjoyed one of the best New Years ever. Thanks, Diva.

Sunday, 29th January 2006
Naturally one had a lie in after the excesses of the night before; I mean I must have drunk at least one plastic cup of wine! It was not until the afternoon that

the others and I got together for dinner. It was great just to sit there, take time over a meal and relax with friends.

Monday, 30th January 2006

I cycled about the five miles to Shimao, met up with Frau and Native and we then cycled to a ferry south of here and crossed the river. Tied up by the ferry terminal were the rusting hulks of two boats. One was a regular river ferry, a big one; the other was festooned with huge musical notes and two huge steel fabricated guitars at either side. It was covered in scaffolding and so not obvious if it was under construction or the opposite.

At the other bank we cycled way into the city to Fuxin Park and had our picnic in the sun watching the Chinese relax; also being watched ourselves. It was great fun and very warm. Inside the park are the usual Chinese ingredients: (almost litter-free as there is an army of cleaners), people playing cards, Chinese chess, mah-jong and kids blowing bubbles with soap. There was a group of children colouring in small "windows" with a sort of rubber solution. They were quiet, diligent and well-behaved. No-one threw any, spilled any or squirted at each other – so well mannered, or disciplined?

We cycled on through familiar and unfamiliar streets, dodging taxis, cars, other cyclists, scooters and trolley-buses, with me blowing kisses at amazed, delighted Chinese girls aboard! They just love to see us out and fooling around – almost any face, wave or friendly gesture makes them smile.

We ended up at yet another DVD shop and scored again – I picked up a copy of the entire set of the Monty Python TV shows.

We cycled through some of the old town still left standing, but marked for demolition and saw some amazing sights. Really we needed to be walking; there was so much of disappearing Shanghai to take in. (Photo p.XVI).

Tuesday, 31st January 2006

Today I managed to eat in the Pent-Ox café, and then looked out at the grey day before me. It was not too wet, but it was cold; maybe the appalling weather forecast for the week was coming true. We hope not – a week here in grey smog is not what the doctor ordered. I took off on my trusty bike for the ferry we used yesterday. I managed to retrace the route except for one wrong turn; I ended up going down a cul-de-sac, but at the end was a gap in the fence and a new stretch of tarmac beyond. Naturally there was a "security" hut by the gap. I could hear someone moving around inside the window-less box and his bike was outside.

The gap opened up onto a very new road, complete with signs and street lights, on the outer edge of a new development of high-risers. I rode on, hoping that the route would open up at the other end and I could reach the ferry terminal that I could see beyond the next fence. I was wrong, but before I had to re-trace my steps, there against the side wall closest to the river was a group of several tents and lean-to hovels sheltering the displaced of Shanghai. There was one man sweeping up the pavement outside his lean-to made of waste building products and the ubiquitous woven plastic tartan sheeting. He hardly noticed the rich boy on the fancy bike; I was an irrelevance to his lifestyle, too far apart. I refrained from the urge to capture this pitiful sight on camera and turned myself around.

On the other side of the river I again retraced the route of the previous day, wanting to capture some of the disappearing slums on camera before it is too late. I managed to find the rusty, broken trike I remembered, stuck in the framework of a ruined hovel. I hope the picture does justice to the scene and the feeling of inevitable community destruction around its silent frame. I managed to photograph a few more old fancy porticos and friezes, some bearing the dates of their creation, the mid-1920s. Passers-by stared as I took my shots in the cold wind – what did they think of some nosey foreigner poking around their neighbourhood? (Photo p.XVII).

I cycled on through to the distinct edge of this particular part of town, which, when Native's guide book was written only a few years ago, was only a two-storey part of the city. And now the high-risers crowd in on the beleaguered Old City, crushing the life out of the communities which have existed for eighty years or so. Yes, the old houses are small, cramped and perhaps unsanitary to our Western eyes, but people and communities live there. I do not know what the answer is, but it sure is not 30-storey monstrosities in concrete and glass.

I joined a Chinese guy on a bike who wanted to race, so I tried really hard and just about gave him the slip down Chengle Lu, before I turned off. Some of these locals on their single-speed bikes, riding with the instep can really get a move on; it's embarrassing as I sit astride my 18-speed expensive machine. They always enjoy the race anyway, whooping with delight as I mock-whip my mount as if on horseback, which seems to transcend the language barrier.

The evening's entertainment was to be dinner with Native, Frau, Winston and Brummie at the "Old Shanghai" again, followed by a session at the Paulaner. We are always so welcome there (as much is consumed) and we were joined by the boyfriend of one of the band, who is himself Danish and a real laugh, as well as the sax-player's girlfriend, who is from Leipzig. It was a real International gathering. We had a great time and had many of our favourites played. The power failed mid-Tina Turner, which can be painful and it was fun to watch the technician fumbling around for the fault as the band took a break.

One inebriated local was desperate to climb the stage and sing his piece, finally making it, much to the consternation of the girls. He was finally removed by the staff, who are very gentle when it comes to trouble, not at all like your average UK bouncer, plunging in and forcibly removing the offender. Thankfully he left later, so he could be ill outside.

Chapter 9

CYCLING TO WORK, THE FASCHING

AND A LOST WALLET

Wednesday, 1st February 2006

Today I had to secure railway tickets for our planned journey to Suzhou. The room phone rang at 11.00am, with news from Reception that there was a simple way to acquire rail tickets – the local office is just across the road! The helpful girl wrote out our requirements; destination, seat type, times and party size and then wrote the Chinese for "Ticket Office" on a sheet of paper for me and gave me directions, with a rider to ask any local if I became lost on the short journey.

On Yuanshen Lu, I was stupidly trying to match the characters on the top of the sheet with something written above the door of the most likely looking building, when sense got the better of me and I asked the only person on the deserted street (as it is Spring Festival week, many people have gone back home). He pointed at the building I was looking at! Inside was a stark, government office-type of room with a series of hatches with times overhead, so I walked over to the 11.00 to 12.00 one. I felt like a "Kilroy" cartoon, as I had to stoop slightly to be able to see in through the hatch and catch sight of the person inside, who appeared thoroughly bored and on top of that had a dumb foreigner to deal with. You could almost hear the "Oh rats, Ping, I've got a dumb foreigner here with a piece of paper", as she talked to her mates.

It was with some relief and a small sense of achievement that I walked out of the office, RMB200/£14 lighter but with four return "soft seat" tickets to our chosen destination, the so-called "Venice of China", Suzhou.

We had decided upon an arty day and to meet up for lunch at K5, or Kathleen 5, on top of the Art Gallery, the old racecourse building. If I had thought, I would have dressed a little more up-market, as it is quite a stylish place to dine. Amazingly, all of us opted for a taste of Europe and a lamb shank, with Frau reminding us that much of this country's lamb comes from New Zealand, where of course sheep had been introduced from our own shores many years ago. And so the world goes around. The others were well pleased with the tickets and the story of their acquisition.

K5 sits in a glass conservatory, with a view across People's Square and the stunning buildings which surround it. We dined well, with a touch of Crème Brulée afterwards and then it was time for a diet of art. The displays of architecture and Chinese modern art were still the same ones I had seen before. The Italian display was worth seeing again and there was time to see the exhibition of cartoons depicting Chinese village life from the 1950s and 60s. To call these detailed, life-like sketches cartoons seemed to undervalue them as pieces of art in their own right; such was the level of facial expression of the heroine in the tale and the people around her, the village buildings and simple farming scenes.

While we were messing about with rocks making Stonehenge, these people were making silks and fine ceramics. When we were making silks and fine ceramics, the Chinese were still at it too. While we were making UPVC double-glazing and central heating, the Chinese were keeping cold with the door open thinking it was healthy.

Having dined on lamb shanks and art, we strolled along the Nanjing Road, which by this time was stepping into its night-time clothes of neon and tungsten illumination. We were approached by the usual sex-hawkers, people wanting us to dine in their restaurant, hairdressers on the prowl for heads to pretend to cut, kids selling illuminated wheels to put under your shoes and others wanting to practise their English. We were encouraged by Rolf to visit the "No. 1 Department Store", which features the only circular escalator I have ever ridden; so childishly we rode up, across and then down, following the steps lower into the basement and off towards the pedestrian underpass below Xizang Zhong Lu, which borders the eastern edge of People's Square.

There is a complete city under the Square, with a massive variety of shops and eateries. Rolf decided it was hot custards time, so he went and bought a six-pack of the tasty sweet cakes for us all to enjoy. We attracted the usual amused and bewildered stares from some locals, with hot, sticky yellow mess dribbling down our faces, well Rolf's, to be accurate. He enjoys his food, and so can anyone within dribbling or spitting distance!

We rambled on along the pedestrianised way, although of the three "Pedestrians Only" Chinese roads I have walked, all have stupid, annoying, tourist buses or trains running along. They all, being Chinese, have to be noisy and feature either a standard honking horn, or chime in a jolly, ice-cream van fashion. It is so unnecessary and it spoils the whole point of a vehicle-free route.

It was time for a drink, so I led us up to U.B.C. Coffee, above the entrance to Middle Henan Road Station and after a wait of about half an hour for our order to be brought to us (very unusual for Shanghai, or even China, for that matter) we enjoyed a reviving cup of Chinese tea. There is such a bewildering choice and even teas of the same name can vary in presentation from place to place. It is a very traditional Chinese pastime to drink tea and discuss the matters of the day, "taking root" as Sharon would say in a tea-shop, but many of the traditional tea-houses are dying out apparently. It is good to see some new ones opening here, although like this one we were in, the label is "Coffee".

We were able to sit and view the hairdressers on the same level and watch as with great expensive, expansive and exaggerated flourishes the stylists removed millimetres from their pampered clients. It was another, most amusing session of voyeuristic enjoyment, looking at Chinese life about us. Or are we just nosey?

We left the comfortable confines of U.B.C. and walked further along the road to Henan Lu, turning right and off towards the Yu Gardens. The lanterns were up and Frau had not seen them before. We would also have some dinner there after a good mooch about.

The YuYuan or Yu Gardens is a tourist magnet and a little false, but day or night is a fine sight. The architecture, the shops, the traders yelling for sales, the colour and people having a good-natured time is always a comfortable place to be. No-one is annoying, too noisy, "grungy", or detracts from the atmosphere as I can imagine they would at home. Yes, there is the spitting and smoking, but people are so well-behaved and just there to have fun. China shows itself off well here. (Photos p.XIX–p.XXI).

The decorations for the forthcoming 15th day of the Spring Festival, or New Year, and the Lantern Festival, were up and as stunning as last year. The only detractors are the constant reminders of the sponsors, Coke or Kodak – a slice of the good old U.S. in the Orient. I do not know if it bothers the locals, busy looking up at the riddles printed on the shades of the Chinese lanterns. Some of these were revolving round as well and people were scribbling down the messages and riddles to solve. A huge amount of work had gone into the decoration and when we emerged at the tea-house in the centre on the lake, even more was to be seen and marvelled at. There were trees with animals sat in them, plenty of images of dogs for the New Year, but none of the out-going rooster. They must be a forward-looking lot.

We walked across the crooked bridge which zigzagged across the water, so to ward off the evil spirits. The spirits were having a hard time of it recently, being bombed out of their non-existence by fire-crackers and other explosive devices, intended just for that purpose and coupled with a walk across the bridge, I felt quite safe from them! (See cover photo).

We bluffed our way up to the YuYuan Stage, with no intention of buying any tea or tea-making equipment that is sold up there; we just wanted to savour the view from the third floor balcony across the Gardens and over to Pudong. The lights and sounds were impressive from here. The girl who drove the lift and hoped to sell us something realised that there was nothing to be made out of the tight rich foreigners and shivered her way into the slightly less cold lobby. Chinese people seem to spend so much time being cold here, with doors always open and like this poor soul, stood outside their premises soliciting for business – in the nicest possible way, of course.

Back down in the melée of people, we could look back upwards at where we had just been and see the huge moving, talking image of Fu Manchu. He was flanked by a couple of others speaking some seasonal Chinese from cleverly-made rubbery faces, with winking eyes to add to the "realism" of the sight. Last year it was just a solitary Fu with a pre-recorded message of "I'm gonna get you", or whatever he says.

A visit to "78" beckoned, as we enjoy the choice in the restaurant there and it was open. After we arrived it seemed that most of the locals left, but it was nearing their bedtime. Unusually we had to pay with the order, but when the food came it was up to the usual high standard we expect. More tea was presented; I had Rose tea this time and thoroughly enjoyed it. We were obviously the subject of much amused banter from the locals before their departure.

We continued our tour with the walk on through the busy streets to the ferry and as ever admired the riverside lights. Once across we walked along the front of all the new developments and as the brand-new "City Shop" was open under the massive City Group tower, we dived in. The temperature soared, not good for a supermarket, but the choice was impressive. It was much better organised and stocked than "Pines" in JinQiao with which we are familiar. Some of the prices were reasonable, but many were hopelessly over the top. Many goods were labelled one price and once at the till emerged much higher.

We then split, with me taking my now normal number 85 bus and the others the underground.

Working and operating together is a big thing in China – people worked in communes, and the good of the Nation was a big driver of change and economic growth. The communities we move through in the poorer areas do obviously know and rely upon each other; they have to as they are so physically close.

So here is a new "Conundrum of the day", about the sense of Community. (We haven't had one for a while. Either we understand more, are asking less questions or not seeing things clearly any more).

I get to observe bus drivers closely now, as I had a ride in the "suicide position" – stood in front of the packed bus behind the massive windscreen. So then why do drivers cut each other up completely unnecessarily in such a way? They must all be mates on the same company, or are they? Or do they (as we suspect), get paid by the number of passengers?

What a night! I retired to bed having called home and then the fireworks started. This was more heavy ordnance; there were some seriously big mortars out there. I could not sleep and rose again to call home once more so that they could feel the power 6,000 miles away. I felt as if I was in a war-zone again. From my balcony I could see explosions across the river; countless sites where sparks were flying. Local to me were some big, big bangs, deep thuds followed by the echoes and then the lighter ones. How could so many people let off so many fireworks? Where did all the money come from?

Back in bed, I counted four echoes from the big mortars as the sound bounced and reverberated off the high-rise blocks in the area. My windows flexed with the energy being dissipated. I was impressed, until I also noticed that the cement yard was adding to the noise. I felt sure that finally the fireworks would subside, which they did, but the yard would be at it all night, as there were ships to unload. I was not to be disappointed and the wretched noise woke me at about 3.30am again. I could always pray for rain; that usually stops work.

Thursday, 2nd February 2006
I made an early start, with a good breakfast downstairs. It was a relief to be up, as the night had been so disturbed. The rain held off until it came time to seek out the number 85 and set off for the main railway station, which I made in about thirty minutes.

There was the usual scrum outside the station, with bodies and bags everywhere. It is not possible to pass into the building itself without a ticket and there are security checks to prevent non-holders from entering. There are also scanning X-ray machines for bags. I took in the size of the massive square in front of the station and wondered how my wife and I had managed not to pop up into it when there were four subway exits emptying into the place!

I met the others, who were also early, but the crowds had been there for some time and the waiting hall was full. It is easy to use Chinese trains at such main stations; the train number is on the ticket, as is carriage and seat number. Look for the train number on the big boards at Shanghai, read off the waiting room number and stroll along. Inside the waiting room are rows of steel seats, (perforated, so the spittle can run through) and join the throng. There was a massive screen showing Premiership football from the UK and speakers blaring out the sound, as if it were not already noisy enough at a station. The screen was made up of nine panels, three of which were in some way faulty. This was similar to the plethora of screens we saw at Chongqing airport showing UK soccer. Why the fascination? There is perfectly decent football here.

There is an illuminated sign showing train number and departure time and over the tannoy it was announced that it was time to board. The masses jumped into action and some ran like hell for the boarding gate. This is because the hard seats are not reserved and so it is first come, first seated. We joined the throng converging on the ticket checking at the barrier gate as we had reservations. It always amazes quite what some people carry on to a train here, much of it in cheap boxes or plastic woven tartan bags and heaved onto shoulders.

Many people will stand for hours and hours on these trains and stories abound of trains so full that people are stood in the toilets too, or their bags are stacked up within. This issue of not being able to visit the W.C. has spawned a burgeoning market for adult nappies (sales are up 50% this year). It is a simple solution to a specific problem. It seems some enterprising people have found a market niche. Making money out of the discomfort, or relief of others, which is an old story.

The train left on time, and was warm and clean. The carriage attendant was polite and marched up and down the double-decker accommodation with her kettle of hot water and selling cups with foliage in the bottom for green tea drinkers. Those who came prepared with a pot noodle type of meal could also be served. She was followed by hawkers selling other snacks and tourist guides for the various stops that the "Nanjing Express" would make. It was all very civilised.

The journey passed through the grittier parts of the city, as trains often do, and soon the cityscape changed for fields, canals, stagnant ponds, rubbish tips, greenhouses and endless new roads and buildings awaiting the newly affluent drivers and owners. New factories stood empty, awaiting new wealth creation industry. Oh, to see that sort of thing back in the UK, but it is not going to happen. The local papers back home are still full of the Chinese plans by Nanjing Motors to restart production at Longbridge, but in my opinion it remains a pipedream. The estimates for car volumes and people employed falls with each new report.

We alighted at Suzhou, and immediately the hassle started. "You want taxi? All day RMB150/£10". Then the price started to tumble as I was not interested. It ended up with an offer to hire bicycles! We had several of these people and one woman walked quite a way with us, once outside the station, offering her taxi.

As I had been before, the others followed me left out of the station to then turn right at the first roundabout. We stopped to watch some fireworks which were going off at the side of the road and then started to cross the bridge over the Grand Canal. This was an engineering feat of canal building to rival the Great Wall, but much of it is now not navigable. It was cut to move precious silks from Suzhou to the Imperial Palaces in Beijing and other places north and south of the city. It is a waterway to rival the Thames at Westminster in width and certainly length. It is now really only used by pleasure craft, but the view afforded from the bridge of the towering gateway allowing access into the city from the Grand Canal was impressive. The city is criss-crossed with waterways from barely two boats wide to the main arteries, which can be two hundred metres across. (Photo p.XXVIII).

Suzhou feels so much more spacious than Shanghai, as it lacks the sky-scrapers of its southern neighbour. The presence of so much water, the many formal gardens and the pagodas gives this place a different feel altogether. Our first stop was to be the Silk Museum, which was a real treat, albeit a freezing cold one the last time I was here with my wife.

The Museum is a Mecca for silk-lovers the world over and is a cheap, but fascinating insight into the production of this amazing thread from purely natural resources. Naturally, like many other industries, such as mining or even humble needle-making back home in the Redditch area, it has its share of horror stories. In the case of silk, the cocoons give up their threads when plunged into boiling water. The thread ends then peel off and float and can be picked out and twisted with others to then form a yarn. Young girls were employed to do this and suffered disfigurement to their hands in the boiling water. We were given a demonstration by a lady who refused to be photographed whilst working. The equipment was simple, just a pot bubbling over a flame, a couple of bobbins and a treadle system to wind the yarn.

Within the same room were complex looms which I had seen working before; I still do not know what all the many strings and rods do. Better minds than mine built these looms, yet my family background was the cotton mills of Lancashire. My grandmothers and great-aunts worked in the mills and the "Pogson Shuttle" was a renowned piece of weaving kit; not as it is today, a pseudonym for giving the kids a lift all over town.

Meanwhile, back in Suzhou, the rain fell as we wandered in and out of the museum grounds, admiring the ancient silk gowns and other clothes on display. Hours of work went into the production of finery for the rich to sport by people who were paid a pittance; so no progress on that front then.

Plastic mulberry leaves and plastic silkworms were scattered about to show the various stages in the development of the raw material, with several varieties of worm and subsequent moth giving rise to differing silks. The colouring and treating of silk to give it sheen was also shown. The skills of silk production go back many years and were a closely guarded secret, with the penalty of death by torture being meted out to any transgressor unlucky enough to be caught.

Although they were not working this time, Sharon and I had seen the ladies making quilts from silk on our visit last year. This is achieved by soaking the cocoons, skewering the wet case over a spike and sliding it down over a cone. This spreads the cocoon out and more water is added. The slit, now a sort of circular mat of silk is further teased out (where the worm goes I do not know) and pulled by hand until it makes a piece of flat matted threads about the size of a pillow case. These are then spread out over a table and formed into a duvet-sized sheet with the addition of more "panels" of stretched cocoons. Once a decent layer is built up, the duvet can be covered in a bag and quilted. Various thicknesses are created from 1.5 to 2.5kg for a double quilt and prices range up to £45, which is not bad for a handmade natural product. There is little waste and maybe the worms are fried in the works canteen!

Once quilted, we walked across the street, dodging more fire-crackers just laid in the cycle-lanes and plonked on the railings, barely missing passing scooters and cyclists, to see the Northern Pagoda. This was very impressive the last time, but was closed for refurbishment – indeed it had looked quite tatty a year ago. The result was looking very promising, but not worth a visit this time, so we wandered on towards the "Garden of the Humble Administrator". Humble he may have been, but not the garden bearing his name. This is a World Heritage Site; one could tell as the road outside was a dirt track, building materials were strewn everywhere and that familiar "it will be great when it is finished" feel came over us. We were joined in our stroll there by "Ding Ding", a passing local, whose hobby was cycling around the streets, looking for Johnny Foreigner to talk to. We suppose that as many traditional Chinese houses or apartments are so small, that the pursuit of pastimes and hobbies cannot involve much space. So his hobby was outside.

Ding Ding accompanied us for much of the way, asking about the various pronunciations of English, in which he was quite fluent. We went through Australian, American and Oxford. He knew quite a lot about our country and the language, without ever having stepped outside the confines of China. When we asked him what he wanted to do when he finally left education (he looked in his late twenties) he replied that it depended upon what the bosses decided for him. He appeared to feel as though he had little control over his own destiny, a common thread here.

The "Garden of the Humble Administrator" was eventually reached via the dirt track, pounded hard by the passage of many bikes, scooters and visitors' feet. Entry was RMB30/£2 and it still rained, but there was no extra charge. The garden was not at its best, but was still impressive. Someone, no matter how humble, had some real vision. Despite the weather, we roamed around the vast treasure of pavilions, rocks, pools and bonsai trees; it was all the usual classical Chinese garden art. In spring it must be quite something to behold, but in the grey February afternoon, there was little colour on the trees and plants.

It was hard to tear ourselves away from the cold wet garden, especially as there was a cold, wet walk ahead to find the next bit of inspiration. It was time to eat, so we decided to stroll through the city in search of a restaurant mentioned in Native's guide book. Naturally we could not find the address or the place itself, so we plumbed for the most likely looking place to eat. This was to be a real find, starting with the tea-boy who wielded one of those long-spouted copper kettles, from which he spurted hot water at one's tea-cup. The spout is almost a metre long and very narrow, giving a satisfying jet clean across the table from a pace away! We enjoyed a good meal, although the complete duck floating in broth, its head lolled to one side, put the fairer one in the party off her meal somewhat.

We left under a cloud, as it was still raining, so it was time to hunt for a decent loo, with a certain fast-food chain featuring a red-headed clown looking the most likely. The rest of the street thought the same, so the queue was long, but this possibly pointed out the customer's need for clean toilets, not that they were when she got there!

Next door to the golden arches was the biggest temple in the city, with a most impressive roof structure, featuring a double span. The entry fee was a steep RMB20/£1.40, so one cannot worship there if one is poor, thus cutting out a massive chunk of the population. Apart from the smoke, the noise around the temple was akin to that from a fairground, with various stalls vying for business. All this commercialism next to a place of worship always surprises me. A plethora of praying accessories, good luck charms and deity models were available, just to ensure one's passage to the next life.

The place was wreathed in smoke from the spent joss-sticks in the hopper, adding to the murky atmosphere. They were also burning massive candles, up to about 150mm in diameter and red, of course.

The temple itself was similar to many we have seen here, but was just bigger than most in terms of the central building. Inside was the usual deities; pick whichever one you feel like praying to appears to be the scheme. I must find out more about this religion.

Friday, 3rd February 2006

Today's was a simple shopping job, so I went on a DVD hunt at the Ka-De and the shop opposite the Xiangyang market. The prices appear to have risen slightly in view of the approaching clamp-down. On TV the other night was a film of pirate Chinese DVDs being shredded on the pavement in Beijing, as a warning to all. In the Ka-De was one of those loud Annoying Americans who in common with much of his countrymen was "stressed out". It was quiet and peaceful like a library before he came in.

As usual I enjoyed the cycle ride in itself. Do I get "smoked out" less often or does there seem to be less smoky vehicles about. I wonder if the Shanghai government war on smoke is working?

Further DVD and CD hunting was done at the local Da Dao DVD/CD shop – for my patronage I was awarded a plastic "Loyalty Card"!

Another interesting snippet is the rise in the popularity of cosmetic surgery here, but that brings with it claims for compensation when the results are none too good. There were 20,000 complaints last year! Just as a guide in case you need a quick nose-job, they run at US$2,500 here.

So the "compensation culture" is creeping in even here. I heard of a group of residents who lived on the second floor of some block of flats who had been burgled and were claiming off their neighbours below. Those on the ground floor had installed anti-burglary steel cages which are quite popular over here as "extensions" to meagre room sizes and serve as places to hang washing, meat, mops and general junk. So those lower down were protected but argued that the miscreants had used the cages to climb up to the second floor!

Saturday, 4th February 2006

Today was nominated a cultural day, and with Native, Uncle Dick, Rolf and I decided to meet in the Shanghai Museum for lunch. At RMB20/£1.43 for curried pork, in smokeless surroundings, this is one of the more pleasant places to eat.

Lunch over, it was time to cough up a massive RMB20/£1.43 for the museum entrance. We selected our first exhibition as the Bronze castings. These are so fine, dating from way back in the 19th Century – BC! They would be impressive had they been made after the birth of Christ, but nineteen centuries *before!* This took some believing. We reckoned that we should not have the casting problems we are currently seeing in the Chinese made parts at work, if this was the standard all those years ago.

Ceramics from all over country of such fine detail were in the next hall, again showing skills of staggering dexterity and quality. No wonder people pay such money for fine Chinese porcelain. It has been fine art for centuries, with clear regional styles and colours.

We strolled up to the display of minorities costumes next, which is a blaze of colour and again demonstrates some extraordinary craft skills from across this vast country. The show of ceremonial masks impressed me no less for a second viewing, as Sharon and I had been here last year. People still wear some of the traditional costumes in some of the far-flung corners of the Chinese Republic as day-to-day wear. Here in Shanghai you could be forgiven for thinking (in summer especially) that local costume is pyjamas. Even in winter jim-jams are worn, although they are quilted against the cold and a body-warmer is considered optional.

We also popped into the furniture display and there were many interesting pieces, especially the lounging beds for the whole family, which often had some form of crude heating device below to warm the cockles. There were cabinets inlaid with the finest mother-of-pearl, small stools so carved that there was barely any wood left and throne chairs for important officials.

Most impressive was the imported show from America of one chap's collection of minerals, including diamonds. I did expect some level of high security here, but it was the same as all the other halls, just a dusty old guard in an ill-fitting uniform keeping an expert eye open for notorious cat-burglars and Pink Panthers to show up. What was slightly annoying was the Chinese habit of standing in front when one was looking at a cabinet. I know it is just their way, but once you have seen twenty black heads squeeze in front of you, it can be quite tiresome.

The diamonds were continually surrounded by pushing, shoving small people and even peering over their heads it was hard to see more than a couple of sparkling stones in the lights.

On the way out, we shopped for inspiration for the artist, Rolf, and he bought a few postcards of Chinese views to turn into paintings, which he does rather well.

We then walked along the Huahai Lu to Shanxi Lu and turned left off there to Xinhe Lu DVD shop, which is nearly as good as the local place on Pudong Da Dao.

There are many small shops on Shanxi Lu, and I diverted into one to look for Converse boots for my daughter. They had a certificate in the shop – could this be an official outlet? I very much doubt it! According to the manufacturer's website, there is only one in China and it is not this place.

Tonight I enjoyed a long talk with family via Internet Telephony; what would we do without new technology? I did not fancy going out much, so I was a couch potato.

Sunday, 5th February 2006
Today, we were obliged to go to work, as we had to cover one of the days we had taken over the Spring Festival week. Not everybody is back yet; some have travelled thousands of miles to be with family for the festival. A real problem is using the toilet on the train. The corridors are so full with people that movement is apparently virtually impossible. Hence the aforementioned sale of adult nappies............ Oh, no, please.

There was no Hooray, as he was one of those who had travelled on the bulging trains, although the distance involved to reach his village in the next province of Shanxi was only 1,500km; but the slow trains are very slow and he then has two connections to make at the other end.

People stepped straight into the working groove; there was little apparent gossiping about the holiday, unless they saved this up for the lunch-time walk.

Shanghai has realised its environmental problems with vehicle exhausts and the headlines to a recent article in the local paper reckon that one third of all the city's vehicles will be taken off the road if the authorities have their way. The emissions standard they are aiming at to begin with is the Euro 1 level, which we left behind when catalysts first (and I believe erroneously) became standard fit in Europe. We would have all been better off following "lean-burn" technology.

The plan is for mobile testing, as it is recognised that regular inspection is "not as mature in China as some foreign countries". Chinese law sets a yearly inspection, but many of the taxis and buses I have used could not have passed a test without the exchanging of a certain amount of readies.

According to CCTV, there are 40% of vehicles on the road which exhaust twice the EU1 limit being used as the start point for legislation and 2% which are ten times the EU1 levels.

Monday, 6th February 2006

Today feels like a Tuesday, but no such luck. The usual Team Meeting was held, and information was given out by Gary; but one key piece was not there, seemingly held by another but retained. Why? Gary always does try to impart as much as is possible, but others try to hold him back.

Amazingly, we are still on about the same things but at last there seems to be some progress on tax – we have an agent! Ring out the bells! There is also a change of plan on the Health care provider – this is just like Rover days when one could not keep up with whoever was the provider. Just like the Rover days, we have no input either.

Tuesday, 7th February 2006

Here is a quick interesting story about how these people work. A tall Brit we know (who speaks fluent Chinese) is standing in a bank queue. He is ushered to the front by Security because he is big and Western, so he starts conducting his personal business. A local leans over to find out why he has been moved up the queue and asks how much does this foreigner earn, so the bank employee ruffles through his papers and tells her!

I had a good meal and chat with Rolf and the boys at the Mawdesley, where we were treated to watching a "Team Pep-talk", given by Nelson and directed at the "Terracotta waitresses"; although they have now ditched their brown uniforms in favour of black trousers and white blouses. They are so easy to amuse, so whilst Nelson was being serious, we were not, as we were sat behind his back, facing the girls. We would love to know just what he said to them.

There is still a pecking order to where they stand around the room, with the youngest being volunteered to stand outside in the cold and welcome guests or solicit for business.

Later, I decided it was time to shop, so I went in search of a silk quilt. Carrefour was very quiet after the masses bulk-buying before the Spring Festival and so it was a much less fraught experience being in the shop. The vacuum-packed quilts at the airport were RMB720/£51.40 for a standard double, at Suzhou in the Silk Museum they were RMB600/£42.85 and I secured a king-size for RMB399/£28.50. Sounds like the kind of retail investigation my lovely wife would be proud of; I just hope that the Carrefour quilt is a quality job. We will not know until we are snuggled up underneath.

Wednesday, 8th February 2006
Bad news for Biggles – I discovered that I had no wallet when time came to pay at the East-West. Maybe I had lost it outside, but a check revealed no sign. So I borrowed RMB100/£7.14, raced back to work to check, but it was not there. As cloning cards is a problem, I cancelled my UK credit card and wondered how I might sort out the Chinese ones.

We resisted these cards at first, but like many things here, the Company decides and that is it. One of our objections at the time was how to read statements, general communication and sort out problems. So here was a problem. I decided to wait; having discovered that when I returned to the Pent-Ox, someone had reported the wallet found and would return it the next day. I hoped they would.

Thursday, 9th February 2006 (Warning to parents – rude word in this account)
I popped into the Admin office and was informed by a cheerful colleague that losing my bank cards would be no problem. Stunned, I pondered this further, but it seems that although they are my cards and I applied for them, the account can be accessed by my employer!

Today's conference call was as amusing as ever, and naturally rambled on over the hour, into our own time, when all I wanted to do was return to the Pent-Ox and check on my wallet. One cracking quote from Brummie referred to his visiting a transmissions test facility out west of here. "You weren't very impressed?" was the questioning statement. "No", he responded.

"It was three hours flight there, three hours back, three hours delay and three seconds to find they are shit!" This was a frank and considered assessment from our Solihull representative.

This evening Rolf and I had decided upon a gym session at his place, followed by dinner at the Coffee Beanery. We changed in his place, turned on the heating for our return and sprinted to the next building and into the cold, dark gym. I must have overdone it as my back was very painful later on. Moral of the story – don't leap into an exercise regime until you are ready and start slowly.

Assertion – this is a window-dressed society, all front and tatty round the back where impressions are all important.

Evidence – at the group meal the Chinese select the most expensive dishes to impress, even when they really have no special taste or nutritional value at all. We have often been faced with dishes like shark's fin soup, which is a real let-down; give me a bowl of Baxter's Scotch Broth or Campbell's Tomato anytime. The one time I had snake you could have fed me much better with a far cheaper bowl of prawns or chicken. Snake tastes like spicy chicken, anyway.

It was great to have my wallet returned to me, sadly short of the cash, about RMB500/£35.70, but the low-life thief had left the cards, including the travel card, which had some money on it. Being re-united with one's wallet is so good, even when it is somewhat lighter.

Friday, 10th February 2006
As usual, Friday was Test Meeting day, the time when we find out just how good a job we are doing out here, and how good Chinese parts are, or not. It is also a good cultural exhibition, and the more so because of the presence of Waldorf and Statler, as in the Muppet Show. These two older engineers are truly revered by the younger guys, but after one or the other have made a hugely powerful-sounding point, veins bulging on their necks and faces, always loud and impassioned, we ask for a translation. A short statement usually preceded by "I'm not sure what he said, but…….." is then given to us. We are convinced that part of what they say is vitriol aimed at our engine or ourselves and how we should not be there, but when the technical contribution is translated, it is usually irrelevant or wide of the mark. So much for revered engineers.

After reporting the loss of my wallet yesterday and being met with a smile, today I walked into the Admin office with the returned cards and asked how to cancel them. I should not have expected it to be simple; this is after all, China. I had cancelled my UK card so easily by phone. The process was to take the cards to the nearest Bank of China branch and with my passport as ID, hand them in. I also had to fill in application forms for new cards, no automatic replacements as back home, oh no. That would be too easy and not enough paperwork would be involved.

I left work early to be able to make it to the bank and decided to try the bus which stops outside the office and runs down Pudong Da Dao, the 573. I had only walked a short way down the road and one turned up. I was ushered to the back as this was conductor-operated. I finally made my intentions and destination plain, coughed up the RMB3/20p for the 8-mile trip and was invited to sit next to a local on the very narrow seats. He was very chatty and friendly and we passed a very pleasant time, looking out over a sun-drenched Shanghai. The route was familiar and I was dropped a short distance from the Pent-Ox.

The bus was a fairly new one in Shanghai terms, but had the noisiest rear differential (the bit that sends drive from the gearbox to each wheel) I have ever heard. I would be very surprised if it had any oil in whatsoever. The noise was particularly offensive as in my dim and distant past I had supervised a team of people machining and testing the principle components of a differential and we were fanatical about creating a quiet gear pair. That was Land Rover in Birmingham, not China. It was so loud I had to have my ear right by my new friend's mouth to hear clearly – not the sort of closeness I relish with a strange man.

I reckoned the nearest Bank of China was by the Pearl Tower. I positively flew my bike down the road and triumphantly turned up at the counter. Bassey from Admin had helpfully written an explanatory note for me to hand in and instruction to take my passport. It is a shame that in my hurry this vital piece of information did not register sufficiently for me to take action. The girl in the bank looked at me as if I was stupid, which was correct. I asked what time they closed, decided I had enough time to thrash back to the Pent-Ox and return, which I did, slipping under the shutters as they closed above me. I was locked in a bank with a bevy of pretty women. Life's hard sometimes. They all found me, my sweaty face and lack of Chinese language, hugely amusing.

To me, this trike represented the dying Old City, forgotten and left behind by progress. (Photographer, I. Pogson).

Some Westerner with a feel for the old neighbourhoods had painted this in red on some of the boarded-up buildings. (Photographer, I. Pogson).

The classic architecture of the YuYuan and its surroundings has thankfully evaded the bulldozer......so far. (Photographer, H. Routledge).

Essential wear for Shanghai-pyjamas. Here also is a Traffic Assistant (seated right) and men playing mah-jong. (Photographer, I. Pogson).

The YuYuan always provides a surprise – this time an all-female orchestra playing instruments made from porcelain. (Photographer, I. Pogson).

A Chinese Tea Ceremony above the Yu Gardens shows the hand made tea-balls blooming into this magical shape, called "Romeo". (Photographer, I. Pogson).

*As close as you can get to a Chinese Father Christmas; this massive head "spoke"
greetings from a moving mouth! (Photographer, I. Pogson).*

*Lanterns aplenty at the Festival in the YuYuan, fourteen days after the Spring
Festival. Each has a riddle inside. (Photographer, M. Billington).*

In order to make a wish, a coin with red and gold streamers attached is thrown into the (man-made) Money Tree to gain prosperity. (Photographer, M. Billington).

On our cycle to the seaside, these toilet pans were for sale on some waste land. You could also buy recycled doors too, for privacy! (Photographer, M. Allen).

So this was where all the waste polystyrene went – to make floats for the fishing fleet. (Photographer, I. Pogson).

You can imagine how an estate agent would describe this bijou riverside residence with private slipway and sea views. (Photographer, I. Pogson).

Recycling, the Reliant way. These two three-wheeler trucks had just been stopped by police in Baoding city and are typical of the rag-and-bone type of collectors you see everywhere. We have lost this level of work in the UK as we become more affluent. (Photographer H. Routledge).

Sarah at Luna. She loved this place and the music. I was so proud of her and the way she adapted to the rush of city life. (Photographer, I. Pogson).

Recycling with friends. This pair were trundling along Biyun Lu in the posh area. Police often discourage these people from using the roads in this part of Shanghai as they make the place look untidy and may offend Westerners. What a way to build resentment; they don't bother us. (Photographer H. Routledge).

Ashley on the Great Wall at Simatai. Very soon you leave the crowds behind at these altitudes. The Wall goes on forever. (Photographer, I. Pogson).

Sharon and I visited the more "Tourist-friendly" re-built Wall at Badaling in February 2005. (Photographer, S. Pogson).

This chap was working with a harness – it just wasn't fastened to anything. Note he is pulling the air-con cover towards himself and oblivion! He is 6 floors up. (Photographer, H. Routledge).

Lujiazui Park is a favourite place for wedding photos. It was cold, so she had boots and plenty of layers on! (Photographer, I. Pogson).

Sharon took a shine to this young chap entertaining the passers-by on the busy Nanjing Lu shopping street. (Photographer, S. Pogson).

A novel way of airing your clothes whilst working on-site. Hang them over a sewer inspection hole! (Photographer, H. Routledge).

推动循环经济，防治环境污染
争创生态园区，建设和谐社会

Push the circulation economy,
Prevent and cure pollution of the environment,
Contend for creating the ecosystem park area,
Construction harmonious society

The streets of JinQiao are littered with these exhortational signs - why do they not check the grammar first? (Photographer, I. Pogson).

The Stock Exchange building was visible from my apartment, but from inside the architecture is amazing. (Photographer, I. Pogson).

Suzhou - the Venice of China - is criss-crossed with canals and are a great way to move around the city. (Photographer, I. Pogson).

On our first trip to ZhouZhuang the water-taxis were again a great way to see the sights. (Photographer, I. Pogson).

Cousin Catherine strolling through a quaint ZhouZhuang (Watertown No. 1) setting. (Photographer, I. Pogson).

On the "mid-level" shops in Hong Kong, Sharon, Jessica and Ashley.
West meets East. (Photographer, I. Pogson).

From our hotel (the Bishop Lei), the view of Hong Kong was stunning by day and
overpowering by night. (Photographer, I. Pogson).

Eternity locks are bought in the temples; you have yours and your lover's name inscribed and lock them to the temple for everlasting love. (Photographer, M. Allen).

Chinese modern architecture and half-empty stands at the motorcycle version of Formula 1. There was no-one there at the previous day's practise.
(Photographer, I. Pogson).

And now to sleep, perchance to sell an abacus! A suitable way to end a photographic tale of China. (Photographer, M. Allen).

In late 2006, the demolition crew had almost flattened Longbridge North Works. I ran a facility in here for some time. (Photographer, H. Routledge).

There was a flourish of forms and swiping of redundant plastic while my as yet unused cards were consigned to spending history.

The yard had been busy last night, so I used the telescope on loan from Gary to do some snooping around and see what was going on amid the piles of cement and lime bags. It was not really necessary, as the stupidity of it was obvious with the naked eye. The yard is laid out as a grid system, with alleys at right angles to each other, around the tarpaulin-covered piles of bags.

The driver of the tug with two empty trucks behind drove across the yard, past the alley down which his colleagues were working, down the next alley towards me, then right across the bottom of the yard and up the working leg. He then did a "U" turn. The problem with this was that the bottom alley, closest to the Pent-Ox, is the one with all the service duct covers which rattle and is the part with the worst pot-holes. Why drive further than necessary, to then shake, rattle and roll, causing an immense amount of noise over the broken surface? This had gone on all night. Surely the driver did not enjoy the noise and bumpy ride? He wasted time and energy. Would it occur to him to change, or is he instructed to always use that route, so he will not change? (Photo p.III).

Saturday, 11th February 2006
It was a beautiful day for a bike ride again, so off I shot to Puxi to meet up with Frau and Native so I could use Frau's experience in the purchase of hair-pieces to take home and use on our Murder Mystery evenings. Sharon wanted a couple which were whackily different from her normal luxuriant brown tresses, so the order was a black "Cher" number and a funky pink/blond bob. The market area where these are sold is a maze of stalls on four floors, with all sorts of bric-a-brac available, with some good finds hidden away in the corners.

Some of the stalls offer stomach-churning dried lizards and other delights for supposed medicinal use. A form of sea-worm is dried and bound together to form weird star shapes, for some unknown purpose. An apothecary is a good old-fashioned word to describe the riot of dried colours and shapes for sale to cure every ailment.

We then trooped off in search of dressing up gear for the forthcoming "Fasching" party at the Paulaner Brauhaus in Xintiandi, where we are required to appear as pirates for the evening. Frau will create eye-patches and make us up, so we needed parrots for shoulder adornment and anything else we could muster. Black and white head scarves were decided by Ubergrüppenführer Frau to be necessary as well, so these were sourced from the market too. The parrots were actually soft toy roosters from last year's New Year animal and so we haggled down to RMB10/70p each.

A drink was in order following all this retail nonsense and we adjourned to the local Starbucks. From its comfortable confines we could watch as the crowds milled around as a snake of grey heads wound its way through the sea of black – another bunch of touring Westerners. A Chinese guy impressed the tourists by unclogging his nostrils, created a sticky mess on his fingers, was unable to shake the glutinous mess off, so scraped it on a nearby polished brass railing. Later on some locals were seen to be sat on said brass railing. The moral of the story is – anywhere is fair game to deposit – Beware! Tissues are available widely as well, but just imagine the paper consumption if everyone in China used them, so the guy was helping the environment, in his own way.

We split up and I returned by the ferry. On the way I was determined to take some photographs of the neighbourhood in the throes of being demolished by a crane and wrecking ball. Some children were playing on the pile of rubble by the dormant crane, as it was parked up for the Spring Festival week. I shouted to gain their attention and they responded by brandishing steel rods and pipes recovered from the wreckage of their neighbours' homes. Chinese kids love to be on film and will pose readily. I took a shot of some boarding up against the shattered remains of a house with the English words "The last Goodbye" sprayed thereon. A trio of Irish visitors stood by as I took my shots and engaged me in conversation, lamenting the demise of old Shanghai, wondering along with me where these poor people were to end up, as surely they could not afford the new apartments going up all round. They were also searching for the YuYuan, which was only five minutes walk away and they had a map. I offered to show them, but they were tired and on the way back to the comfort of the Shangri-La hotel. We met up later on the ferry and debated the non-existence of flocks of seagulls. We could only count six or seven of these normally ubiquitous birds. Still, six or seven is better than none. It is more than I saw last year. (Photos p.XV–p.XVII).

I met up with Brummie in Super Brand Mall and we dined at Zoë's, watching the goings on around us, which mostly centred on the amusing fashion sense of the Chinese. It is mostly the girls who amuse, they seem to get dressed in the dark of their rooms, picking up whatever is lying on the floor at the time. The result is often a clash of colours, even to my masculine eyes.

We later had a session at "O'Malley's", the Irish bar to watch the Six Nations Rugby for Ireland versus France. The place was full of French supporters in fine voice who drowned out the smaller Irish contingent, especially as for the first half it was a French walk-over. Something was given to the boys from the Emerald Isle in the changing rooms at half-time, for they came back with a real vengeance. Perhaps given another ten minutes they would have won. It was interesting to see how little the French supporters drank (nothing in some cases) and how much the Irish sank.

Sunday, 12th February 2006
Sunday was another sunny day, so another excuse to cycle and shop. I had "orders" for North Face jackets, so I sped out on the normal route into the city. As usual, I was quicker than most and am becoming quite adept at cycling the Chinese way around red lights and keeping going. Being with them at this level gives ample chance to observe the way they act on the road.

Assertion No. 1
Though one should not generalise, the Chinese have no sense of impending personal danger.

Evidence – Observe any local lighting fireworks, especially in the close vicinity of cars. Observe the lack of gloves, goggles and children unprotected. Observe them returning to lit fireworks which are slow to start, with glowing cigarettes.

On the road, they will cycle or ride straight on at junctions, without turning their heads to the side at all. The world only exists just in front of the leading wheel.

Watch them turn right out of a driveway onto the main road without a look left. On-coming traffic must sound their horn or stand on the brakes. No matter how many times I see this, I still find this the hardest one to accept.

Watch them step out in front of a speeding approaching mad Westerner on his bike, without a glance left. This even occurs when they push a wheelchair out into the road.

Watch them jump off a bus at the stop, straight into the cycle lane, when it is the on-coming cyclist's job to make a noise (ideal Chinese pastime!).

See the photographs of the air-con maintenance man at work. (Photo p.XXV).

Seat belts are not worn, despite official requests.

Children are stood in or on the front seats of cars; their little delicate heads close to the windscreens.

Children are often stood on the running boards of scooters; their necks in line with the top of the steering head, with no helmet.

Increasing numbers of them drive and make mobile phone calls, which makes them as dumb as UK drivers, but not as skilled or aware.

Assertion No.2

They cannot walk, ride or drive in a straight line.

Evidence – Walk along the pavement with a local and they will lean on you as they attempt to wander. Leaning back generates an equal and opposite force, with the result being closeness with one's Chinese friends, and a straight path.

Jump into any taxi, bus or ride down any cycle lane. They cannot look behind or to the side without then wobbling or steering that way.

Today started with a smile when I unwrapped my Valentine present and card from Sharon. There were some suitably amusing boxer shorts and a pair of pyjama trousers with "Superman" logos all over. The card was homemade, naturally, and the envelope was sprinkled inside with punched shiny hearts. I laughed to myself and enjoyed the feeling of thinking about her even though she is 6,000 miles away. 30 years on and we are apart, but closer than ever.

Today was really busy at work; the guys are busy writing project briefs for suppliers and asked me to check them. I am sure that few of them have ever done this sort of thing before or even know anything about the components for which they are responsible. At least they asked for my help. I will now attempt to give it, in the best possible way to ensure that they listen and learn, but not so I put them off asking again.

Wednesday, 15th February 2006

Tonight was dinner at Frau and Native's with Winston and Gasket. It is really so much more homely in their apartment, with a woman's touch compared to our cold, bare rooms. Dinner was excellent, a good chilli job and we whiled away the hours in pleasant conversation, taking the Mickey out of everyone and everything. It is interesting how we have all adapted to life here, but all still share the surprise at daily events which are so different to back home and can still maintain a sense of humour about it.

Today's conundrum (haven't had one for a while) – why in a country with a known and worsening power shortage problem do you see so many electric radiant heaters keeping lobby areas warm, yet with the doors open to the outside? The security guards at work tie the front doors open, so the whole building feels an icy blast coming up the stair-well, and they have such a heater behind their desk. On the way back tonight, I saw a group of security guards in the gatehouse of an estate, all sat in the doorway of the place, with a huge reciprocating radiant heater pointing to the outside! Why?

These people love to be cold, as most any door is left open and I am quite fed up with shutting the window in the Gents. The icy blast heads straight for the ever-open doors to our office. One day, I was stood doing my thing, thinking that I should have shut the window before starting, when a gust blew my tie against the side of the urinal and it also became difficult to maintain my aim, the wind was so strong! It is safe to say that the tie was in the wash as soon as I arrived back to the Pent-Ox. Why must the window be open? Ajar is fine, so that is how I leave it. At the other end of this corridor, some clown leaves the emergency exit wide open too, probably a smoker, as the smoking room is at the other end by the toilets. This latter room has a wide open window, which just lowers the temperature even more and blows smoke back into the building.

The other thing is their aversion to washing in warm water. Every time I go to wash my hands, the tap is turned to the cold side. I slide it over to warm and ensure they are clean. It also warms my hands up in the icy blast from the window. No doubt in summer this will be reversed!

Thursday, 16th February 2006

Words cannot begin to express the many experiences we have here, just being driven around. I have noted before that every junction is a game of chicken, with a "who dares, wins" attitude to road safety by all users. Often, a cyclist trying to ride straight across a junction will be "leaned upon" by a right-turning bus passing through on red, as one can here. They will run parallel for a while, and then the bus will win.

Today's minibus driver this time was no exception. Nosing onto the road, he caused an on-coming vehicle to slow rapidly. He decided to loop his seat belt across his lap for show in case any police were about, so he obviously knows he is not going to crash, and therefore I should have been assured. However, he displayed the same cavalier attitude to his driving that everyone here does, with erratic lane changes, accelerating hard when there is nowhere to go, dabbing the brakes as if he is preparing to brake for the hairpin bend at Mallory Park Race Circuit and jumping lanes just to gain one car length, only to lose it later. Just before our final destination, he overtook a pootling minibus and then jumped on the brakes straight after. It is hard to relax in any vehicle here.

Once arrived at the foundry, which was our destination, we were met by an engineer and set off through a cold foyer (naturally the doors were wide open), a cold lift and corridors to the meeting room, where the heating was turned on, but the door was left open. Neither our local engineer from the client company, nor the foundryman wanted to change the product, as that meant work. We were, however determined. A few years ago, when we had resourced this particular component to Poland to save money, we were not allowed a change to improve the product. Now was our chance. Through a lot of discussion, drawing and standing firm, we won the day. Then lunch, as it ever does in China around 11.30am, intervened.

We were led to an empty dining room, which was thankfully warm enough for shirt sleeves, much to our host's amazement, as being Chinese, everyone keeps their coats on over winter until given official permission to disrobe. The food was simple, but good and came served on individual plates, not all piled in the centre for us to pick from.

Lunch over; we had some time to kill before the next frustrated rally-driver came to collect us to return to JinQiao. We were offered a tour of the facilities, so we duly accepted. Walking back from the canteen, we strolled past tree sculptures (Chinese do not walk fast, especially post-prandially). These were almost bits of driftwood painted to resemble snakes, dragons, birds and other creatures. There was a whole collection of these pieces of art, a welcome diversion from cold metal engineering which was our subject for the day.

Inside the cold workshop (the doors were open and it was about 5°C outside, even sheltered from the wind) we were shown into a toolroom, if one could call it that. Tools were being made and worked upon, and it was a room. It was dirty and dis-organised, but everyone was working.

One pair of workers came past with a (naturally) overloaded pump truck which they then moved under the gantry crane, as it really was a pile of steel too heavy for a humble hand truck. No-one was wearing hard hats, but lifting went on.

We were trying to look into the moulding tool for our part which was open on the floor. For some reason, the foundry engineer thought we needed it opening up. Now such a tool looks like a big rusty box on the outside, with pipes for the hydraulic fluid down the edge. Within is the cavity for the part shape. It was quite easy to see what we needed without any bother, but opened it was going to be.

This was achieved here by the simple expedient of blowing compressed air into the hydraulic fluid connection through a purpose-made steel extension on the air-line.

Now it is elementary engineering that any hydraulic circuit is a loop, so if you pump air into one end and the other is open to atmosphere, then any residual fluid will spray out of this latter end. It seemed to come as some shock to the "blower" that this happened. He jumped out of the way as it came pouring out of the connection and looked in dismay at the pool forming on the floor. Winston and I, who had both foreseen what was about to happen (as we are fitted with the action/consequence gene apparently missing here) had already made ourselves scarce. We were, however, running out of places to hide, with the lifting of steel already having sent us scuttling for cover.

The hapless blower looked at the forming puddle on the floor and went off in search of the official watering can, which was obviously used to collect waste or escaping fluid. He put it under the nearly empty mould tool, now merely a dripping connection. The horse, as they say, had already bolted. The air was heavy with atomized hydraulic fluid.

The return journey was just as fraught as the outbound. Our driver was one of those cool, one-handed types, who was also confident of not crashing, as his seat belt was fastened behind his body – not much use in an incident.

This evening was a Team Meal, which was held at the restaurant under Diamond Court. We were conveyed there by Smiler in his VW Satan (Santana

215

to you; to us they were the devil's creation!) It isn't that his driving is bad by any local standards, but his observation and forward planning would not pass a UK test. We were waved down into the subterranean car park of Diamond Court and there was a classic Chinese "ditherer" in front, a person who could not decide which way to go when two options for parking bays were presented – to the left and to the right. Without a horn, a flash or any warning, and also whilst turning his head to talk to his passengers, our man just drove alongside the car in front, as its wheels were turning left and sliced across its bow. There was no angry exchange, no expletive from our driver; in fact I would be amazed if either driver noticed. This is driving in Shanghai.

We were shown to our private room and as usual, the food was excellent and the toasts or *ganbeis* ("Down in one") were flowing. We were treated to a couple of speeches where our presence and help were acknowledged and I think applauded. For a while, a warm glow of *entente cordiale* spread through the yawning cultural gap.

It must have occurred to you, dear reader (and I accept the charge) that I spend quite some time on subjects lavatorial. Perhaps this is my natural Northern humour infiltrating the diary, or just that a measure of a society can be taken from its basic human facilities.

Anyway, the point here is that the lavatories at this restaurant feature a "flunky", who resides in the Gents and hands out warm face flannels to customers who have just washed their hands. I hope they are used once and then laundered. This time I was in need of a contemplative sit, so I approached a cubicle, entered and turned to shut the door. I was just about to despoil when there was a knock at the door. For a second or so my mind was in turmoil. What to do? One does not normally accept guests in a cubicle, but here was someone begging entrance. I obliged and opened the door. There was our man, flannel in hand. I must have looked like the stupid Westerner, for he bowed and gestured to the toilet seat. I must have still been looking bemused, so he laid the flannel on the nose of the seat, bowed again and withdrew.

Hurriedly, I locked the door and stood contemplating the now clothed seat. Whilst undressing I had a Eureka moment and decided that the device was to prevent my private parts from becoming soiled by the germs lurking on the plastic upon which I was about to perch. My Father's phrase "Clever these Chinese", came instantly to mind, so I set about to do what I had entered the room to do, all those lines ago.

Upon completing my session in the "thunder box" (another elder Pogson phrase), I wondered what to do with the cloth. I am quite a tidy chap and always keen to clear up after myself (and others quite often, which comes from having three children), so I gingerly lifted the flannel and carried it outside. There was the flunky, smiling and ready to receive the gift which I bore. He accepted it with a smile and bow, placing it in his laundry basket. I washed and was supplied with another (hopefully clean) to dry my hands. A basic human function carried out with style.

Friday, 17th February 2006
Test meeting day dawns again – a real treat for a Friday morning. Today's was no exception; a presentation was made by a local engineer, with graphs and charts and everyone listened. Our translator was not available, nor her stand in, so we had one of the managers help us out. He left after half an hour for another meeting. We could actually sit there for two hours and not be asked anything; our opinion is not sought. Despite all the platitudes at the Team Meal last night, in the cold light of day, we are ignored. It does appear though, that it is up to us to make our opinion or our factual knowledge known by speaking up. Sadly there were no heated arguments this time, but a really valuable contribution from Waldorf, of an idea which had not occurred to me, which was nice.

The meeting had its normal interruptions of mobiles going off and people leaving, not shutting the door as they go and carrying on loudly in the corridor. The boss was in and out, providing the usual exhortational encouragement.

I caught the shuttle bus today to the prototype build shop, just a mile away. The driver was characteristically asleep. He had removed his shoes and the insoles from them were draped over the dashboard, being warmed by the sun. The smell was not just awful, it was deafening. It made me retch somewhat and I then had to sit with the odour for about five minutes. Never has Shanghai air tasted fresh before!

A delight was this excerpt from an e-mail which shows that some of our local colleagues do relish help……….

"Please be as more strict as possible with me. Although I have many defects, I want to be an eligible and excellent engineer. So if you find any defect of me, please tell me and I will improve right now."

We can only wish him well and help as much as possible. He even says "Excuse me" when one is talking and he needs to butt in!

Native told me today that he has learned from his new Chinese teacher that we have been asking for a particular dish wrongly all this time – we have been asking for "ya row" (a flat "row", as in row the boat) when we should have been saying "ya ro" (a short "ro" sound)! We were ordering duck feathers ("row"), not duck meat ("ro")! This language is a killer.

Saturday, 18th February 2006

Saturday evening began in fine style with the arrival of the team (Frau, Native, Winston and Brummie) for dressing up as pirates to go to the Paulaner "Fasching", which is a German beer-festival. We had decided to respond to the challenge on the tickets and dress up, as there was a prize of a flight to Europe for the best-dressed character. Brummie's two lads and one of their ex-girlfriends also came along but remained normally dressed.

We had bought some "parrots", which were soft toys of last year's rooster character (whereas this is the year of the Dog) and these were mounted on wire coat-hangers upon shoulders. Frau had made pirate hats for the creatures and name-labels for them and us. We all had matching head scarves and stripy socks, with the odd bit of jewellery thrown in and facial hair painted on by Frau. I added the "Cher" style wig and we looked a right bunch of dodgy sea faring deviants. Lock up your cabin boys, we are coming!

The event itself was held in the Paulaner in Fenyang Lu, one of three Paulaners in the city. It is a very grand old building with three floors and the splendour of past owners showing through. The seating was on benches at bare pine tables and an excellent buffet was laid out in the vast conservatory. Food and drink were "all-in" on the ticket price. It was good to see so many people had dressed up in the spirit of the event. Teutonic people were out in number. And they were noisy.

Being a German occasion, there was lots of standing on the benches and swinging tankards, singing. I didn't know that there were so many German drinking songs, which all sound the same! Is that all they do? The band was great, apart from having to play all that rubbish oompah music; but they did do a good medley of proper rock songs, the singer looking very much like Tina Turner and appearing in many different costumes.

Around us various funny people were made even funnier by the costumes and consumption of alcohol. Several not very good-looking wenches who thought they were hot actually looked ferocious, so I did not ask them for "eine kleine Tanz". Another table behind us was filled with Germans dressed as Chinese guys, who later were seen to be involved in a little dance floor fracas, with some fists flying! They had drunk a lot and were Germans, so not much better than the Brits for a peaceful time. I cannot imagine the locals doing the same.

We ate and drank our way through the night and enjoyed the exotic house dancers on plinths scattered around the room. These girls were quite animated, the more so when anyone was watching, but the novelty seemed to wear off for many watchers after a short while, not that I was one! At one point they waved fireworks about to add to their allure (I think) and the result was a very smelly restaurant.

Sunday, 19th February 2006
After the excesses of last night, I was not an early riser, but mooched about in the apartment and then took off for Puxi, determined to do a goodly amount of shopping. Every time I go out and report home what I have bought, I am faced with another set of "orders". Cycling past the demolition sites between the ferry terminal and YuYuan, it is amazing that people are still living and trading between the piles of rubble. I have never seen any actual knocking down in progress, but each time I pass by there are less places standing. I do hope that the demolition does not cross over the main road, but I am sure that the spread of high-risers will continue until they completely surround the YuYuan itself. (Photo p.XVI).

Into haggling mode, I tried out my best price in the wig shop again and also on a couple of rabbit fur scarves, but I must be losing my touch. In the end, though, you are often arguing about RMB10 or 20, but it is the principle which is important, which is to have a laugh.

Monday, 20th February 2006
Monday Team Meetings are useful for finding out who is due to come over that week and see everyone in the "family" out here. Guests must wonder about the issues we debate sometimes, as they are very domestic and hum-drum, but living long-term in a place gives a certain perspective and set of needs.

Today the air was full (for those of us in the know), hanging with anticipation as we knew that Gary would announce his departure. His public reason for going is that he has had a better offer he cannot refuse, doing work for which he is more than qualified. Privately I suspect he would voice opinions shared amongst all of us that we are not allowed responsibility or to be even heard and listened to at times. It is a sad day; we shall all miss his wise counsel. He can be annoying at times, with an uncanny ability to want detail and involvement some days and others not. He can also home in on people when the focus should be elsewhere. Overall, a good solid Welsh bloke who could manage companies with all his limbs bound, better than some people I could mention when theirs were fully functioning.

Tuesday, 21st February 2006
We took a taxi ride tonight to Zhangjiang, the end of the metro line. The driver must have watched the 70s kids' TV cartoon "Whacky Races" for his driving style inspiration. From within the car, it was positively frightening. We mixed it with the big green "Yutong" coaches taking employees home. The drivers of these leviathans take no prisoners and view the cycle lanes as their own private bus lane. None of this waiting at traffic lights nonsense, they are away as if they are on two wheels. We arrived safely at the destination, as we had scheduled to go swimming, but the baths were "closed until match!" Was there some competitive event scheduled?

It took us some while to understand that the pool was being repaired and we were not waiting for a swimming match to finish, but that the pool would re-open on 1st March!

Every time I dismount from a bus, I go all "Green Cross Code" and look along the cycle lane right, then left, then right again, as I do not want to be mown down. I may be stuffy and English, but I would prefer to be stuffily undamaged. Dismounting from the 85 bus tonight, I saw a "silent death" electric moped approaching at speed, with no lights on of course. I waited for him to fly past and put out an arm to arrest Winston's progress. A second or so later, we witnessed a man who was stupidly not looking up the bike lane for oncoming danger (like most locals), being run down by the moped. The noise of crunching plastic, steel and bones was audible over the roar of the traffic. The rider of the moped was ready to speed off, as the victim nursed his injuries.

Wednesday, 22nd February 2006

Today is a grey day weather-wise, but full of laughs to brighten it up. Clegg reported that one of the crash cars had to be moved (to the crash test centre prior to being slammed against the barrier) a distance of some 50 miles. For safety reasons, a crash car is usually built dry of fluids and ballast is added to the car to simulate the weight of the wet bits. (These include oil, fuel, battery, brake fluid, coolant and so on). As no lorry could be found to move the car, the Chinese were going to fill it with fuel and drive it. Our man begged them not to "wet" it, but to no avail; they knew better. The car had no front seats, either, which were to be fitted later, so they proposed driving it whilst sat on a beer crate. Jokingly, Clegg suggested that they put the seat belt on, so the driver did! It just shows how little understanding of vehicles these people have. A seat belt only works when used by a properly seated person.

Thursday, 23rd February 2006

Today was the first day I managed to cycle to work. It is so satisfying not to rely upon someone else. I have all the room I need on my bike, no-one hawking up to spit from the driving seat, no stupid moves are made out of my control and I can make good progress without having to stop at every light. All I have to do is pedal and watch out for suicide jockeys on the road. I managed to make it to within 500 metres of work before someone pulled a stupid stunt in front of me. No-one here looks behind on a bicycle; they just go. Slowing down to avoid someone going backwards seems almost a cultural impossibility. There is little giving of way in this city, just push, push, push.

During a meeting, there was a sea of cultural issues worthy of note, but little of substance from the main purpose of the session. It was lucky then that the Departmental Head had asked Marvin to present his monthly report to the engineers, as it was a fairly bleak outlook. He gave it to them between the eyes, hoping to find something there to receive the message and react. What he did not expect was them to home in on an important side issue, rather than the principal one of "PANTS" (Parts Are Not To Specification).

On purpose he tried arguing with the local who wanted to talk about quantities. The chap next to me wrote "He is a very strict teacher" on his pad and showed it to me. I replied by writing "He is speaking from facts". He was only trying to help, and as always has the engine's best interests at heart. Sadly, the Departmental Head was not there to reinforce the message and it is questionable how much notice the people took of our man, who spoke eloquently. Interestingly, just as Marvin was getting really passionate, the meeting somehow broke up. I don't think they could stand the heat. They seem to argue heatedly between each other, but when we raise the heat, they shy away, or just smile or laugh nervously and annoyingly.

For the evening's entertainment we boys stopped in for a "Peter Kay" evening. We do not do this very often; I suspect if there were a bunch of ladies out here then they would be in and out of each others' rooms all the time. Needless to say, we cried with laughter, especially at the "Four Tops" and the "Biscuit dunking" sketches.

Friday, 24th February 2006
Not a lot happened, so I will just report that Rumble believes that the most heard Chinese phrases in the office are "Wu bu je dow" or "Wu ting bu dong". Although I may have mis-spelt these, they mean "I don't know!" These are often followed by "Ni shwar she ma?" – "What did you say?" They could always ask us; that is what we are here for!

Saturday, 25th February 2006
Saturdays gives one a chance to lie in, so I did.

Sunday, 26th February 2006
Today we gathered at the Mawdesley for a small celebration of the impending marriage of Nelson to the original "*piao-lian*", or beautiful girl in Chinese. We had made a small collection for them, as is traditional here and Brummie had sorted a card and red envelope for the money. We all were given a free drink by the lucky groom. She still is an attractive lass, but came in wearing a dodgy 1960s style twin-set and yes, horrible thick yellow tights.

Celebration over, I had to hot-foot (or hot-pedal in my case) to the river, catch the ferry to Puxi and on to the Fabric Market for some silk, requested by Sharon. This was a risky mission, as it was rather like asking her to go to the bike shop and pick up some bits. Would I source the right shade of blue? Would I know what I was looking at? In the end I got it wrong, but only realised once I had made it back to the Pent-Ox.

And now – a Competition for "Dumbo of the day". The choices are:

- Mobile moron girl
- Mobile moron chap
- Glass-carrier guy
- Crasher cretin

This has been a hotly-contested event. Any day of the week, there are contenders for "Dumbo of the day"; there is no shortage of people doing stupid things here. Some are the same idiots as we have in the UK, but some are specialist Chinese entries.

Mobile moron girl is an example of the former category. People do it in the UK, but being Shanghainese, she added her own slant to the stunt. Rather than finish her doubtlessly vital conversation, she pulled out very slowly from the apartment block, one hand on the wheel, crept into the road without looking and I swerved around her. She then continued down the middle of the road at walking speed. A mobile chicane.

Mobile moron chap added a new Chinese style to this activity, because he was on a scooter. He was holding his phone to his ear, riding therefore one-handed. His pillion passenger was helping by holding the rider's helmet in position just over his head, ready to slap it in place when the call was over. It is indicative of these people's inability or unwillingness to stop for traffic or vital calls. Life is so busy and urgent. Stuff the safety aspect. The helmet was also ready to be slapped on if a Policeman was spotted, I suspect.

Glass-carrier guy was nearly the winner today and a Chinese specialism. He was transporting a sheet of glass on the running board of his scooter. It measured about four feet across by three high. It was wedged against his belly. A slice of Shanghai man, anyone?

Crasher cretin was the clear winner. He was on a scooter with a child riding pillion and he was a real horn-blower; I could hear him coming behind me. A white van passed me by, indicating right and moving slowly towards the kerb. It was clear to me that he was intending to park at the side of the road at the next gap in the parked cars. I say obvious, because I am observant and mistrustful of white vans. Seeing a narrowing gap about to form between the van and the last parked car, I slowed, moved to my left and prepared to overtake the van. On my inside, Hooting Crasher sped past and rammed himself into the now small, wedge-shaped gap between the van and the car. He collided with a satisfying clang of metal against metal. He could not fall over as he was jammed in the gap. Dumbo of the day.

Today's conundrum is a simple one. It was prompted by a "Traffic Assistant", and policeman booking a scooter rider at the traffic lights. I stopped at the red light and a following cyclist squeezed between me and the Assistant, just to nose into what was going on. Any such event always pulls a crowd, as does any police activity. Why put yourself into a position where you could be closely examined by Plod-Wang when you could just keep your nose out and stay low? In the end it was he who attracted the enraged attention of the Law!

Chapter 10

THE MOTO GP AND ROACH BUTTIES

Sunday, 23rd April 2006, St. George's Day – time to fly

We arrived on Virgin VS250 Business Class at Pudong, having had a very agreeable flight in my personal "cot" at the sharp end of a new Airbus A320-600.

At Shanghai I opted to avoid the taxi queue and walked towards the stunning Maglev station, for my 7 minutes 20 seconds of travel, at speeds of 431kph. This trip always impresses me, banking hard around curves at over 300kph and the shock-wave bang as we passed the train in the opposite direction. It is a big status symbol for the city; it must make no money at all as the fare is only RMB50/£3.60 single.

I had telephoned the Pent-Ox from the Maglev, asking if they were expecting me and been assured that they were. How unsurprised I was when I turned up and the receptionist had no knowledge of my arrival! The next bit was even better. The receptionist booked me in, programmed the entry card on the computer and escorted me to a free room. She flashed the card at the lock several times, but door 22F resolutely blinked its red light at us. I tried too, but to no avail. For some reason, at an ostensibly empty room, she rang the door bell. She apologised profusely and asked me to stay put outside the room while she shot back downstairs to check the card set up.

Some moments later, the door was opened by a vision of Latin beauty. She had long dark hair, a perfect figure, a beautiful smile and was rubbing the sleep from her big, dark eyes. We had an unexpected conversation about how I was allocated this room but could see it was certainly occupied and the efficiency of trainee Chinese receptionists. I said that I really must await her return and then I heard the words any red-blooded male dreams of – "Do you want to come inside?" Now either fear, jet-lag or rank stupidity stepped in and the best I could manage to do was politely decline. I am English after all and married too.

Having missed all the excitement, trainee receptionist returned and we went across the landing to 22G, which was thankfully devoid of Italianate beauties, as all I wanted to do was visit the small room, shower and snooze until it was time to meet Brummie for brunch.

Having fallen asleep on the settee, I woke at 1.30pm and felt it was about time to call him, as he should be ready for dining. He was just up and ready to roll, as we had arranged to meet first-time visitors 118 and the Milky-bar Kid in the Super Brand Mall. We had a very pleasant meal together and then it was off to YuYuan for some present-shopping for the new arrivals. As usual it was interesting to see the world through fresh eyes as they took in the sights of Shanghai, starting with the amazing architecture, although Jinmao and the Pearl Tower were shrouded in cloud or smog. The guys were amazed with the spitting ferry and several locals were on hand to show how it earned its name.

On the Puxi side, I was sad to see that the wrecker's ball had been at work and several men were seen swinging sledgehammers on the tops of buildings and at the edges; but they were wearing hard hats, so that was good. 118's wife is involved in Civil Engineering on the H&S (Health and Safety) side, so he was particularly amazed to see how rubble was strewn everywhere across pavements and how wantonly the destruction was progressing. There were still two clothes shops and a butcher trading among the rubble and the visitors were particularly stunned at the open shelves and counters displaying raw meat, flavoured with a gentle film of dust and grime, additional to the normal road dirt. (Photo p.XVI).

I insisted we dive down one of the local backstreets and show the guys how real Shanghainese live – in very close proximity and in some squalour. These are real people in a real neighbourhood being torn up around them. This is sad but apparently progress. It always feels slightly uncomfortable to walk down these alley-ways (*lilongs*) and narrow streets, being as far away from our warm, dry, expensive apartments as we are; it feels like voyeurism. It is however, a must-see for any visitor before these places disappear and it does not seem to bother the locals; they remain as polite and demure as ever. The lads were amazed at the crowded feel, the poor quality repairs to the roofs and walls, the lack of paint, except the ubiquitous faded red and the outside sinks.

We strolled on through the *lilongs* and past the tiny local hairdressers, the community eateries, the outside cooking and the street vendors of fruit, vegetables, fish, meat and sugar cane. Through this press of people came squeezing the usual trikes piled high with almost worthless jumble and hooting scooters. As usual, the new-comers marvelled at the variety and colour of the many stalls and shops crowded into a corner of this Communist country. What is Communist and what is Capitalism? I have lost the boundary somewhere in this city.

We journeyed through the streets until the local shops and alleys opened out into the artificial tourist trap that is the YuYuan, or Yu Gardens. Whatever you say about it, the buildings are always impressive, it is always bustling with life and there are bargains to be had. We threaded through to cross the zig-zag bridge and over to the other side of the lake, passing the famous tea-rooms. As usual, there were crazy tourists trying to take photos across the bridge, which as ever was packed with bodies. We worked our way down one of the many arcades, stopping to allow the visitors to poke about the musical instrument shop, before rounding the corner and seeing the "Wishing Tree", which was being renovated. This is an artificial tree, made from steel mesh, covered in chicken wire netting and then plastered to look like bark. The leaves are gold-painted silk, but today it was surrounded by bamboo scaffolding whilst the workers repaired the scars of a million attentive Chinese wishers. (Photo p.XXI).

The next stop was a shop so the visitors could buy typical Chinese gifts, such as "chop" stamps (carved stamping blocks), a dress for one lad's wife and a jacket. While the chops were being carved, we took the opportunity to look around some of the local art, which is always impressive. It must be spring now as the old guy was back on the street with his one model of a ship, made from polished aluminium sheet. It is most impressive, and he just sits behind it, waiting for the one customer who would make his day. His neighbour was there, carving wooden abacus calculators! (Photo p.XXXII).

Monday, 24th April 2006

It felt odd returning to the JinQiao office after seven weeks away, but there were no flags out to greet me. A few of them came up to me to shake hands, but that is all; there was no instant queue of confused engineers waiting with questions or work for me to do. Native was away on holiday in Japan with his lady, so that just left Marvin and I in the office.

Monday morning is always Team Meeting time and this time it was really headed by Visa, who has taken a leading role following the departure of Gary.

There were the usual half-baked responses to our questions from the UK over the same subjects we have been debating for weeks, nay months now, i.e. tax, health insurance and holidays.

Let and Flower had been to a conference at the new vehicle assembly plant, a five-hour bus ride away down south. They said that the food was good and the short facility visit was interesting, but the small amount of speaking which they could understand did not really warrant the ten hours travelling! Our hosts really do enjoy their celebrations and big meals. They were "excused" the Party meeting, although the local mayor was keen to recruit members!

We often muse over how we can better understand our hosts, but it seems that the more one knows, the more one is confused. In particular our office is a strange clique of people who used to work together at the government test facility and our appearance seems an annoyance. Imagine being back in the UK in a government research establishment which has worked on a cost-plus basis for years, and is now facing cold commercial realities. One day a group of "suits" walk in from a failed private enterprise in another country and tell them what to do; you can imagine your reaction.

Perhaps we should not be surprised, but we have had the guts ripped from our industry back home, yet we are here helping China PLC in its economic growth towards world domination. I am definitely becoming more dark about this whole exercise and have today announced my intention to return home for good in June on or around the 11th.

DIY and I went to the evergreen East-West café. You could see I had not been back long, as the taxi-driver had driven up the cycle-lane (many of them do; it is green tarmac and features a painted cyclist logo, but they still think it is part of the road) and I stupidly opened the door without looking, unwittingly missing an unobservant cyclist by millimetres.

We enjoyed the usual high standard of food and service. Just as we had finished, Mr and Mrs Rolf strolled in, cuddling each other like a couple of teenagers and grinning similarly! He looked a little washed out, as he had been in hospital for some preventive surgery and we were a little concerned as the phrase "take it easy" is not in his nature! He said he was fine and more concerned with his new place of work, which is in the new engine plant, an hour north of where we are. After the sophistication and bustle of our normal environment, he found it "very Chinese" and dusty, being in an old ex-motorcycle factory which was looking a little tired and forlorn. Apparently the food was much worse than the worst of our experiences in the JinQiao staff canteen, and that could be bad. It was so dusty on the floor that they had tried to organise a sweeping party, but all the usual leafy "witches' brooms" did was swirl the dust around a lot. A 45-minute shopping spree failed to produce what we would class as a decent bristle broom. There is definitely a market here for those. Industrial floor-cleaners had been ordered, but would take some time. The concept of putting new machine tools on a dusty floor is an affront to our sensibilities, but to the Chinese is no issue; we used to put them under leaking roofs, so we weren't much better.

Tuesday, 25th April 2006

The afternoon saw yours truly back in familiar territory, in a competitor viewing event. These traditionally are held in the UK with clean cars in a clean well-lit environment. This, however, is China. No attempt had been made at all to clean either workshop or cars. In no time we were filthy. I am sure that most of our colleagues were unsure about why we should be doing the work, which was meant to provide some guidance on how much a new car should cost to build by looking at current market offerings and pricing up the components via quotation from our suppliers. The bosses had said the new car would cost X, where X is a crazily low amount, so it would cost X, wouldn't it? Belief here is absolute, despite evidence to the contrary.

Such evidence is regularly seen here, yet not believed, even when it is material, such as a broken part. How can one not believe such evidence? We see it almost daily. Perhaps what we see as a quality problem, because we know the possible consequences cannot be seen as such by people who, for the most part, do not drive or own cars. I do not know what the logical thought process is and I am not alone amongst my colleagues. If we did know, perhaps we would do a better job, but we are conducting ourselves the only way we know how. There isn't an engineer here who wants to do a bad job and all of us know how it should be done, as most of us have worked in Honda, BMW or other places (Marvin worked at Bentley and Cosworth, for example).

In the afternoon, I slipped out at 4.30 to beat the rush and head for Frank's office at Bestrip, my tame local travel agent. I arrived at Jing'An temple and the massive, high-class shopping mall in good time. Jing'An park was, as usual, full of lovers in various stages of loving, in a very Chinese way.

There was also a massive quantity of catkins blowing in the wind; people were brushing bits out of their hair and it started me sneezing. I strolled into the block where Frank has his "suite" (more like a big cupboard) and the staff from the ground floor restaurant were on their break; the stench of cigarettes did not encourage me to tarry for a bite.

Once back in the park, tickets obtained, I decided to climb up the man-made hill and see what could be viewed from the top, try and see some of the birds I could hear (are they just recordings?) and disturbed more lovers in full flow. I wandered off the hill down extremely slippery rock steps and ventured through the rock "caves". Here in the half-darkness were more adolescents eating each other! Perhaps not the best time to pass through.

Normally I enjoy the Shanghai parks very much; it does not take a lot of foliage to mute the incessant traffic noise. I suppose I should not be surprised to see so many residents enjoying them in their own way.

I decided to travel back on the Metro and headed for Xiangyang Market. When I reached the place, I was hungry so it was time to head for the quiet, welcoming environ of Jenny's bar, where I found a Kiwi and Brit, with whom I ended up sharing PC jokes. PC in this instance means personal computer! We both had our machines out swapping funny videos and pictures, many of which were very non-PC.

I whiled away a very pleasant time and then decided to stroll over to the market, so I settled up and left, having enjoyed the usual chips, spring rolls and fresh orange juice. Naturally, upon stepping outside, the heavens opened and I was not wearing a coat. I shopped hard and slung the resultant heavy shopping bag over my shoulder and turned for home; shame I was only going to the Pent-Ox! Just walking from the number 85 bus-stop to the apartment block I was soaked.

I had arranged to meet 118, the Kid and Brummie at the Paulaner, as it was the latter's final day here for a couple of weeks. I was tempted to stay in as it was so awful, but he's a good mate and the company of all three would be good. A taxi rather than my chosen 85 bus and a stroll would have been much wiser, but what's a bit of rain?

The band were on form as usual and the new visitors to the bar were (as all newcomers we take there), completely transfixed by the girls on stage, with their overtly sexy moves and gestures, followed quickly by a smile and a slice of humour – a winning combination. As usual, they played up for us as we were the most attentive of the audience and understand the humour.

A star turn was provided by an old American guy and a local, who was either a really expensive or really cheap girl. They were like two sixteen year-olds who had just discovered snogging – they were virtually eating each other. This they kept up for a long time, barely coming up for air, perhaps believing themselves to be "hidden" at the back of the bar. On the contrary, they provided such a marathon spectacle that many of the bar staff were watching! There was more to come, as the bloke laid his coat over them and movement could be seen underneath. By this time, word had got around the bar and virtually all the staff and the band were watching. 118 even pulled out his big SLR camera and *whop!* The flash barely caused them to pause, before burrowing down to eating each other again! The girls were singing appropriate songs now; the couple were at it for so long and the girls were making suitable gestures on stage. We were in bits.

Wednesday, 26th April 2006

The day was gleefully spent on more competitor benchmarking, which is right up my street, especially working with Fraggle. We had a good system worked out where he called the data and I recorded and sketched. Always adapting to circumstances, Fraggle was at pains to explain a drive belt routing whilst under the car, so he drew it in the mud on a chassis rail! This the scribe duly copied into the official book. We had a good day and worked well with some of our Chinese colleagues.

All around us however was panic and chaos. Two special cars had been built and they were not working properly. I had often wondered why there were so many squealing brakes in this city/country; we have had the issue more or less licked in the West, but here one's ears are assaulted by the constant howl of brake squeal, which to most Chinese will be one of those things, nothing to get excited about. It pains our more sensitive Western ears, as it is unnecessary. Also not necessary are brake pads which squeal *and* have chunks taken out of them, which is what we found upon examination. As usual, if in doubt we switch back to parts used on the original cars, which to ensure success meant robbing from two UK-built cars.

At the end of the day, it was another Shanghai experience for Fraggle – taking the Bus to Carrefour. I had my card, but insufficient change, so I had to take RMB8 coins for a ten note from a helpful local. It was the usual vehicle for route 790 – a deafeningly noisy bus. My ears actually hurt after only 15 minutes of travel and about three miles! Also, because the 790 is an old Chinese bus, it has quite a high deck as the engine compartment is front mounted (which passengers have to clamber over), and if stood close to the driver it is quite hard to see landmarks, so unless road markings mean something, one has to keep bending down.

Fraggle noted the glazed, eyes-on-stalks, staring face of the driver which showed perpetual terror and his fight with a recalcitrant manual gear-change and a clutch pedal which was not hinged as normal, but was the old-fashioned style which had to be pressed straight down through the floor and only disengaged at the bottom and engaged fully at the top of its stroke. I have said it before, but some of the heavy vehicle drivers here are supermen, like we used to have in the 40s and 50s back home, before we started to catch up with the Continental trucks.

We descended from the bus to the usual stares from locals "Are these *poor* Westerners on a bus?" We scooted around the shop floor, with me pointing out bargains, instructional sex videos, live bullfrogs, terrapins, crabs, fish and cheap whisky. There is always something interesting to see at Carrefour! Whether in its native France, China (or as I was later to discover in Dubai), it is a reflection of the society around the store.

We enjoyed a cheap meal from the massive choice in Megabite, with Fraggle discovering the delights of Chinese style crunchy chicken (bones a non-optional extra) then we moved on to Decathlon for some of his shopping needs. Everyone comes out here with a shopping list, this time it was for a kite for his boss!

Thursday, 27th April 2006
Work was again fun, with more competitor measuring and comparing. To cover one car properly and allow others to do their bit takes some time, but we ended up with a full score-sheet of valuable data, which is more than can be said for some of the other teams.

Friday, 28th April 2006
At the morning Test Meeting, I looked around and checked at the way the Chinese engineers came equipped to a meeting. Those that came with

anything at all, (as some were empty-handed) had at best an A4 diary, but most had an A5 notebook or smaller, in which they made very few notes. No-one came prepared with any information to present, no-one leapt up to the whiteboard; it was all left to the meeting chairman to tell his story, try and raise a few responses and gee people up a bit. No minutes were taken, although there is always at least an agenda for the session.

I have been having breakfast all week with DIY. He was really looking forward to the imminent arrival of his wife and daughter – at least we have found something he does get excited about!

In the evening, it was Cultural Tour time again (I should charge for this and donate to charity!). We met in the foyer of the Super Brand Mall and passed the usual empty shops with no-one buying anything and assistants with no-one to assist. They must be bored out of their skulls and hence are really easy to amuse with waves, funny faces and walks. I led the visitors to the promenade by the river and we gazed in wonder at the illuminated Bund across the brown swell of the Huangpu. They were suitably stunned at the sights. We even saw ten seagulls, not dead and not on sticks! We did however see a number of large bats, outside the Paulaner bar.

We walked down to the Spitting Ferry; I showed the process of buying plastic token discs for RMB0.5 and throwing them in a counting bin, watched by at least two pairs of eyes. We stood in the bow of the ferry to avoid the smokers and tried to avoid the spray of dirty river water. The terminal is still being renovated, but might look good one day. Across the water, we took the usual route down the backstreets where friendly locals tried to entice us to buy from their street kitchens. It does look good and it seems to be fresh.

We walked to YuYuan, across the zig-zag bridge of many turns and passed by the now complete wishing tree. We dined as customary in the "78" restaurant and both seemed happy with the choice.

Fraggle wanted special rise tea, whose leaves stand vertical in water if it is the right quality. We walked into a tea shop and were greeted like long-lost customers, with several of the many staff speaking some English, and with the Chinese character for the tea supplied by a colleague we secured the very article. We were naturally offered tea-tasting, to encourage more spending. As ever, it was huge fun and smiles all around. The shop also sold dates – flavoured ones. I always thought dates had their own flavour, depending upon the variety. Don't tell me the locals have found a way of flavouring one of my favourite fruits!

From the YuYuan, we headed on down the "dark side" of the park and again the boys were impressed with how safe they felt compared to how they would be back home. I led them to the Expo 2010 countdown clock, which marks every second before the event. This point also marks the start of the Bund as it snakes along the river towards the Peoples' Heroes monument. The Bund was stunning as usual, the lights and people strolling, the boats and architecture. We walked all the way to the Suzhou Creek and I pointed out the brooding shape of Broadway Mansions (an Art Deco apartment block) across the water. Naturally the might of Jinmao and the Pearl Tower across the water really impressed. There was the usual flotilla of beggars and hawkers. The boys were rather taken by the sight of workmen disc-cutting paving tiles with a dry cutter, no mask and flip-flops as toe protection. One of them pulled the plug on the lights at 9.00pm, but they kept on cutting in the shadows!

We had only taken a few steps onto the Nanjing Lu (after my warning to be ready for it) and there he was, a thirty-something bloke with a purse and a suit offering us sexual favours from a "clean Shanghai woman".

Fraggle asked if we would see parts of our old manufacturing equipment for sale down this particular Lu. (In-joke, as Nanjing Automotive had bought all the UK factory equipment and stripped it out!)

They were as amused as everyone by the upright display in the "Adult Shop" at the start of the road; some things are just too big as models to be taken seriously. However, an attentive copper was not amused at our hilarity, so we moved on.

We gazed in wonder at this Chinese Oxford Street and filtered into Peoples' Square, where we had to skirt around the perimeter as the gates were locked. Just by the Art Gallery we enjoyed pudding – hot custards! Yet another Rolf and Ian tour highlight at only RMB3/20p each.

We continued down Renmin Lu and passed the Government offices and then the amazing sight of the Planning Office. Descending into the subway I confirmed my complete lack of a sense of direction by turning the wrong way. Thankfully Fraggle deciphered the Chinese characters and pointed out the mistake. We travelled the two stops to Lujiazui, rose from the Metro depths and stepped right into a taxi, which dropped me at the Pent-Ox, before I sent it on its way to Diamond Court.

Saturday, 29th April 2006

Today was a working day to earn holiday for the following Labour Week. The working week has passed really fast, toiling with Fraggle and we seem to have bounced off each other really well.

I had cycled to work – I really enjoy speeding around Shanghai, and like the taxi-drivers I rarely use the same route twice, turning right on red lights to keep moving.

In the evening we met outside exit 4 of Lujiazui Metro. We descended and I tried to explain the new and far less helpful or clear Metro map to the crew, which to my delight included Bean. We only went as far as Peoples' Square and emerged to take in the Art Gallery again and then to walk into the south-east corner of the Park to show them where 500 houses were cleared to make way for the grass, rocks, a lake, swans and ducks. I hope the sacrifice was appreciated. (Photo p.VI).

We strolled across a busy Jinling Lu to the Cyber Mart, where good haggling was put in by me and the boys to secure the usual hard drive and memory sticks.

I suggested we could ride the Metro one stop or walk the Huahai Lu to Xiangyang Lu. The fit boys preferred the latter, so they were treated to a hike over one of the massive pedestrian bridges and the sight of shop after shop selling the marital dream. Marriage in Shanghai is big business – the girls want it all and it is not cheap.

It was a bit of a frog-march as we were short of time, but the Fake Market was reached in good time and being men, they were there to buy and exit quickly. Fraggle was after handbags, so it was down to A41 stall and haggle hard. The imminent closure of the place seems to have sent prices rising to make a quick Yuan before closure.

Goose bought a jacket and some T-shirts, but we nearly lost him as he is so quiet. We resolved to catch the Metro back to Peoples' Square in order to make it to a table in "Kathleen5" restaurant before too late. This is a superb place to eat and we were able to find an outside table, with a truly fabulous view. It worked out at about RMB300/£21.40 per head – expensive for Shanghai, but the location had even hardened engineers waxing lyrical about the "Dan Dare" shape of the Radisson hotel, which looks like a 1960s model of a flying saucer has landed on top. They were enthralled by the view down the Nanjing Road, the expanse of People's Square and the size of what was the old racecourse. I had insisted that we climbed the stairs to see the old pictures of the course on the stair-well and they had grasped the enormity of the place and could now see for themselves where it had been.

We put every effort into enjoying our roast lamb (selected by everyone!) and the sweet to share afterwards. We felt like kings sat up there, looking down on all the masses below. I have never been in such a place in the UK. We felt privileged and as though it were some sort of international adventure, for not a year ago many of us were on the dole.

We left our eyrie replete and happy, and walked down to the underground station, but the shutters were down and the night-time sleepers were lined up sardine-like on the stair-well. We resolved to catch a taxi, so I flagged one down and attempted to ask him to fulfil another Fraggle aim and drive around the 720° slip-road onto the Nanpu Bridge. I finally succeeded, as many of the Chinese do not understand our fascination for something which to them is just a road, and we had an amazingly slow tour over the famous Bridge.

Sunday, 30th April 2006
I opted for the taxi to Longyang Lu and the Maglev to reach the airport, but following the pleasure of this trip, tragedy lay in wait. My itinerary from the travel agent showed my leaving from Pudong (the new) airport and flying back in to Hongqiao (the old) airport. I had checked the times on my itinerary against the ticket, but not checked the airport. I was at the wrong one and they are about 90 minutes apart, right across the city. I must have looked the very image of disconsolate, flavoured with stupid. I was advised to go and change my ticket then go back to Check-in and be put on stand-by. I noted I was third on the stand-by list and as the flight was full, I was going to be buying a later ticket. Would I make the connection at Beijing, or be a day late in Dubai? Sharon and I were to spend the week's Chinese holiday there.

I sat there for forty minutes until the appointed time to return to Check-in. These were not the most fun moments of my life. When I got there several large families were milling around and arguing, so I waited some more time. I shook the guy's hand when it transpired that I was on and away. I ran like the wind to Customs, but there was to be blow number two. Obviously in need of party supplies, the Customs lady confiscated my cheap bottle of gin, which I was taking for our enjoyment in the hotel room in supposedly dry Dubai. I gave them to the officer and said they were a present. I then missed the sign for my gate and went down stairs rather than up two flights and was in danger of missing the flight, but managed to squeeze through the gate.

There was nowhere on the crowded flight for my bags, as Chinese travellers are like Americans and stretch the point on hand luggage beyond the boundary, so my stuff went in the blanket cupboard. I was hot and bothered by now and set the overhead vent to cool me down. The Chinese woman next to me, in her velvet trouser suit, made a show of fastening the jacket, even though the plane was hot inside and then asked for a blanket! What is it with these people? Do their body thermostats not work properly? I know humans have a very narrow band in which we are comfortable to operate, but it seems even narrower with the locals.

The last time I was in Beijing airport was with the family, but no such luck today, although I was on my way to meet Sharon. I bought a copy of an interesting little book, "Following a Dream" by Joanne Braaksma, a Canadian teacher (ISBN 0-9733748-0-2), which was a bit steep at RMB44, but this is an airport. The book is a collection of her letters home from a teaching post in Beijing a few years ago. It was interesting to read a lady's take on China and many of the issues I cover in these pages she had experienced and many of the problems I face teaching Chinese she faced too.

On the next flight I sat next to Mr Wriggle the Nut-Eater. He was rarely still and was surrounded by a sea of discarded shells. We had a long wait for a slot and the airport is expanding, doubling like Pudong to cater for the forthcoming Olympic Games in 2008. We flew off into the night, nuts and all.

Dubai was a surprise in terms of the simply massive duty free shop and the huge quantities people were buying, as I suppose it is the only place one can buy alcohol. I picked up some gin to replace the bottle "donated" to Pudong Customs and hailing a taxi set off for the hotel.

Dubai was so much different to Shanghai, cleaner, more open and with a whole new language of course, with people wandering around in white for the men and black cloaks (*abaya*) and headscarves (*shela*) for the women, though not exclusively. How do the men keep their clothes SO white? They do look very smart in their headscarves (*gutra*), chord to keep them in place (*agal*) and long white ankle-length robes (*kandoora*).

237

The holiday began for me with a shower at the Riviera hotel – the first one built in Dubai and where Michael Palin stayed on his "Full Circle" trip. I had a sleep from about midnight until 4.30am, when I rose to go and meet Sharon off her plane. Dubai is only a small place (big enough for two or three airports, though!) and so a quick drive back saw me waiting anxiously for that first glimpse and hug. We returned to the hotel so she could freshen up and we both dozed, before attacking the breakfast table and starting our first day in Arabia.

I would recommend a holiday in Dubai, there is much to do. We covered all the usual sights, shopping malls and traditional *souks* (or markets), selling gold in one, spices in another and silk in the next. Other souks on the other side of the water sold all manner of fabric and cheap clothes, footwear, food and general goods. We loved the *abras*, or water taxis which cross the Creek, a narrow inlet of crystal-clear Gulf water splitting the city in two. We took an open bus tour around the City route, either side of the Creek and along the coast road to the fancy hotels and palm tree shaped man-made islands sprouting even more villas and more hotels. So we were in searing heat in Dubai, being guided by a set of Philippinos on the top of a Leyland bus made in our home county of Lancashire. What a mix!

We toured the stunning building site that is 2006 Dubai, with the balance of the world's cranes that are not in Shanghai appearing to be there. Whole marinas have been built in the desert and water is de-salinated at some ridiculous rate to keep the roadside grass and tree/flower beds looking verdant.

We also experienced the delights of a desert safari in 4x4 Toyota Landcruisers, which took us out into dunes as far as the eye could see, racing up and down them, sliding on the sand, and all this in close company with three chattering Japanese tourists in our Cruiser and umpteen other vehicles. Totally crazy driving was provided by our Iranian guide. The evening entertainment at a "Bedouin camp" was a bit staged, but the food was good, the local crafts were interesting and the belly-dancer engaging. Sharon even got up for a go – she was good, too. I hid in the shadows, not wanting to be picked.

We had but one day at the pool in a sports centre where I characteristically managed to over-sun myself, but other than that we were on the go quite a bit.

We did enjoy watching the loading of the Arab dhows on the quayside just opposite the hotel from the comfort of our air-conditioned room. This was done from piles of goods left out overnight on the quay – and nobody touched any of it! The dhows were loaded mostly by hand, with the odd crane and boat-mounted derrick. Men swarmed up bouncing gangplanks and bamboo ladders like stevedores of old. We watched for hours.

We had heard that women should be covered modestly, but anything seemed to go, especially in the malls where it was a competition to see who could look the hottest. We were warned about shows of affection in public, and tried to keep to this one. Worryingly, many of the men we saw were holding hands.

All in all, we had a thoroughly great time. It was with a heavy heart that I waved the love of my life goodbye at the end of the week.

Monday, 8th May 2006
It was back into Shanghai via the old Hongqiao airport for me, having had the best of times in Dubai with Sharon; my own favourite travel companion. The flight from Dubai to Beijing had been delayed and was populated with odd Chinese people who displayed their oddness by not coming through the barrier into the departure "lounge", one woman complaining that there were insufficient seats! You are going to be sat down for the next seven hours, missus! Enjoy stretching your legs. Other returning locals were characteristically late; others just hung about outside the barrier, diving in and out of the toilets and generally being a pain. I have never before seen so many people leave a departure lounge for the lavatory.

Amazingly, I walked straight into a taxi at Hongqiao, as they seem to have finally devised a system that works. Our driver was reasonably smooth and competent, delivering me safely to the Pent-Ox. It was noticeably cooler in Shanghai than I had been used to and quite a relief in a way.

I arranged to meet up with Winston at the old East-West, where the food was as good as ever and a real welcome back to the Orient, with a slight Western flavour. No-one else was about and this may have been because the Company has now found a new hotel, closer to work in which to shove visitors, so we are now spread over Diamond Court, Phoenix Mansions across the road, the new Sunrise Glory Hotel, ourselves in the Pent-Ox and the long-termers in Shimao Lakeside. We put the world to rights during conversation and I caught up on the local news. I asked, not expecting anything, how the morning team meeting had gone. As we are now "leader-less", there had been no meeting. Who could fill the massive void left by Gary?

Tuesday, 9th May 2006
Back to work again, so it was the usual 7.45 meeting in the "Robby" (the letter "L" is officially pronounced "R" by Chinese people) to wander across the road to catch the next taxi. We are now on "speaking" terms with the lady Traffic Assistant who usually talks through her whistle, as they all do, but always beams when she sees us, because we see her and smile, not having a clue what she is saying, but we all end up smiling, so that furthers international relations.

I strolled into the office and no-one greeted me at all. Welcome back to China, it's time to go. I am becoming sadly dispirited here, I am so glad I am flying out in five weeks time.

Today I was sat in a taxi at the lights and the car to the left had dilly-dallied about in typical local fashion, seeming to want to turn right, but not in the right turn lane. It amazingly stopped at the lights, but straddled both lanes. The policeman on duty instructed the driver to pull forward, straighten up and reverse back into the middle (straight on) lane. Reversing is something not natural to a Chinese driver and usually requires two or three external "assistants". The car duly completed the manoeuvre and was made to drive across the junction. The copper now turned his attention to a flat-bed pick-up truck in the right turn lane. Documents were demanded of the driver and then the officer strutted to the load bed to count the bodies packed therein. I stopped at 10, because we were moving off by now, but it is a regular thing for trucks to have men and women packed in like cattle.

Wednesday, 10th May 2006
This coming Sunday is the Shanghai Moto GP, motorcycle racing, the Formula 1 of the two-wheeled world. There is a good dozen of us at work interested in bikes, so I began arranging logistics.

Then out of the blue came an "engineer" with a question. "What was he on about?" I thought as he walked away. He had asked about a specification for some writing moulded onto the top of an engine cover. Well that depends on what you write, I told him (dimensions, font, etc.) and he seemed even more confused (not unusual here). I told him to use the same specification as the one which covered the lettering on the lower half of the moulding. He explained that he did not like that script, so I suggested he changed it. He then repeated the original question. Sometimes we are at the opposite ends of the communication spectrum. He asked me for pictures of an earlier cover which had "Rover" moulded in the now blank space. "Why would you want to have Rover there? I asked. He didn't, but still wanted the details about the lettering.

Someone asked me how long I had been in the industry and I proudly replied, "Twenty-five years!" I hoped that this assertion of a quarter of a century of knowledge would elicit a deep and meaningful session, but it was just a polite or nosey enquiry. Perhaps this frightened the questioner, but I doubt it.

The evening was to be a bus ride home in the sunshine (but stood up) with Dr Diesel and we enjoyed our 14km ride for RMB3/20p. The Doctor said he had been on one bus where it was so packed that the driver could not re-open the doors at a stop. Someone shouted from the bus to passengers wanting to come aboard that they had to kick the doors to "assist" them to open. The drivers' motto seems to be "We never knowingly leave anyone behind". More light was shed on this at buttie-time today, when we had been discussing bus travel and the story was that the drivers are paid by the number of passengers they cram in. Absurd, but it fits in and explains why they cut each other up, race between stops and blare their air-horns at one another, slower traffic and indeed anyone in the way.

For a change, the bus did seem to have some oil in its transmission and back axle, but there was something serious banging about under the front floor and the engine was squealing away. Never mind, it was still moving and could carry masses of people.

Thursday, 11th May 2006
A couple of the long-termers are taking closely taught Chinese lessons and reveal that the language is very short on certain words. Chinese has no tenses as we understand, using modifiers to give a sense of past or future. There is no conjugation of verbs and only one word, which we would understand as

the infinitive used in all cases. There are no cases for nouns and little male/female distinction. A simple phrase such as "If I had not taken my coat, I would have been wet" would flummox them completely. If one thinks in one's own mother tongue, then if Chinese has no future tense as we understand, no wonder they seem to have trouble planning! We believe that our colleagues think we are really stupid as we cannot understand Chinese, and they play on it.

Tonight I left work on my tod on the 573 bus, (spotting a passing male cyclist still wearing long johns in 27°C temperature!) which was driven fairly well by a horn-happy bloke, who had probably had his anti-depressant drugs for the day; he seemed quite laid-back apart from his horn-finger.

I was considering walking down the Da Dao to a new café for tea, but ended up being super-lazy and brave at the same time. I ventured into the newly re-signed "Western-style food" restaurant, which is the same place where breakfast is taken. In the evening, I have never seen anyone go in there, except for locals at big organised events. It usually seems deserted. So I felt that I would brighten up the place a bit being the "Lone diner" and went in. I was about to pick up a plate and walk around the tureens as one does in the morning, but the girl spoke a quiet "Mayo", (literally "don't do"), and gave me a "Table d'haut" menu. The "Curried beef with egg and bread" looked promising, so for RMB23/£1.55 I thought it could be OK, so I ordered and sat down.

What came was a plate of chopped onions with a fried egg, a plate with two small pieces of a baguette toasted and a pudding-sized bowl of about 2 litres capacity, filled with thin curry water, a mountain of spaghetti and lumps of beef. The waitress then helpfully proffered chop sticks to eat this unlikely combination – later on I demonstrated the correct and logical tools with which to eat strings of pasta – a spoon and fork. Naturally she just laughed. Have you ever tried to consume spaghetti with pointed sticks?

Not a good meal really, for a chap who should avoid wheat and can have bad breath consuming mint. Still, I was on my own and hungry; I would monitor the consequences.

As I was dining, a man with two small children came in, sounding German, but speaking English to the two infants, one of whom was in a pushchair. It took him a full five minutes to make the three waitresses and one chef understand (or at least I think he did) that he wanted chicken with rice, but in two separate piles on the plate. Undaunted (must be the Teutonic blood), he then tried to make them understand his need for a glass of water and "a piece of bread, not toast". These are simple needs – I had received my (warm) water as I waited, despite not asking for one! In order to ensure that the bread was not engulfed in flame as mine had been, judging by the colour, he had to walk into the kitchen and rescue a slice on its way to the blowtorch, or whatever welding equipment they use to toast the bread. He wisely used the journey to avail himself of a drink from the fridge, as asking for an orange was obviously going to be a long job. I left just after his eldest infant had hurled a pot to the floor, smashing it in fine style. I only went in for a simple meal and came out badly fed but amused.

Friday, 12th May 2006 (thirty days to go before I deport myself)
Amusing translations pop up all the time – here is one for a Sales Department Manager's job:

'Sales department manager: Often lucky peak Welcome the national new old user to come to discuss the service
The company pledges: If the expensive unit comes our place not to buy the arrival of shipment, my company hopes to undertake all economies loses'.

Now why don't they ask some nice English person to translate into the Queen's best? Should we offer? The Government wants to eradicate poor translation in advance if the Olympics.

Friday evening promised to be very agreeable; meeting Mr and Mrs Rolf, Native and Frau for a meal at "The Moon River" diner. This is a new American-style place within "Thumbs Plaza", a complex of restaurants, where the architects have really tried to create something Western, but with a Shanghai flavour. The diner is run by a genial tubby American, but what I could not work out was why within an American diner, with the first item on the menu being "Eggs Benedict", there was an MZ motorcycle bracketed to the wall.

This is a two-stroke single 250cc machine, which probably never entered the States as it would have been outlawed, being two stroke and made the wrong side of the old Iron Curtain! It was also at head-gouging height, should one be silly enough to stand up under it and catch one's scalp on the brake lever!

Another odd thing was the ice-cubes in the urinal! What were they there for? Naturally they dissolved with urinal use; very satisfying and very childish. We have seen this before here, but is not quite as weird as the "massage bar" in town, where one receives a massage whilst drinking, and apparently continues the massage in the lavatory, when stood at the urinal, where a flunky pops along behind and administers the treatment. So surprised was one of the lads that he turned around and soaked the masseur's shoes!

It was good to see Rolf again, as he is now stationed on his own in the new engine plant as it fills up with equipment. But did the Chinese bother to clear the floor of years of dust before putting brand new, expensive equipment upon it? No. Did they then start to dig up the floor? Yes. For an engine plant, cleanliness is the first and most important issue. Dirt destroys engines. Back in the UK, visitors were always impressed with how clean we kept our building, despite its age. It is a lesson they need to learn and they can do it, because other plants in their group are clean.

We retired, *chez Native,* as I was keen to attack a bottle of Chivas Regal, which had been delivered to the office for me as recompense from my travel agent, Frank, for sending me to the wrong airport on his itinerary. What customer service! I shall recommend them again.

Saturday, 13th May 2006

As I had arranged tickets for the weekend's motorcycle Moto GP, it was a shame to waste the stub for today's practice, so I set off to watch. I decided to go there using the public transport to see if it worked. I used the Pudong Ave. underground station, which is one of the new ones with sliding doors in a full screen across the tracks, like some of the Docklands stations in London. There were two places I could catch the free shuttle service to the circuit and I was determined to see if this magnificent piece of Chinese organisation would work.

It would have helped if I had organised *myself* properly, read the timetable and set off earlier. The journey to the pick-up point was a lot longer than I imagined and by the time I arrived and spent ages trying to find the buses, the service had finished for the day at 12.00 noon! Dopey, or what?! In my defence, it would have been much quicker if I had gone to the other pick-up point, as I discovered later. We have often found local advice to be way out (the Pent-Ox receptionist had advised me badly). So I took a taxi to the circuit, which cost me RMB150, including motorway tolls.

Once at the circuit, I remembered the layout, but was amazed at the quiet, empty stands. There was no-one there! Fortunately, it was cool, so I did not need to worry about the sun; in fact it rained a bit during the first part of the 500 session. The noise of the bikes was amazing and the stand for which we had tickets was by turn 1, at the end of the start/finish straight; the one with the big BMW badge and the almost 360° turn around it. I sat there mulling over the transformation of swamp-land to track, and the two years it took to build. There is still evidence of the swamps around the circuit.

The young Spaniard, Pedrosa had put in a blistering performance as one of the youngest riders, (if not *the* youngest at 20 years old! He is just older than my son!) He was pipped to pole by Texan Colin Edwards, who was having a good day's work. A small screen on the infield showed the latest results and on race day was to be useful in relaying the action from the far side of the track.

I enjoyed myself as "Billy-no-mates" (a loner) for the afternoon, but what I would have given for a little company, such as my son or the members from the BMCC at home (Bromsgrove Motorcycle Club).

I managed to catch the shuttle coach back to Shanghai Stadium and work my way back to the apartment, and then went out shopping for a hard drive for my boss, and haggling with the stony faces in Cyber Mart, the electronics market. One of the risks of cycling the way I do is "dodging the flob" as fellow cyclists spit whilst cycling along. I must be lucky not to have been splattered so far.

Feeling that a pair of cheap binoculars would be useful at the track, I sped off down Jinling Lu, across the ten-lane junction that is under the Chengdu elevated section of the inner ring road, and headed for the Xiangyang market. I haggled for some binoculars, a case and a laser pointer/torch for RMB100/£7. I probably paid too much, but I was in a hurry as I had not eaten yet.

On the motorcycling theme, other amusing stories happen to all of us here, almost every day; if something funny does not happen in a day, then you have been asleep or wandering around with eyes shut. One such tale was the one about taking four hours *not* to change two exhaust silencers on two scooters! These are slip-off, slip-on silencers which only need one pinch bolt and one bracket undoing. In order to replace the silencer with the "Performance" part, three holes in a bracket require to be elongated, the work of a few minutes with a drill or appropriate file and a vice in which to hold the part. However, this is China and the vice was the edge of the kerb and the drill might as well have been a six-inch nail, as it was so blunt; but this device's failure to cut was not recognised by the operator.

Previous to this, a big-bore kit had been fitted to the same machines. The cylinder barrel and piston arrived and the shop assistant attempted to insert the piston into its bore. For those of you who have never done this before, it is an operation requiring either the right tool, to compress the cast-iron sprung rings, or some strong fingers. It is vital to prevent the rings, which are hard and very brittle, from breaking by easing them gently into the bore of the cylinder barrel. In a production environment, we use a sleeve with a generous tapering lead to squeeze the rings into place. In the workshop, there are tools to assist and it is possible to use thin steel strips or "feeler gauges" to squeeze the rings. In Chinese scooter shops, they use a few hacksaw blades, the odd feeler gauge and then when all else fails, bash it on the pavement. Naturally, the rings broke and the liner cracked. The parts were later hurled back at the hapless supplier representative as being no good, despite tell-tale concrete dust on the liner and piston skirts!

Other percussive engineering stories abound here. A "Chassis engineer" was seen with a hammer, bashing the front damper and spring assembly on the floor to make it fit, with more tell-tale concrete dust marks. We have all seen percussive engineering with Birmingham micro-adjustment sticks (big hammers) performed on parts at home, but at least there the person doing it usually either knows they are doing wrong, or can be reasoned with via education or just simply disciplined for being a thug.

Pollution is a real problem in any developing economy; Britain has polluted its fair share of rivers, sea water, ground and air, but we now all know better and we do have access to the right disposal places. Here, many people are so poor they have more pressing needs than saving the planet. Pollution equipment is often monitored by the authorities, but may be turned off as soon as the inspection is passed because being clean is often costly. As I flew over Beijing, one could hardly see the ground until the plane dropped really low, due to a brown scum of dust and other particles across the sky.

One colleague's girlfriend, who we'll call Belle because she is concerned about her waist, (which is perfect), has had a medical at which she was advised to stop smoking. She replied that she did not, but it was the effect of living in this nation's capital.

There are some German cities which will close to traffic should the pollution index rise above a certain level. This level is itself 300 times lower than the current level in Beijing.

We still go on the odd factory visit (it is not in the culture here to regularly visit suppliers) and in one the team was shown proudly around the metrology room, with banks of new measuring equipment on the tables. None of it was, however, plugged in. In a similar situation at another plant, the UK visitors were shown into another measurement facility. Not only were the instruments not plugged in, there were no sockets in the room to facilitate this supply of essential power! Our check lists ask us to look for certain types of equipment to be in place, but not to conduct an IEE Wiring Regulations study! It pays to have eyes everywhere and to question everything.

Another gem is our continual insistence upon the use of the correct fluid in automatic transmissions. These auto boxes are complex highly engineered hydraulic devices, depending for their smooth function upon a very specific type of oil. We insisted that the local team buy some, but it is expensive, so they refused. We reminded them repeatedly that use of the wrong fluid would cause severe problems in the boxes, maybe even complete failure, which as the cars were to be tested at a remote location could prove expensive. We suggested that having the right oil was preferable to changing gearboxes in minus temperatures, but they still insist upon not buying any. When we suggested draining oil from some spare boxes to then use on the test cars, they even dismissed this and poured it away! Why do these people ignore our advice, which they are paying for handsomely? Their own engineer (with a whole 6 month's experience) had said we do not need the special oil!

Sunday, 14th May 2006
Today was Moto GP day at the Shanghai circuit and we had arranged a mini-bus and driver to convey us the hour-long trip. We met him at

Diamond Court and as he spoke no English, Jonas, one of the eternally helpful bell-boys, resplendent in his red uniform, stepped in to translate. We explained that there were three to pick up from Shimao Lakeside, and we knew the way, but he insisted upon riding shotgun. We even had a Shimao resident in the bus, who does know where he lives. Nothing was going to stop Jonas from helping, which is an endearing and often annoying feature of our hosts.

We turned left out of DC onto Biyun Lu and took off down the road. We had only driven the short distance to Carrefour when he slowed to a crawl. We all protested and asked why, but it appeared as if the bell-boy was mistaken in knowing where Shimao lay! We issued instructions in Chinese for the place, which were ignored by the driver repeatedly until the bell-boy had spoken to us and then translated for the driver's benefit again.

We collected the others and had to insist upon dropping the bell-boy off. Perhaps we misunderstood him and he wanted to skive for an hour! We had only travelled 500 metres when the driver's mobile rang and he stopped in the middle of the road and answered, following the call with a sudden U-turn and headed back to DC. Sadly, in the 500 metres, he had forgotten the way there and following our repeated appeals made an incredibly dangerous 270° turn, nearly splatting a taxi and driving right across a busy junction. We were by now wondering what the problem was and whether we would arrive in one piece or not. He then tried to turn into the "No Entry" of DC, but we stopped that little game and directed him to the entrance. He kept sticking one finger in the air and shouting "one more!", but I was (as organiser) racking my brain as to who we had left behind. We drove round the back of the Court and there was a lonesome European. No-one recognised him. It turned out that he had heard a bus was going to the circuit and as we had a spare seat the bell-boy had ordered the about-turn!

This was a good start to the journey and it became readily apparent that the mini-bus was either sat on its bump-stops at the rear or had no suspension or damping to speak of. It was as rough as they come, but transport. The driver had kindly supplied water bottles too.

Unlike any trip to a UK or European circuit, there were no lines of bikes pulling stunts, showing off or simply being cool. There was no queue to gain entry and no atmosphere at all. When we did spot a decent bike (we probably saw ten at most) there were excited shouts! We are so starved of bike hardware here in scooter world.

The circuit has plenty of space and concrete around it so there was an impromptu display of stunts such as wheelies, stoppies (balancing the bike on the front wheel), spinning the bikes around the rider's leg and so on. Back home this would have been broken up by the H&S police, if it had even been allowed to start, but here there were no barriers and people inches from smoking back tyres.

Once seated in our mostly empty stand seats, we had a fantastic view of the start/finish straight, the exit of the pit lane and the huge turn in front of us, which then fell into a goose-neck and down hill under a bridge. We watched the 125 and 250 races from here, not believing how the riders could be flying full tilt along the straight and then not appear to brake before dropping onto their right side and knee into the massive corner.

In the 125 race, there were elbows and knees banging as usual, and they stormed off like angry bees, but again, how did they make the bend? In the end, it was Kallio (KTM), Pasini (Aprillia) and Bautista (Aprillia).

The 250 race was naturally noisier and faster, with some close racing and another Aprillia win, with Barbarosa dominant as he had been in practice, followed by Dowizioso (Honda) and third Aoyama (KTM).

We moved for the main 500cc race into a stand nearer the track and the pits, which was a superb spot. The noise for the 500s was amazing, with Honda V5 engines and Ducati twins bellowing out their tunes – all music to our ears. (Photo p.XXX).

We were sat by some Americans, which is fine but why do they have to re-write history? As you know, dear reader, I have no real problem with Americans, except for the fact that they seem to only be happy when the streets are full of "fast food" restaurants and look like downtown Chicago. Like many nationalities, they are OK in small doses; too many Brits and its not long before there are drunks in the gutter, too many French and there is a demo or riot and so on. It is the desire to change history which really grates. Hollywood makes a great habit of this, with no apology or credit to those who really made the history in the first place. In this case, the race was being led (unusually) by Colin Edwards, the "Texas Tornado". He was followed by a rapidly closing young Spaniard, 20 year old Dani Pedrosa and then by two more Americans, John Hopkins and Nicky Hayden. Our local red-neck supporter was jumping up and down, whooping and hollering away with many a "Yi-hah" shouting "USA, USA, 1-2-3. Go USA". We all grinned at a) his grasp of the race situation being played out right in front of us and b) his mathematical skills.

In the 500 race, we were all blown away by champion Valentino Rossi's scything through the field; at one point he was making up three places per lap, then two, before he suffered problems and had to retire. He thought he had a chunk missing from his rear tyre, pitted to change on lap 17, and went out again to find it was the front. What a showman – on the warm-up lap he exited the pits and stood on his pegs to wave at the tiny crowd. There is a man who knows how to appeal to his supporters.

It was such a good day, the racing was tight and fast, and I still do not know how those guys made it around the bend at such speed, but we saw them! The start was as usual a sensual overload, with colour, noise, speed, the air torn apart by exhausts and the smell of unburnt hydrocarbons in the Shanghai spring sunshine.

Sadly, as the racing atmosphere is provided generally by the fans, there being so few of us (and no-one even had an air-horn), that there was little atmosphere at all. The local radio reported that the Moto GP circus may by-pass China next year as they did not make any money. The riders were out there risking their necks for a handful of fans. I took a photograph of one Chinese family who enjoyed a long picnic on the grass below our stand throughout the whole of the 250 race! It was typical Chinese food; loads of fruit and vegetables, some cakes and drinks, the women in their horrible short pop-socks and high-heels, the men in their suits and smoking.

In the end the result was Dani Pedrosa (Honda), Nicky Hayden (Honda), Colin Edwards (Yamaha) and John Hopkins (Suzuki), who gave himself and the Rizla team their best result for ages. Pedrosa was only in his fourth race at this level.

There just is not the grass-roots motorcycling interest here. We saw easily twenty bikes over 250cc all day in the car park, so you can compare that with the thousands which turn up in the UK, US and Europe. Someone said that the Shanghai authorities have only issued 100 big bike licences recently and have stopped issuing any more because so many of the 100 are already dead. Makes you think, doesn't it? Please be careful on your bikes especially in China.

Monday 15th May 2006

With no new appointed team leader for us Brits, Visa took the chair, although as he had been away on holiday, he had little to tell. If someone came in to these meetings several months apart, they could be excused for thinking that time had not moved on, as many of the same issues (tax, health insurance, food at lunch-time) had not been sorted out. We had the usual amusing debates and people offering opinions, but few facts – are we becoming Chinese?

A classic at lunch-time was the sight of a cockroach escaping from Tup's sandwich tray. He tried to swat it, missed and it landed on the floor where a deft stamp consigned it to the insect afterlife. Instead of being totally repulsed, the enigmatic bearded Tup examined his buttie for further invertebrates and finding none, consumed the rest of his lunch. The lad was obviously hungry. We looked on in amazement, as this is the second such creature, although the first live one, in our lunches provided by the Mawdesley.

It is about time we had a non-job of the day, so here is one from Rolf. He asked me "how many Chinese displays of flowers on those wicker/bamboo stands does it take to open a motor accessory shop? – Answer – 120!" One hundred and twenty flower displays for a shop catering mainly to men. This could surely only happen here. His next question was "How many Chinese does it take to operate an *automatic* car-wash at its Grand Opening? – Answer – 16!" In China there are jobs for everybody; they provide a full service, not one spotty adolescent who shakes his head if the car-wash breaks on the second vehicle because it has a roof-rack and a tow-bar. To cap it all, the signs outside proclaimed "Autro.com" and "Autromobile", although later in the day the errant letters had been removed.

Tuesday, 16th May 2006

Today provided much chance for amusement as it transpires that (allowing for translational errors) the Company has "normalised" Chinese emloyees' salaries and there have been winners and losers. One chap has seen his salary cut to a quarter of its previous level and he is understandably not a happy bunny. He had vented his spleen via an open e-mail to all. This was frowned upon and a Boss just stood up with no real warning and read a hasty communiqué from HR about the ill-advised nature of such slants at one's employer. This caused the most excitement we have ever heard. There must have been one in our office who was aggrieved, as he was very vocal and his face full of vitriol. I stood up and told them that it was pointless to rant at the Boss, as he was just the messenger. This produced a few laughs and seemed to coincide with the break up of a near-riot.

In another of those Chinese moments, with clear physical evidence a child could see, we were having massive trouble getting through. The component was shouting its message loud and clear to us and as we had seen this problem back in the UK and solved it completely, we felt we could help before it became a big production and Warranty issue. Pushing water up hill must be easier. All we wanted was for the component, a pulley, to be made round and flat across its width. Why, oh why had the supplier chosen to mould it the way it had? The obvious way to mould a pulley is in two halves, split across the edge of the belt running surface. Not here, oh, no; it had been split in two halves like one might cut a cake, across a diameter. There must be easier ways to make a living.

Lunch brought the spectacle of humble staff from the Mawdesley, apologising about the extra, living protein in Tup's lunch yesterday and hoping that two bottles of Coke would help us to forget the image of the running roach. The meal was eaten to the sounds of crunching effects and insect jokes. Some could not stand it and left.

After dinner in the Mawdesley, the original manageress is now back in the driving seat, as Dennis and Nelson have been moved on or out and a much brighter, quieter bar greeted us, with many new, but overall less faces. As we were on our second drink, we were invited to sit down for a free "welcome back to Shanghai meal!" Someone was feeling guilty about roaches in the bacon sandwiches. It was all too much and I had to have a walk to the new DVD shop at Shimao just to shake some of the food down. Naturally, I was recognised in the shop; why should I not be in this city of seventeen million people? The girl who did see me had given me my "VIP Card" in the DVD shop on Pudong Da Dao where I live!

The night was very noisy – the dockers were at it again loading bags of cement. I was so frustrated; I stood on my balcony screaming abuse at them, berating them for making so much unnecessary noise, which must have deafened them too. It was way over 90db for me, I reckon; it certainly drowned out the TV at one point. I have whined about this before; it was the usual issue of driving along the back road closest to me, where the surface is broken and then up towards the working pile. The noise was like someone banging an empty skip with a steel bar – the tug driver must have been deafened; I was! Someone must have told him that the process is to drive along the back, so he does. The process must be followed.

Chapter 11

AUDIT SKIPPING, TIDDLING TIPS

AND WATERTOWN TRIPS

Wednesday, 17th May 2006

New bars to visit are often a topic of conversation. What suits one does not, however, suit all. I prefer Jenny's, where no-one bothers you beyond the normal courtesies, and there are no Karaoke machines, rooms upstairs or girls trying to have you buy them drinks, rubbing your arm and saying how handsome you are. I know I am not, and I find it a bit strange having girls touch me like that; it can be quite enjoyable, but it is all an illusion and completely false, but it is their job to extract money from you. My job is to spend my money on my own wife; at least she's honest enough about my looks and doesn't cost a bomb. I was rumbled once in the early days of my time here, had my ego stroked as well as my arm and it cost me dearly. My drink was spiked and two "heavies" turned up at bill time, so I lost. Beware as in these circumstances, alcohol can be charged by the millilitre!

Other discussions often come down to the subject of driving. Even those of us who have been here over a year are still amazed at the lack of skill, observation and surfeit of luck that these people have on the roads. Why are the gutters not lined with injured pedestrians? They ride bikes and scooters on the pavement and a habit which really appals me is that of riding or driving at night with no lights on.

Rolf reported an incident with a woman delivering two bottles of gas on a bicycle, (obviously with no brakes) that was cut up by his taxi-driver and she had to dismount the bike to brake with her feet and try and stop the heavily-laden velocipede from hitting the taxi. Rolf said that woman, bottles and bike ended up in a heap inches from his door. It always happens on his side! She didn't become particularly irate; she had probably had it happen before and viewed it as her turn again, perhaps.

Rumble turned up today to show me a wrapper from an ice-lolly. The picture on the front was of sweet garden peas. This is indeed what it tasted of and the colour was bang on, apparently! I believe there are sweet corn flavoured ones too. I think they will go on the "Miss" pile, thanks.

He was in a bar last night with DIY, and Flat-bed wanting a quiet drink and within seconds the girl serving had opened with the usual gambit (they all seem to have a similar script) – "I've seen you before". She hadn't, as they had never been there before, but she gave them both the same treatment. This was followed up by the rest of the sentence, which she must have been practising – "in my dreams". The boys were too polite and not keen to enquire further as to the nature of her sleep-time thoughts.

The day passed quietly, although I believe in my absence at lunch-time there was another round of arguments about the salary normalising.

From the taxi today, I could barely see the wheels of a lorry in the smoky distance. When we neared the over-loaded blue tipper truck, the driver must have accelerated (well, pressed the throttle pedal; these vehicles are so slow) and the back of the vehicle almost disappeared in a haze of thick, black soot. At 20 metres distance, the wheels were completely obscured by the smoke. I will not miss this aspect of Chinese life. Even the locals are complaining now, and the City does have plans in place to curb this menace.

The news is full of typhoon Chenga, which is ripping up from Hainan Island and the Philippines, where it has killed thirty-some people and is heading our way. This is the first one of the season and is a real deadly mix of wind and rain. It has already claimed eleven people on the mainland; the devastation is enormous.

Other interesting items are the completion ahead of schedule of the 3 Gorges Dam. The last massive flood-gate will slide into to place tomorrow and the last few thousand cubic metres of concrete are being poured as I write. It will generate 80 billion kWhr per year, enough to power the lights in Shanghai, perhaps.

The Sino/Japanese talks about the contentious South China Seas gas reserves have broken down again. International Law has it that the gas belongs to China, but that of course is not good enough as far as the Japanese go. A country like theirs, with no real natural resources needs all it can grab.

Thursday, 18th May 2006

I found Post, my new boss and Gap were running a course today for vehicle auditors, so as things were slack in my office, I asked if I could observe, as there was every chance of learning something. The quality auditor in a car company can be the most important defender of quality standards, like the team headed by the venerable Tony Wood in Powertrain, or the powerful QZ *mannschaft* in BMW.

We had a dry run through the audit process, from selecting the car, recording its details, the pass through the water ingress test and on to the checking of the car itself. We then moved on to the vehicle workshop for a demonstration of the process in real time and a chance for the local auditors to have a go. One of them was already an auditor from VW, but we were keen to see how good he really was. To be fair, he asked some good questions and when Gap said he should be able to do one part of the audit in ten minutes, the chap timed him! In the end he took 17 minutes, but it has been some time since he has completed one.

I have spent a few days in the workshop, but this one became more and more bizarre as the day wore on. The door to the shop is a steel roller-shutter, which is slow in operation and incredibly noisy, sounding like a giant set of finger-nails scraping down a board. This rose slowly to admit one of the prototype cars built over here. The noise of the door was deafening, and the car purred to a halt next to us, wipers still going. Two guys leapt out, opened the bonnet, connected a meter and poked about hopefully. They set the revs to about 3,000rpm and held it there. At this point, Gap was starting to have to raise his voice.

The next interruption was the raising of the door again to admit the works van, which chugged in and sat with its engine running for a few moments next to us, dripping rainwater. By now, the smell of hydro-carbons and other fumes in the air was becoming rather heavy.

We were then joined in the workshop by a troupe of youngsters and one older lady, who proceeded to assemble a skipping rope and two teams jumping through said rope as it was rotated. I was aghast, and had to ask the translator what on earth was going on. She replied that they were to feature in a marketing promotion for the company and would demonstrate youthfulness, team-play and their skipping prowess. Having watched them for a while, I reckoned that they needed lots more practice. What was amazing was that no local seemed to find this at all unusual.

The door had only just groaned shut when it was on the way up again, this time to allow an early mark one VW Santana to roll in, chugging away and really belching out exhaust gases, laced with unburnt hydro-carbons from its manually choked engine. At this point, Clegg walked in, drew himself up at the sight of the skippers in his workshop, told me not to worry about my health and went on to ask how he was expected to build cars in such an environment.

The mark one was kept running for a while, stinking the place out and I could feel my brain cells being poisoned as I stood there. Gap bravely continued, his voice by now at maximum volume without shouting. He was so professional. The driver of the Santana now proceeded to attempt a "U" turn in the workshop. I watched, willing him to hit one of the big pillars, knowing he would, being a local. I was rewarded with a big crunching sound as he bounced off an unforgiving lump of concrete. Another worker leapt out of the office and proffered assistance. This helped to complete the turn without fetching down the ceiling. They then left the smoking wreck running, whilst they filled it with spare wheels! I was seconds away from walking over; and berating them suitably for being uncaring, when thankfully the key was turned and the smoking VW was silenced.

Friday, 19th May 2006

These are a couple of amusing notices for the record, reproduced verbatim. One is an invitation to go dragon boat racing, the other was posted in our apartment:

iMandarin Dragon Boat Festival Race,

The Dragon Boat Race is part of a larger Chinese cultural tradition that goes back 2,400 years. iMandarin Training Center holds the third Dragon Boat Festival for you and your friends. Why don't you **Learn something about the Chinese folk custom and enjoy the splashy sport and team spirit!**

Totally under the Chinese traditional atmosphere, avoid city stress and relax yourself, have more funs and refresh yourself. **Come on, seat limited, register in a hurry!!!**

Actually, I fancy a go, but will need a couple of cans of evil cola to kill off any bacteria from the water.

In our apartment was this:

Dear Residents,

Because it is becoming more terrible with typhoon now. Please take care of your room facility such as windows, gas, electricity and tap if you would out this period time.

Please don't be hesitated to dial the following telephone numbers if you have any problem.

I will try not to be hesitated.............

The Test Meeting was the usual weekly opportunity to see how the project was progressing. The man in overall charge came into the meeting, an hour after it began, set his (tiny) note-book down and his mobile went, so off he went again for a further ten minutes!

Back in the UK, a person at this level would be banging the table (really or figuratively), ensuring that everyone realised his or her responsibilities. Over here, table banging would be viewed very dimly.

As usual, it seemed to be one man asking for support and receiving very little. I did not feel any heat or tension as there would be back home. I have sat in meetings with Production Managers in particular, who would use all manner of abuse, taunts, threats, the doubting of one's parentage, offers of dubious sexual acts or favours, just to ensure people realised that the job must be done properly.

Rolf is at the new factory where the line is being installed. He is impressed by the speed at which it is being done, if not the dusty conditions in which it is being erected. He is also impressed with the fact that "his" toilet is being constructed. He and Spit were concerned about the "hole in the floor" type of facility which was not to their rather genteel liking and also that the food was of dubious quality and often cold. Cold drinks were not plentiful, either. So a fridge and microwave have been installed in Spit's office and even Rolf's chair was delivered as he could not get himself comfortable in the cheapo ones at the factory. So occasionally we are looked after and complaints are acted upon. His lunch was brought in by one of the ladies the other day, followed by a "waiter" in shirt, waistcoat and dickey bow, bearing his burger and chips! Now he would never have had treatment like that in Longbridge.

Back to the Test Meeting again, very few notes were taken, the agenda was there, but I could not follow it, no minutes were issued and no-one came in to present facts; it was more like a conversation. The only heat was provided by yours truly. As I entered the room, I noticed that two senior guys were smoking – against Company rules. I pointed at them and loudly stated "They are smoking!" In an instant the evil sticks were extinguished and the cap put on the "ashtray" which is an old tin of tea, but still with a plastic cap, full of dog-ends. I often crush them and throw them away, but one can become covered in ash!

My interpreter this time was not the usual Oil but the lovely, down-trodden Kelly, whose technical knowledge and interest in the meeting is much greater, so I understood a lot more about what was going on, and did not have to keep asking. She still "filtered" bits I should not hear, I am sure. As in a meeting anywhere, it is some of the asides which really give an impression of people's feelings and intentions and I could not catch these; she probably missed some too. It is so much easier to understand when the interpreter is good and willing (Kelly), not playing with her mobile phone (Oil), otherwise thinking of her out-of-work interests or stroking her leg absently.

It is a truth here, that if a boss is paid at one level, his team are paid commensurate with that. If a boss is considered superior in some way, she/he and the team are rewarded similarly. The current issue of pay and "Normalising" is still rippling through the place, with Hooray and Test-Bed still in deep depression – the latter was even seen filling in a GM application form! I hope he is successful, but he still does not know much about engineering. His name comes from the fact that he had to ask me what a test-bed looked like!

Friday night's entertainment was a meal with Frau, Doo, Native (barely better from his nasty Shanghai cough) and the Doc. We dined at the "Old Shanghai" and as usual, it was good food, great service and smiles all round. We virtually cleared all the plates (very un-Chinese) and had a sufficiency. After this we strolled down to the promenade to admire the illuminated Bund across the river, with new laser lights off one of the old bank buildings stabbing out like green fingers from the top. I began humming the "Close

Encounters" theme, as it looked so much like "they" had landed on the roof. Loads of people were out, giving the place its atmosphere and something my home town cannot compete with. I will miss this free sight hugely when I've gone. (Photo p.VIII).

We pottered along to the Paulaner bar, as the Doc wanted to see some pretty Philippino girls (though he hotly denied this) and we were greeted by Armand, the manager as the VIPs that we are! We were ushered to share a table with our old friend Manfred. It was good to see him again, such an amazingly well-travelled man. From a village of 4,000 people near Salzburg, here he is, 27 years in Shanghai, an Indonesian wife and daughters with four nationalities (two from their parents, one from their place of birth and one from Pittsburgh, where they live).

He flies all over China and the East, with he says, a very loyal and hard-working set of employees – the single men will turn up at the weekends and work for free! He has people who have been with him for 10 and 20 years. He remembers the time when he first came to Shanghai and he had to have an interpreter, a Party Official shadow and a chauffeur, even when there was no car! The country has changed, although as I keep observing, Shanghai and the cities are not wholly representative of the country, where 800 million of the people are peasants.

I have to admit, I'm becoming a little bored with the Paulaner and its expensive drinks, and I'd like to see some different places before I hang up my visa.

As usual, there were the amusing Chinese "dancers" gyrating to some rhythm other than the one I was listening to; but I am no twinkle-toes, so I suppose I should not comment, but why not, as it is so funny? There was a fashionably hip local Shanghai girl, very full of herself, coolly dancing by her table, her body language saying "look at me", but *out of time!* So she collected no cool points whatsoever. There were some very competent Westerners giving it some jive, and they were smooth as silk on the floor, with what appeared to be local ladies who were good too.

The Doc and I were the last to leave and headed for the midnight bus, but just missed it at the ferry terminal. So we stood around in the balmy evening air talking about work and China, which fascinates us both. He is becoming something of an expert on the bus system and selects a new destination to visit each weekend. Once on the bus, we had one of those Shanghai moments, where a local plastic bottle collector was sat on the bus, playing "Scarboro' Fair" on his flute. He was looking appealingly at us for loose change, I think.

Saturday, 20th May 2006

To me, summer has come. Last night was the first when I could not settle down under the duvet and be comfortable, so it is time to dispense with this cover and make do with a sheet or my cotton dressing-gown (Chinese, of course). It is close and hot.

It felt like a laze around, write and shop sort of day, but I only left the apartment after mid-day. The heat hit like a steam iron. I cycled slowly for me (still quicker than most locals) down to the ferry and across to "Best Friend's Music" for some more guitar supplies for my son. A woman was cycling along with an umbrella as a parasol, supplies of more portable shade behind her on the bike. A young man in plastic pink flip-flops pedalled a tricycle along with a young girl in the load-space at the back – take your girl for a spin on the work's trike! It is amazing what these people carry – Clegg saw a delivery boy with some mouldings over his shoulder which were drooping so much that he had to be very careful not to let them catch on the road. He probably had no brakes, either.

When I found the new "Ka-De" shop, you could tell that there were Americans inside, as outside were waiting their drivers in large Buick Regals or people-carriers, engine and air-con running. That meant noisy people and possibly badly behaved kids within. I was to be disappointed, as that was exactly what I found.

When I left the cool confines of the shop, there was an MG TF in yellow in the street outside – a real car amongst all these fakes.

Passing by the park, there was the usual bevy of brides and wedding photographers, some of the girls wearing jeans/long johns underneath the pretty dresses and massive amounts of make-up. This is a very special day for a Chinese bride and very expensive. The more imaginative photographers and couples will visit a park or green space; others have been seen at Carrefour and outside the East-West! It is a whole day set aside for photography and make-up; there are rarely many guests and usually a poorly attentive groom. Many local girls complain about how inattentive and unromantic their counterparts are here.

I stopped at Jenny's for spring rolls, fresh orange and a photo of myself with the bar owner; she runs a clean, quiet place where one is not bothered, but the food is good and the sports channel always on the TV and the music hand-picked.

It was time to fulfil another North Face jackets order, so I went along and picked up four, with no need to haggle; she knows what I will pay. This could be the last time.

Once back it was time to shower and change, then out to Frau and Native's for dinner, with a noticeable temperature difference 30 floors up, where it is so much warmer in summer and cooler in winter. We had a very agreeable time together and Frau's own book is coming along well, perhaps I should ask her to illustrate this meagre offering?

Sunday, 21st May 2006 (21 days until I return home, but who is counting?)
I had another lazy start to the day, reading a good book and eventually cycled down to pick up the ferry near the new Jasper Tower this side of the OPT. It plies across the river north of Suzhou Creek and the city has a quite different atmosphere over that side, which is more Chinese, but less busy.

I was aiming for Qipu (pronounced *Shipu*) Lu, where we had been given to understand that there were very cheap clothes on sale. The route I took saw me struggling through throngs of shoppers, most of whom seemed to be walking towards me, so I tucked in behind some stupid woman driving my way! It was slow progress. I decided to take the opportunity to weigh my bike in preparation for shipping it.

This caused much amusement when I motioned to the owner of the weighing machine that I did not want to know my weight, but the bike's! Everyone around seemed amused or bemused – foreigners! I returned to the throng, but it was still slow behind Mrs Dopey, so I picked up my bike and carried it over the obstructions, behind some scaffolding and away. This also caused amusement, judging by the "Look at the foreigner" type comments I could barely understand.

When I finally found Qipu Lu, the road was up and awaiting new tarmac, barriered off and so sellers crowded on a thin line of tiled pavement with their wares. I wanted some goodies for my girls and hopefully I picked some appropriate gifts. The area showed massive contrasts, with really shabby buildings surrounded by a new mall plopped in the middle.

I dined alone, having tea in the new "Tête-à-Tête" café just up the Pudong Da Dao, where RMB45/£3 secured chicken with free small bones! I will never get used to the way they just chop chicken up on the bone and then cook it.

Monday, 22nd May 2006

There were the usual old recurring domestic issues to debate at the Team Meeting, and also project matters as cars were to be built and that was important.

As we were wrapping up, the Department Head popped his head through the door which was ajar, beckoned me out and muttered something, but "questions..... interview" was really all I heard. In his pen was a young man in a smart suit, who rose to greet me. I think I was introduced and the boss left. I assumed that I was to interview the chap for a role in the department, but I could be wrong. So I thought quickly, asked him some preliminary questions, ascertaining that he was 25, had a degree in Engineering from Tongi University in China and a Master's in Automotive Engineering from Bath in the UK, where he had studied.

In order to have something to talk around, I picked up a piston and connecting rod assembly and laid it on the desk. I also fetched a digital vernier calliper measuring device, so we could discuss quality and what it meant to him. It became apparent that he literally did not know what way up the assembly sat in the engine, or what it really did. He had never measured anything with decent kit, either. Bath University must be selling Master's degrees or giving them away. Perhaps I could attain one; something I had dismissed as unnecessary to my career years ago.

As the time came around for lunch (11.30 in this part of the world), I asked if he had a meal ticket, or needed a drink. He replied that he did not in either case, but I told him that I had a hot meal to eat and managed to find the only bloke left in the "Marie Celeste" office, who agreed to take him to the local restaurant, where all the locals eat. I told him that I would be back before him and would be sat at my desk.

Following an amusing telling of the story in the Brit's sandwich room, I waited for him to return. Although he was little more than useless to the project, he had a good attitude and his English was fluent. In these respects, he was as useful as some of the people already there. We sat and reviewed his project thesis, which was centred on the electronic control of suspension damper valves, for no less a client than Jaguar Cars. "Have you ever been to Jaguar, or spoke with anyone from the Company?" "No", he replied. "Ever been in a car plant or supplier factory in the UK?" "No", he said. This guy was all theory and computer skills, but no knowledge or experience of cars. I asked if he had a bicycle and did he do his own maintenance? He had sold his bike and did not have the tools or wherewithal to maintain a cycle. I countered that I had been fiddling with my own mechanical devices since I was about ten. I had lost count of the number of engines I had built. He was impressed, but that did not help his cause. This, I explained was the difference between UK engineers and Chinese.

His thesis was fairly boring, and could have come out of many a text book, but I believe he actually conducted the experiments himself, judging by his lack of enthusiasm about recording the data. Once I had exhausted my questions, the boss returned finally and we joined him to report. As I was describing what we had done and not making any qualitative judgement, I was closed down and the applicant was dismissed. The candidate assessment form was produced (it would have been useful to have had one before I started and in English) and we discussed the scoring. I did not believe we would take him on. Poor soul, but at least he knows what he needs to brush up on.

It is definitely coming up to summer – the water heater has not only been turned off, but it has been unplugged too! So if one needed hot water it's tough. The hot air hand-drier has also been de-commissioned! Official summer may start this week, as we look certain to have five consecutive days of average daytime temperatures over 22°C! Roll on the free ice-cream at 35°C plus. Maybe the blokes will dispense with the long johns and vests now the government has declared it officially summer.

As usual, Rolf had some amusing stories to tell from his "ex-communication" at the factory in Baoshan. "His" new toilet had been fitted and he was looking forward to giving it a trial run. He was hoping that a larger privacy screen might be grafted on now that his "throne" raised him up somewhat!

Tuesday, 23rd May 2006

The excitement today was signing-off test cars before they left the workshop. This is a traditional chore for engineers back home, as one needs to be as sure as possible that before an expensive test is commenced, that the vehicle is fit to begin. A sign-off sheet is provided with each car and any observations or rectification work is noted. If all is well, the sheet is duly endorsed by the engineer responsible for that part of the car.

We then road-tested the cars, which gave Native his first trip behind the wheel of a car in China since receiving his licence. We felt quite liberated, off on our own, with a great car, free fuel and a whole city to explore! It is amazing how quickly this place changes in character. One moment you're bowling along a wide six-lane highway, with manicured bushes and trees either side, the next creeping through what I must call a village scene, with stagnant pond, cramped housing and stalls (or people's front rooms!) selling anything from tricycles to hot water bottles, sunglasses, taps, DVDs and pyjamas (of course, for summer evening wear!). It was really great going as and where we wished; the difference in lifestyle between us two and the various trucks full of workers in the area was astonishing, but we can't change the way things are. At least they waved cheerfully at us – back home we'd have probably been given at least one finger gesture. Here they do not seem to feel open resentment across the wealth pools.

We quickly ascertained back at the "workshop" that the car was OK; no leaks. I use quotation marks around the word because there are very few pointers to the fact that vehicles are worked on there. The toilets are free of any running water to flush or wash and the smell is consequently over-powering. There are no paper towels or few other wipers for spills, and there are very few tools as these appear to be jealously guarded by the few "fitters" around. It is even hard to find a pen and paper in the "office". Perhaps it is a virtual workshop and I have not really been there. At least on this day there was no-one skipping. As for any of our local colleagues being there and learning from us as we investigated, we only had the benefit of two of them for a short while. This should have been a chance for loads of them to watch and learn.

Again it was a quiet night in the East-West. (Vegetarians, please skip this paragraph). It was a chance to hear more funny stories from the others, such as the local riding his scooter down the road with the carcass of a pig slit from throat to tail, split open and flapping on the seat behind the rider, trotters skipping along the tarmac. Blood was sprinkling around behind him. Food hygiene is not a Chinese strong point.

Welcome back veggies; sorry about that, but tales have to be told. Another amusing one was from Rolf and Spit who were commissioning (proving our equipment at a supplier) in Italy and had fifteen Chinese around one Italian machine tool demonstration engineer. He found it so trying that after a few days of this, being peered at, leered at, jeered and questioned endlessly, took himself to his sickbed! The exercise really needed four at the most, but no, fifteen had to be there and none of them had any clue at all what was going on.

Normally in the West, you generally pick a few of your best people, (not fifteen at once), who can learn the ropes and then follow the facility to your factory and instruct the others. Most sensible people follow similar principles.

However, as you may have gleaned from these pages, culturally we and the Chinese are poles apart and they must be much smarter than us, as they do things differently. After all, our company did go down the tubes and they are building theirs up! So their attitude to the vital commissioning phase is different; perhaps we had it wrong all these 100 years.

Wednesday, 24th May 2006

Mid-week already! It was time for a long-awaited conference call with a tax expert. We duly assembled in a brand new "conference room". Normal logic would have it that people are going to be talking and listening in such a room, will need access in this modern age to a telephone socket, maybe a network port, some power and lights and maybe not to be disturbed by the one next door. So the ceiling did not stretch across the whole of the room and there was a massive gap in the wall between us and next door. In this adjoining "conference room" was the noisiest bunch of locals I had ever heard. One of the team had to go in with a message of "peace" for them, which went somewhere along the lines of "Shut up you noisy lot", with an appropriate gesture. Our neighbours became very animated and excited – sometimes it is as though they are the only beings on the planet; no-one else matters. Usefully, The Bottom joined us for this call.

Accessing a phone line to dial out or be called upon in this building is a lottery. Back in the UK, all our conference rooms are quiet, have data ports, working projectors and conference phones. This is simple, basic equipment that any international company should have, especially one with two or more nationalities who need to communicate regularly with "home". Visitors are often amazed at the laid-back way we accept or work around these inconveniences without rushing or panicking. We have seen it so many times.

A highlight of the day was DIY coming to my desk to tell me that there was a protest (he claimed) by the locals outside. (He claimed it was about what I have said about them in this account!). He beckoned me to the window and outside across the road at the Whirlpool washing machine factory was a real, live, Chinese protest! There were six or seven blokes sat cross-legged on the ground in the blistering heat, preventing any lorry movement in or out of the gates. All the waggons were lined up in the street and the drivers were enjoying a game of cards in the shade of the lead truck. There was no noise, no chanting "We will not be moved" in Shanghainese; in fact a quiet do all round. A lone copper came on his motorcycle outfit, but appeared to merely observe. So the Chinese do dare stand up to authority, but quietly.

Wednesday night is as you may have gathered, traditionally a night out here for us, but I really did not fancy another session down at the Paulaner. Besides, my boss's boss, One, was due to be there and has a habit of making one feel very welcome to have one more, and one more and………. Hence the name. He is very sociable, but I cannot keep up with most of them here as I am such a lightweight drinker, so I slipped off with Rolf and Doo to the familiar surroundings of the Moon River Diner.

The "Unpleasant Section"
There being ice-cubes in the urinal again, it has moved me to record what are hopefully some useful tips for gentlemen visiting the lavatory abroad.

Tiddling Tips
- Check you are in the right room – no urinals, no blokes and you are possibly in the wrong shop. Exit and check again. What are you wearing? The correct attire is vital when choosing a tiddling venue.
- Is there a flunky within? Are you to be watched whilst urinating? Some men cannot hack this; if you are one of these you will have to tie a knot in it and seek alternative sites.
- Will said flunky merely keep himself to cleaning duties or as at the Diamond Court restaurant be keen to give you a hand towel upon completion of your job? Or even, on the case of entering a cubicle for a number 2, a towel for the seat.

- Will he (or she in really liberated clubs) give you a neck massage whilst one is stood to attention? Can you deal with such an intrusion?
- Is there a window open (as they always are at our office), and will the wind blow one's tie onto the urinal sides? This is prevented by tucking the neck adornment into a pocket or holding it with the thumb of the unoccupied hand.
- Are there ice-cubes within the receptacle? Then choose your aiming point carefully, as spraying willy-nilly (pun intended) at a many-faceted shiny feature can cause random splash-back; not good if wearing light trousers. It can be fun and not a bit childish when faced with "the cubes" to see just how many one can melt, but aim carefully! My true, unexaggerated record is three and not seven as I may have claimed at the time.
- Is there any soap or water available and why are there never enough dryers or towels for a busy loo? The act of drying takes longer than washing, so why are there more sinks than drying facilities?
- Ladies, you have fun spending pounds on extravagant shopping trips. We men can have fun for free. If one is Chinese, or even French, then no facility of any kind is really required and a leak can be taken in any convenient corner.

  (On a subsequent visit to the Gents at Munich airport, the ever-practical Germans attempted to solve the problem of men missing the urinal. This was cunningly achieved by incorporating pictures of flies or spiders into the ceramic glaze of the surface near the waste hole. This ensured that any man was bound to aim at it! When it did not wash down, one concentrated more – I know I did!

.....................end of "Unpleasant Section"!

I am sure that the area in which the diner is located took its inspiration from the set of "Bladerunner"; it is all screens, noise, lights and adverts everywhere. It is possible to eat in a different spot every night and not return to the same place in three weeks. I asked the lady proprietor of the place what part of Canada she was from, guessing that she was probably American. So it turned out to be, but as Canadians are offended if you assume them to be Yanks, (and does not appear to work the other way), it seemed like a good way to start a conversation. I enquired about how easy or otherwise it was to train the locals. She rushed to their defence, but admitted that she had to be on the premises most nights bar a quiet Monday, in order to supervise.

Thursday, 25th May 2006

Today began well with a debate with our Bottom. We had many frustrations and questions prepared. We waded through the issues like they were treacle. One was on smoking, which is always an emotive issue. It is Company policy for no smoking in the offices or working areas and that special rooms are available. Someone then asked why there was an ashtray on the table in front of us. We concluded that smoking here is a socially *inclusive* thing among men especially, much as it was in the fifties and sixties back home. Most of the women we know hate it, but are ignored. The ashtray was later to find itself being propelled through the open window into the bushes one floor down.

At the end of the day we had a torrential downpour and it is a well-known phenomenon that taxis here dissolve in the rain. Like a big welcome oasis, outside sat the Diamond Court bus, laid on for those infrequent important visitors who had by now all left! So I strolled in as if I were a DC resident again and took refuge from the downpour. Not wishing to be a lonely rider, I called up some of the others to alert them to a non-dissolving free lift back. In the end, none of the six people on the bus were residents of the Court!

An interesting piece of news is that China exported 228 million mobile phones last year, a massive 56% increase over the previous one. Their export value increased 45.7% to US$20.6bn, strengthening China's position as a global mobile phone manufacturer. Electronics exports accounted for one third of the nation's US$250bn exports.

At the other end of the socio-economic scale, a 2,000 year-old tax on China's peasants is being lifted this year, once a basic staple of government income. In Mao's time, it accounted for 40% of fiscal income and now only 1%. The country has recognised the increasing gap between rich and poor, town and countryside and is scrapping farm taxes. The ruling Communist Party believes that further unrest is certain if something is not done to patch over this gap.

Agricultural tax amounted to about RMB300/£20 per family and has been in place since the first Emperor imposed the burden. This may sound a small amount, but I am only too aware that I can eat this at a restaurant in one sitting and it represents more than 10% of rural per capita income.

Peasants interviewed on the TV tell of now being able to send their children to school for this amount and being able to then spend more on fertiliser! Such is the difference between the haves and have-nots in this vast country. We do see a distorted view of China in Shanghai.

Moves like this are window-dressing really and a recent riot in southern China saw several people shot dead by paramilitary police. There are many ways local authorities can extract sums of money from people with little voices, from breaching the one-child policy to snatching land for re-development.

Friday, 26th May 2006
Today's Test Meeting showed Native, who had not been to one for a while, that these sessions have moved on considerably since the early days. The agenda comes out religiously and attendees are regular. We had the lovely Kelly as translator, who is good. It took some while for the smoke to clear from a previous meeting, but no-one dared light up whilst I was around.

There is much information which is not in dual-language, despite the instructions from the management that it should be, so the services of a good translator are essential. One amusing translation on a problem record was *'Piston assembly stricken and ablated'*. I suppose it was, looking at the photos.

We had an absolutely mad taxi driver this evening. We are used to crazies, but this chap was certifiably insane. He will kill himself or someone else. Why do these people keep accelerating into brake lights, and pull out, as this driver did, into the path of a BMW? A self-important Beemer driver is not one to move aside, so we had to dive in at the last moment and we breathed again. That was by no means the worst point, oh no. He was hammering off the Yan'An elevated highway down the slip road, towards the brake lights, still accelerating. A bully in the coach in front nearly swiped us like an annoying fly on a horse's back.

Friday night in Shanghai – aren't we the lucky ones to be here? We planned to visit the mis-spelt "Shufle *(sic)* Bar", where there were to be three bands on the bill. Inside, it was not the spit-and-sawdust sort of venue I expected, but fairly clean, (even the lavatories were). The acoustics were good: with a high concrete ceiling. We were too late for the first band and the RMB40/£2.90 entrance fee usefully (if you aren't me) included a beer. I had, however, to pay RMB45/£3.20 for a Scotch.

The clientele was quite heavily local, but there were a good number of Westerners, especially girls there. Winston and Taigh had seen or heard enough by now and the big lad was hankering for the Paulaner. The music here was not really his style, being too close to heavy rock/punk and too far away from Abba, so they were off in a taxi. Brummie and I stuck around for the main act.

When they opened up, it was clear in a few bars that they were very comfortable with themselves, their style and the material and made good music look easy to play. The delivery was passionate and the sound excellent. I was definitely going to have the CD this time. We jigged away on the spot for the whole set. Why have we just found good music just before I leave? To be fair, the venue is new and has something to prove. There was even a flunky in the toilets, to add that essential Chinese touch – hey, get off me!

We watched all of the final set by the inappropriately named "Honeys" (we did expect girls) and left, me with CD in hand, to meet the others at the Paulaner, although I was going to bale out at the Pent-Ox, as I had consumed enough whisky for my small capacity. Winston called us in the taxi to warn us that the roads were being blocked off, which he suspected was part of a practice for the impending visit of Vladimir Putin. The city had "practised" with fireworks the other night – any excuse for noise and tonight it appeared to be rehearsing the road closure programme. There was consequently chaos on the elevated sections and we were advised not to head for the tunnel by the Pearl Tower, so we headed for the Dalian tunnel further north.

Saturday, 27th May 2006

Following in the footsteps of The Doctor, we decided to visit Zhouzhuang, otherwise known as "Watertown No.1", to the west of Shanghai and one of the many water-towns on the edge of the many lakes in this part of the world. The Doc had discovered that the bus station was near gate 25 of the massive Shanghai Stadium, on the southern side of the city. I had been there when I went (or tried to go) to the Moto GP. There we would find the ticket office, tax-free shop and coaches for many different destinations. It was amazing just where you could reach from the city in a day; trips to go white-water rafting, see mountain scenery, caves, waterfalls, parks and of course water-towns.

RMB140 secured a ticket, which included town entrance and coach travel. It was as easy as pi, once we had a note written by one of our translators. It read "I wanna *(sic)* go to Water-town No.1", and this translator insists she does not speak English with an American accent – she even writes with one!

To kill time between buying the tickets and departure, we had a look around the shops which circle the stadium, one of which was a model shop (Native happy) and a Giant bike shop (cyclists happy). There was also a complete bicycle shop dedicated to folding bikes of all sorts. The Giant shop was massive, with anything from a super-heavy modern "Chopper" with feet-first style and two chains to go rusty, to carbon-fibre dream machines. We drooled a lot at magnesium wheels, lightweight hydraulic disc brakes and left!

So 10.30am saw Frau, Doo, Native, Rolf and I on coach number 3 in car park number 4 setting off for our destination. As usual, typical Chinese efficiency prevailed, with numbered seats, air-conditioning and on-time service. Sadly, also typically, we had Dodo the driver, demonstrating a digital throttle approach (on, off, on, off, etc), so we were nodding away for miles. His playing of the brake pedal was similar, with frequent dabs for no apparent reason. Perhaps he plays an organ in his spare time. We were ready to relieve him of his duties and drive ourselves.

The nodding journey took about 90 minutes and we began to see water after about an hour, as there are many lakes here. The usual half-built tourist attractions started to appear by the side of the road and empty apartments as well (no shortage of housing here, just places poor people cannot afford). We were deposited in a car park and followed the rest of the group (many of whom had been asleep for the trip as usual) into the town. We did wonder how or if we would recognise the coach upon our return! We were singularly under-whelmed by the appearance of the town, as it appeared no older than five years; very pretty, but not the ancient water-town we had expected. We followed the crowds like sheep, past new cafés and watering holes, desperate for our RMB, but onwards we plunged, down narrow alley-ways and backstreets. Really, without locals to follow we would have had trouble. Tucked away down an alley we passed through a "Ticket check point" and were relieved of one tear-off ticket portion.

Shortly after, we emptied out into a street bordering one of the many canals on which the town is built. This was full of shops and people enjoying the sunshine and scenery. The buildings were no more than two-storey places, with gondolas carrying the tourists along between them, and some of the gondoliers singing to their passengers. The shops sold the usual gifts we expect: silk-ware, hats, fans, jade rubbish; but some crafts and food were specific to this part of the country, it is noted for pig's knuckles in a very red sauce, smelling very appealing and even looking so, but we resisted. There were craftswomen and men showing old-fashioned skills (as they do in these places back home and in other countries) such as coopering, blacksmithing, shoemaking (very small Chinese multi-coloured ones), sake-distilling and basket weaving. All over were grannies sat on small stools waving those wooden toys about, which are shaped like a table-tennis bat with a hole in the centre and a ring of pecking birds around the periphery. We bravely avoided buying any of these, except the sake! The bakery was a place of delightful odours and tiny buns.

We lunched in what looked like a very dodgy canal-side café, but no-one was coming out throwing up, so we wandered in past the usual tanks of just-alive fish. We took a table right by the water and enjoyed the passing gondoliers who were at face-level, so we were able to enjoy jocularity and waving with them and their passengers. Who was laughing at whom? Does it matter, as everyone was having a great time and no-one (apart from the tour guides with megaphones just doing their jobs) was annoying? Back home there would be some miscreants just out to create chaos and disturb the ambience of the place. The food (as is often the case), came at random moments, so we had to remind the staff about our drinks and cancel some dishes as we were full. There must be some very well fed birds and fish near there. Talking of which, we were able to see a (just for the tourists) boat full of tethered cormorants being "exercised" by their handler. These birds used to be employed by fishermen who would constrict their throats to prevent them from eating their catch.

Our gondola ride was excellent – corny I know, but when in Rome......
and it is a great way to see the place. Cunningly the trip runs to a point in the town where one has to walk back past many, many shops, requiring considerable reserve to avoid buying tat. Sun-hats with rotating windmills on the front, unisex hats which are made of folded paper and look stupid on either man or woman and more silk pyjamas! I made a couple of purchases of shirts which took my fancy, but had to buy an XL and I am not a big chap, stripping off in the shop to frighten the locals and try them on. I haggled hard for RMB50/£3.57 each. (Photo p.XXIX).

273

We wandered off down a distant alley and found ourselves on the edge of the "public" part of the town, near to the boat yard where a gondola was up-turned out of the water, so its construction could be seen. We saw a local builder carrying his yoke with two plastic pails of mortar swinging from his shoulders. He did not either notice or care that he was slopping with each step. Each slop would go off quickly in the sun and need to be chipped off, but then the Chinese do seem to like to make life hard for themselves.

We returned to the coach park and amazingly by showing our tickets, but not without some debate amongst themselves, the drivers organised us all onto the right vehicle! I was sat in front of the noisy, open-mouth chewing local, but I managed to turn native and sleep for a while. Back at the Stadium, we marched off in the direction of a shopping centre and headed for the Italian restaurant on the fifth floor. This turned out not to be cheap, but great food of typical Italian fayre, served up by not-very-Italian-looking Chinese staff, who were great.

We all dined in style and agreed to meet up the following evening for hot dogs and Formula One, which was to be the Monaco round.

Sunday, 28th May 2006
I had decided to cycle to Puxi to look for a digital vernier calliper, so I set off down the Da Dao, which is being hastily made-over in advance of the Russian Premier's visit. Shop fronts and signs are being boarded over and evened up to look tidy, but shoddily, if you look closely, not that Putin will notice. He must be travelling from the Lujiazui area to the Naval College up the road, so it all has to look good.

I took the last ferry before the OPT and crossed again to Puxi. The architecture over here is different and was the area occupied originally by the Japanese, before they took complete control in WWII. It is far less busy than the area to the south of the Suzhou Creek, but really interesting nonetheless. My aim was to cross over the Creek to Beijing Lu East and the plethora of engineering and tool shops there.

I found one and tried with a crummy drawing to make myself understood. Once I had done so and it was apparent that there was not one in stock, I was told to wait the regulation "5 minutes" and I awaited the arrival of whatever delivery service came along. I amused myself watching a tiny tot scrabble about on the floor, and try to use a broom twice his height; and obviously I was a celebrated foreign visitor as the child was presented to me by a proud father. I felt obliged to pick him up and look him in the eye. Good job I had the old cycling mitts on, as the child felt damp at the rear and as is often typical, no nappies were used and the back of the pants are slit open. It is great here sometimes. He began to crease up facially, so he went back damp to Dad.

When the measuring device was finally delivered by scooter, I haggled and haggled, was shown the list price of this special Shanghai-made device and realised that I could do almost as well back home! So I declined and left, probably leaving behind a cursing shop-keeper.

I popped into Carrefour for some sausages, wine and other supplies, including a pair of bathroom scales for just over a pound Sterling! That would serve us all to weigh bags and know we are over the limit *before* we check in at the airport!

I arrived at the appointed time in Shimao Lakeside and gained entrance without a key-pad code by diving into the basement, catching the lift and surfacing inside the block, then opening the door from within to admit my bike. As usual, a great time was had by all.

Monday, 29th May 2006
The news carried an interesting report this morning on the dust clouds besieging the capital, Beijing. I saw the results of these the last time I flew there. The dust is from the surrounding farms as it is so dry and from dust-storms further north. The proposed solution is "Preventive Farming", whereby attempts are made not to strip the ground of all vegetation and keep some cover in place. I hope it works. I have been to Los Angeles and Dubai, where the dust looks like a brown cloud in the distance.

Also on the news was a piece on a Japanese monk who is on his third pilgrimage around China, stopping at various sites of Japanese cruelty and bloodshed, some marked with monuments, to apologise and pray for his country's actions in the past. Also there was a piece on an ancient 50sq.m. map on display in Beijing, showing that Taiwan "…belonged to the mainland in the past". So that proves it, then. These two items are the most regularly featured topics on CCTV, China National TV. No-one said propaganda, or brain-wash, but it's close.

Also featured was another regular, a coal-mine disaster. Some of these mines operate for a year after their safety certification has expired, work far more hours than they should, have far too many men below ground than can be supported, and generally function on slap-dash safety procedures. The central government investigator was vitriolic in his assessment of the shirked responsibilities of the local officers and was baying for blood. Thousands of men perish in these places each year in avoidable incidents.

Brummie, Hug and 118 went for their driving test today, such as it is. It comprises a 100-question multiple choice session, with prior notice of the questions and answers provided! On the wall of the Test Centre was spotted the following:

Regulations for driving licence holders:
- *For any driving one must still have both thumbs attached and three fingers on each hand.*
- *For manual cars one must have two legs, one of which must be within 5cms of the length of the other.*
- *For automatic cars, one must have a right leg at least.*

This is the Chinese being as practical as ever, except there is no practical test for our boys; it is assumed that because they are Brits that they can drive, I suspect. The locals navigate around cones in a car park.

I used the weighing scales to check my bag and I reckon even with all the purchases I have sent home with others, I will still be close to the allowance. And still my family ask me to buy goods! I will have to leave certain things behind such as old shirts and a pair of shoes, but I planned to do that anyway. I'll bag them up and stick them by the bin so that one of the "borrowers" and bin-riflers can have them.

Tuesday, 30th May 2006
Just another Tuesday dawned in the usual haze of smog and other airborne pollutants. Life is becoming rather warm in the morning and I reckon I can hold out only one more day before it is air-con switch-on time. The UK is still being rained on and we are bathed in hazy sunshine.

The start of the evening's entertainment was provided by 118 who drove us to the Flying Fox pub in a UK-built test car! It is amusing to see him drive like a deranged local, only quicker, with a vehicle having some real performance and dynamic ability, which is more than can be said for most of the cars on the road here.

The Fox is starting to feel like a British pub, with most of the clientele being Westerners and an Aussie landlord, Guinness on tap and black pudding on the menu, which I devoured with glee. The all-day breakfast looked good, but was too much for me, so I just enjoyed the black pudding on its own. We whiled the night away, with 118 well into his stride, guffing on about Lancaster bombers, a particular passion of his.

Wednesday, 31st May 2006

The end of another month approaches and I am looking at 11 days sentence remaining out here. Winston has signed for a further 12 months and if his contract turns up tomorrow, then Brummie will do so too. They are welcome to it. Lunch-time today was the last day of lunch supplied by the Mawdesley and another chance for us to sit together and moan about how the project is panning out.

Many of our colleagues are starting to disagree with us; today one decided that he did not subscribe to some facts presented by British engineers; he had two months experience, theirs combined was over twenty! They could have been wrong, but it was fact and not for debate. Even when shown the error of his calculations, Johnny local was still unconvinced. How do we make progress with attitudes like this?

We keep impressing upon the locals just how important it is to check parts and not accept poor quality. However this is a culture that always accepts that the supplier knows best and is not to be questioned too hard. Add to this the very real lack of knowledge about European quality levels and there is much work for us to do.

I was set for a quiet trip on my own back to the Pent-Ox, then next it was "down the East-West" with the transmissions team, and then a benevolent AJ offered to take us to Monty's restaurant, whose speciality is steaks. Frau, Native and he collected me by taxi from the Pent-Ox. We endured the heat and fumes of the Donglu tunnel under the Huangpu, which is thick with fumes at the best of times and any delay under there is a real gas, in the true sense of the word, hence my preference for crossing by the Metro.

We were deposited on the Huahai Lu, and walked down the all-tile Yandang Lu – this road must be treacherous in the wet! I had never been here, although it had been heartily recommended by old Gary. It turned out his comments were entirely accurate and we had a fantastic meal, with the best steaks we have eaten in Shanghai, maybe even for a long time. The restaurant is in a really stylish old Shanghai residence and the ambience conducive to a relaxing repast. We were serenaded by a trio of Philippinos, who opened by our table with Roy Orbison's "Pretty Woman", just for Frau. They were really good. I asked for "Horse with no name" by America and they gave it some stick when AJ requested "Hotel California" and I reckoned that they topped that with my next request – "Massachusetts", complete with Bee-Gees-style vibrato.

The "show" started with a small bowl of salad, prepared at the table in a glass bowl and spun on a bed of ice within a bigger bowl, which was quite stylish! This set the tone for the quality of food to follow and the care with which it was prepared. We certainly dined in style.

Following our meal, it was time to show AJ around the place and so I led on towards Square Park at the corner of Jinling Lu and Huangpi Lu. This park used to be a thriving community of just under 5,000 families, but they were all cleared away to make room for the park, which features such delights as white swans, real live ducks and a red plastic dragon boat. The "before" photo on the information board, compared to the real "after" sight is staggering. Where did all those people go? It is rumoured that many farmers are being turfed off their land and livelihoods by the authorities in Beijing just now to make way for Olympic Games activities, with little or no compensation. That appears to be just how this place works, or doesn't.

We journeyed on up Huangpi Lu to cross Renmin Lu, which divides People's Square and we turned right and east at the Art Gallery and onto Nanjing Lu, at which point Frau and Native left on the Metro for home, AJ and I carrying on to show him the lights. The brooding '30s' edifice of the Park Hotel looked even more forbidding than usual, but that really is the only dark spot on an otherwise blindingly bright road. We were just out of time to see some of the more outlandish illuminations, but I think he got the idea. We were naturally offered "clean Shanghai ladies" before we had gone more than a dozen paces on the pavement of this stunning road. We were busy, so we passed on the offers; the girls could not have afforded our bodies, anyway!

We dropped off the road at the Middle Hennan Road station, re-appearing above ground at Lujiazui to pick up a waiting taxi and drop us off at our respective apartments.

Thursday, 1st June 2006

The new month dawned with a promise of rain and a slightly cooler day. It was also destined to be a good day for engineering. We had to visit the build shop and listen to a noisy engine, which had been "rattling like a bad 'un" only the day before. Naturally, with an audience of four top Powertrain engineers, it purred away! We turned our attention to the next car and this proved to have an unidentifiable noise, so we opted to raise the car on the ramp (having to push it there as there is only one battery in the build shop to go around!) Once clear of the ground and the consequential echoes, and with the engine bay under tray removed, we could much easier identify the source of the noise. AJ demonstrated a technique well-known to all of us and borrowed a long-shank screwdriver to touch the engine, stick the blunt end in his ear and pin-point the noise.

This was sheer wizardry to the watching local fitters, true black magic and they were further impressed when he demonstrated his clip-off tie, which he always wore following a particularly nasty near-strangulation when his regular neck-tie was caught up in a drive belt. We followed this up by showing the audience how a damaged component had been fitted to the engine by them and was causing the noise. Just occasionally we are worth our salt! Engineering can be so rewarding at times.

An amusing workshop story was from Clegg, who had asked two of the fitters to go out for petrol and fuel up two freshly built cars so that they could be moved (still sharing one battery!) The men came back and moved the first vehicle. When Clegg sat in the second car, having swapped the battery, he was told that it would not start. When he asked why, he was told that it was dry, no fuel. He asked his boys if they had been for fuel as he asked them and they replied that they had. "Did you fuel the cars?" he asked. "Yes, that one", was the response. "So you did not put half in that one and half in this, then?" "Er, no", came the considered response after some discussion in Welsh. It was pointless to ask any more questions, so he sent them out for some more. "But it's raining" they countered. "Then take the van!" he said, exasperatedly. An hour and a half later, they still had not returned and car number two was still stationary. No wonder he has little hair on his head.

Later on in the day, we went out in a car to check the new automatic gearbox change-points, as we have to set these points in the control software. We were minding our own business, with 118 driving us along and a bus just bullied its way out of a side road and drove at us. Fortunately, our top Lancaster-loving pilot managed to hurl a quick right and avoid the clown in the bus. The bus was stopping for no-one and nothing, which is typical of these cowboys; they just use the fact that their vehicle is bigger than yours and you would come off worse in a straight fight. I have seen them driving down bike lanes to get the drop on the traffic – they are deranged, a bit like 4x4 drivers at home, only worse and not really concerned for their own safety.

Friday, 2nd June 2006
Nine days to go. Catherine, (who is the daughter of my godfather, Uncle Jeff), arrives tomorrow with her mate Julie. I haven't seen Catherine for many years – I hope I recognise her. I doubt I will manage to write much as my spare time will be filled with seeing them and being out and about.

Chapter 12

LAST VISITORS AND REASONS
TO BE CHEERFUL

Saturday, 3rd to Sunday, 11th June 2006

My last week in Shanghai was as I suspected, taken up with being a host to my glamorous visitors, Catherine and Julie. I showed them Watertown No.1 as it is so good and we covered all the usual Shanghai sights. They had an amusing time trying to reach Suzhou by catching the train from Shanghai South Railway Station. Naturally, it had been demolished, the signs were in Chinese, and many of the locals did not (or could not) read them so there was a huge gaggle of travellers looking for a station which was no longer there. Chinese opportunism was represented by a fleet of coaches ready to take the lost group onwards. For a small fee, of course! (Photo p.XXX).

The girls had a great time, being seasoned globe-trotters and not worried by being in Eastern climes. It was a shame I had to wait until my last week to rush around with my only visitors (except for immediate family) but we had a great time.

I had carefully arranged my farewell party by booking a large table for all my colleagues and various ladies. We all arrived at the restaurant but they looked busy, with about fifty seated hopeful diners waiting. I enquired of my booking, was told that they took none and there was no room for us! This is China after all. Plan "B" was hatched (move elsewhere) and we all had a great time. It was touching to see how many came to make sure I went home!

Farewell, all.

TWENTY-SOME REASONS WHY I WILL CERTAINLY MISS SHANGHAI, CHINA AND THE CHINESE

1. The people with whom it has been my pleasure to live, work and share hopes, dreams, fears, ambitions, good times and bad, especially the Powertrain boys and wives.
2. Clear, swept cycle lanes.
3. Cheap stuff.
4. Haggling for the cheap stuff and having fun doing it.
5. Fresh fruit juices.
6. The Bund, especially at night.
7. The majestic Jinmao Tower.
8. A feeling of security in the city.
9. Slim people.
10. Easy smiles.
11. Cheap, plentiful taxis.
12. Little graffiti.
13. Crossing the river at night on the Spitting Ferry (but see dislikes no. 1 and 6).
14. The keen desire to serve in service industries.
15. Proper recycling.
16. 4,000 years of amazing history.
17. They view Engineering and Manufacturing as important. We are, but sadly Maggie Thatcher managed to convince the UK that we weren't.
18. People feeling so relaxed, they shop in their pyjamas!
19. A country so vast one can visit places +50°C to -40°C and see the Great Wall, The Forbidden City or visit Shangri-La.
20. The amazing night-life.

21.   The trust in us to be able to download programmes onto our desk computers and have Internet access when few of the Chinese do. That was denied us in the UK.

22.   The "Welfare" when the temperature rises above 35°C. If this happens the cleaning lady brings boxes of ice-cream from the Nestle factory down the road! HR make the decision based on the thermometer and choose from the catalogue of tasty ices!

THIRTY-SOME REASONS WHY I WILL

NOT MISS SHANGHAI,

CHINA AND THE CHINESE

1. Hawking (either attempting to sell stuff or coughing up phlegm).
2. Spitting, following the latter.
3. Pushing or leaning on or over me in queues, in fact an almost Teutonic inability to queue.
4. Giving me no personal space; I am English, after all. Where is their cultural sensitivity?
5. Bad breath (in combination with Number 4 is lethal after a night on rice wine and dumplings).
6. Intrusions (e.g. when one is already talking to another directly or on the phone).
7. Smoking, even when and where it is prohibited. The only safe place is inside airports. One is gassed as one leaves the Arrivals Hall.
8. Slurping food and drink, even dry food. How do they do it? It is just not necessary. Nor is eating with the mouth open. (This goes for Americans too).
9. A uniformly low standard of unplanned, unobservant driving. A game of chicken at each junction.
10. The over-use of horns to hide personal inability to plan driving.
11. Noise; everything has to make noise, from the street cleaner truck to road signs.
12. Bureaucracy (such as three forms to fill in at Customs).
13. Lack of any perception of imminent personal danger and the consequential absence or mis-use of PPE (Personal Protective Equipment).
14. Pollution (fly over Beijing and see for yourself).

15. Poor maintenance (bicycles to aircraft).
16. The curse of mobile phones everywhere.
17. Open doors and windows in the depths of winter (and summer when the air-con is on).
18. Sitting there in coats with the windows open (thankfully only in the autumn and winter. Oh, and part of spring).
19. Engineering know-it-alls who demonstrably don't.
20. Ignoring my 25 years of experience in automotive engineering.
21. People (non-job holders) pointing where to go when it's obvious or one-way.
22. Thick, yellow (or green) tights, especially on the women.
23. Wearing short, ankle-high thick pop-socks with smart sandals (as above).
24. A combination of the above two dislikes – yes!
25. Fat, spoiled, nosey kids (a recognised problem here, even by the Government).
26. Sneezing with no attempt to catch the sub-sonic spray.
27. Asking me if I'm cold when it's 20°C and I am in shirt–sleeves and they are still sporting a vest.
28. Staring, especially towards a foreigner with a cycle helmet on, with an obviously but comparatively expensive bike and shorts on when they are still in vests and long johns. One just has to keep up appearances.
29. Pointless censorship (see the reviews of the Rolling Stones concert in Shanghai; people can look up the lyrics online or buy the albums... come on, Beijing).
30. Their "ways" with animals. (Watch them hold a dog or see film of their zoos).
31. Advertising everywhere; buses, taxis, lifts, Metro trains, buses, bikes..... You cannot escape screens shouting at you. There is a pair in my apartment block, which for many weeks were slightly out of synch, which really hacked me off, as they were loud, too.
32. Doing things when you expressly tell them not to as it will cause problems or unmitigated disaster. It would be OK if they learned from this.
33. Saying "Wei?" as they answer the phone. Sometime they will use this telephonic greeting several times – I counted seven once. Why not

just say one's name like "normal" people? If they answer on a bus, they almost give themselves a headache shouting "Wei?" over the din of the vehicle and passengers.

34. Extremes of weather, with bitter cold winds in winter here in Shanghai and "fry your head" heat. Long johns and vests are worn, even into the hot weather, with summer clothes finishing abruptly for all upon returning from the October Golden Week, even if it is still warm.

35. Marble floors are a menace with the slightest wet spot, but slippery marble is used outside under fountains which often have no bowl; they are just flat open spaces which happen to have a water feature. Also to be found outside buildings.

36. Living by a noisy 24-hour docks where they have individual ability to reduce the noise but don't, because they are simply stupid.

37. Having to explain the obvious when the physical evidence is in front of us.

38. Smoky, polluting trucks and buses. The sooner emissions regulations are tightened, the better. Some vehicles are being taken off the road, but not enough for my liking. The place would stop if my wish came true!

GLOSSARY

It may be useful to explain a few places, terms and *Chinese* used here:

Bei – North, as in Beijing.

Bianjin – the park beside SBM, beside the *Huangpu* River.

Biyun Lu, the road on which sat Diamond Court, the Mawdesley and the other cafés such as the East-West.

The Bund – similar to the Embankment on the Thames. It is on the Puxi bank of the Huangpu.

Cybermart – electronic superstore at Hong Kong Plaza, south western corner of People's Square.

Diamond Court – DC is where I first lived when with Powertrain, earlier in 2005. Also "home" to other visiting colleagues on Biyun Lu in this narrative.

Dong – Chinese for east.

East-West – a café/bakery opposite DC.

Huangpu River – splits Shanghai into two.

Jenny's bar – near the Gift Market and a haven of no hassling.

Jinling Lu – the street of many music shops, at the south side of Peoples' Square.

Jinmao Tower – The biggest, the majestic one and only. 420m, 88-storey, with offices up to floor 50 and the Grand Hyatt hotel upwards thereafter.

Jinqiao – (Green Bridge) the area where we worked.

Lotus Supermarket – several outlets in the city, but I patronised the one under the Super Brand Mall.

Lu – street.

Lujiazui – the financial district of Pudong.

Mawdesley, The – our local bar in JinQiao, opposite DC.

Nan – South.

Oriental Pearl Tower – The OPT is a massive landmark in Lujiazui Park. It
is a TV tower of incredible beauty – see photos.

Pent-Ox Metropolis – "Home" for the period of this narrative.

Paulaner – "Bavarian beer-houses". There were three in Shanghai; the one
in Bianjin park was "ours".

Ping – i.e. Joe Soap, Mr. Smith, or anybody whose name I don't know. Also
Wang, Fang and Zhong.

Pudong – The new area of Shanghai and east (dong) of the
Huangpu River.

Pudong Da Dao – the road on which stands the Pent-Ox.

Puxi – The older area of Shanghai and east (*xi*) of the river.

RMB – Remnimbi or Yuan, the Chinese currency. At the time of this diary,
although pegged against the US dollar, it sat at about RMB14 = £1.

Spitting ferry – one of many; this plies the Huangpu at Dongfang Lu

Stuart – my friend also working for a Chinese car company, whose
experiences were similar.

Super Brand Mall – exactly what it says on the wall – 8 floors of it.

Welsh – "It's all Chinese to me".

Wang – see Ping.

Xi – West.

Xiangyang Market – the infamous fake or Gift Market on the *Hua Hai Lu*.
(Now moved and split up to several locations).

YuYuan – The Yu Gardens, a collection of amazing traditionally-styled re-
creations of typical local buildings built around an actual garden and
the "Temple of the City God".

Xintiandi – once a group of ordinary Shanghai alleys and houses, now an
up-market area of bars and shops. Also site of the first meeting of the
Chinese Communist Party.